Tourism and Cricket

TOURISM AND CULTURAL CHANGE

Series Editors: Professor Mike Robinson, *Ironbridge International Institute for Cultural Heritage, University of Birmingham, UK* and Dr Alison Phipps, *University of Glasgow, Scotland, UK*

TCC is a series of books that explores the complex and ever-changing relationship between tourism and culture(s). The series focuses on the ways that places, peoples, pasts and ways of life are increasingly shaped/transformed/created/packaged for touristic purposes. The series examines the ways tourism utilises/makes and re-makes cultural capital in its various guises (visual and performing arts, crafts, festivals, built heritage, cuisine, etc.) and the multifarious political, economic, social and ethical issues that are raised as a consequence.

Understanding tourism's relationships with culture(s) and vice versa, is of ever-increasing significance in a globalising world. This series will critically examine the dynamic inter-relationships between tourism and culture(s). Theoretical explorations, research-informed analyses and detailed historical reviews from a variety of disciplinary perspectives are invited to consider such relationships.

Full details of all the books in this series and of all our other publications can be found on http://www.channelviewpublications.com, or by writing to Channel View Publications, St Nicholas House, 31–34 High Street, Bristol BS1 2AW, UK.

TOURISM AND CULTURAL CHANGE: 41

Tourism and Cricket

Travels to the Boundary

Edited by
Tom Baum and Richard Butler

CHANNEL VIEW PUBLICATIONS
Bristol • Buffalo • Toronto

Library of Congress Cataloging in Publication Data
Tourism and Cricket: Travels to the Boundary/Edited by Tom Baum and Richard Butler.
Tourism and Cultural Change: 41
Includes bibliographical references and index.
1. Cricket. 2. Sports and tourism. I. Baum, Tom. II. Butler, Richard
GV917.T59 2014
796.358–dc23 2014008999

British Library Cataloguing in Publication Data
A catalogue entry for this book is available from the British Library.

ISBN-13: 978-1-84541-453-5 (hbk)
ISBN-13: 978-1-84541-452-8 (pbk)

Channel View Publications
UK: St Nicholas House, 31–34 High Street, Bristol BS1 2AW, UK.
USA: UTP, 2250 Military Road, Tonawanda, NY 14150, USA.
Canada: UTP, 5201 Dufferin Street, North York, Ontario M3H 5T8, Canada.

Website: www.channelviewpublications.com
Twitter: Channel_View
Facebook: https://www.facebook.com/channelviewpublications
Blog: www.channelviewpublications.wordpress.com

Copyright © 2014 Tom Baum, Richard Butler and the authors of individual chapters.

All rights reserved. No part of this work may be reproduced in any form or by any means without permission in writing from the publisher.

The policy of Multilingual Matters/Channel View Publications is to use papers that are natural, renewable and recyclable products, made from wood grown in sustainable forests. In the manufacturing process of our books, and to further support our policy, preference is given to printers that have FSC and PEFC Chain of Custody certification. The FSC and/or PEFC logos will appear on those books where full certification has been granted to the printer concerned.

Typeset by Techset Composition India(P) Ltd., Bangalore and Chennai, India.
Printed and bound in Great Britain by Short Run Press Ltd.

To the memory of Mike Grover with thanks for his contribution to the literature on tourism through Channel View Publications. His presence will be greatly missed.

Contents

Tables and Figures — ix
Contributors — xi
Acknowledgements — xv
Preface — xvii

Part 1: The Development of Patterns — 1

1. The Changing Boundaries and Geography of Cricket — 3
   Richard Butler

2. Looking for Witney Scrotum? Cricket, Tourism and Images of England — 17
   Brian Wheeller and Robert Maitland

Part 2: The Homes of Cricket — 35

3. Rupertswood and Sunbury: Commemorating Cricket and the Birthplace of 'the Ashes' — 37
   Leanne White

4. Nostalgia at the Boundary: A Study at Lord's Cricket Ground — 52
   Denise Cardwell and Nazia Ali

5. Development of the Rose Bowl as a Venue for Cricket and Other Events — 73
   Joanne Parrett

6. Cricket: Biology and Bali — 84
   Steve Noakes and Alan Wilson

Part 3: The True Costs   **99**

7   Cricketers as Tourists; Analyses of Culture Shock, Travel Motivation and Learning   103
Philip L. Pearce

8   Sport Tourism as a Means of Reconciliation? The Case of India–Pakistan Cricket   120
John Beech, Andrew Rigby, Ian Talbot and Shinder Thandi

9   On the March with the Barmy Army   136
Paul Emery, Warwick Frost and Anthony Kerr

10   An Ethnographic View from the Boundary: India vs England, The Fourth Test, Nagpur, December 2012   153
Tom Baum

11   Recollections of a Coarse Cricketer: Ninety Nine Percent Boredom, One Percent Terror   168
Richard Butler

Stumps   179
Richard Butler

Subject Index   182

Tables and Figures

Tables

Table 1.1 Test match countries 7

Table 4.1 The Ashes 2001 – England v. Australia 62

Table 4.2 The Ashes 2009 – England v. Australia 62

Table 4.3 Thematic analysis of questionnaire SPSS categories of evaluation 63

Figures

Figure 3.1 Sunbury is branded the 'Birthplace of the Ashes' 43

Figure 3.2 The Rupertswood display at the Sunbury Visitor Centre 44

Figure 3.3 Some of the Ashes information and memorabilia displayed in 'The Smoking Room' 47

Figure 3.4 A plaque commemorating the Ashes re-enactment in 1995 48

Figure 8.1 Chronology of India v. Pakistan cricket matches 123

Figure 9.1 Two members of the Barmy Army   137

Figure 9.2 Barmy Army members in 'uniform'   139

Figure 11.1 Coarse cricket Canadian style   171

Figure 11.2 Kwik cricket at Eden Park   176

Contributors

Nazia Ali was awarded her PhD in tourism studies from the University of Bedfordshire (UK) in 2008. Her doctoral thesis examined the interrelationship between Pakistani ethnic identity and participation in tourism amongst the Pakistani diaspora living in Luton, UK. Nazia has published in areas relating to tourism, identity, migration, researcher reflexivity, worldmaking and events design. Nazia's research agenda is largely ethnographic, operating within an interpretive framework to investigate tourism's relationship with such characteristics of identity as religion, culture, nationalism, race and diaspora. She is currently positioned within the Division of Tourism and Leisure at the University of Bedfordshire in the UK, and teaches on the undergraduate and postgraduate tourism and event management degree programmes.

Tom Baum is a Professor in the Department of Human Resource Management of the Strathclyde Business School in Glasgow and a specialist in the study of human capacity development in hospitality and tourism. Tom has worked in over 45 countries across five continents and more importantly, he is a cricket fanatic and is proud father of the current Scotland under-19 wicketkeeper!!

John Beech is an Honorary Research Fellow at Coventry University, United Kingdom, International Professor at the Russian International University in Sochi, Russia, and Visiting Professor at the University of the Applied Sciences in Kufstein, Austria. His research interests are in Sports, Tourism and Events Management, and he specialises in the economic impact of sports mega-events and their planned and emergent legacy, and in the finances and mismanagement of football clubs. He has published widely in these fields in the form of academic journal articles and textbooks.

Richard Butler is an Emeritus Professor of Tourism at the University of Strathclyde. His principal research interests include the development of tourist destinations and the impacts of tourism. He has published 17 books on tourism and resources management. He is a founding member and former president of the International Academy for the Study of Tourism and past President of the Canadian Association of Leisure Studies.

Denise Cardwell is currently undertaking a doctoral research degree investigating the concept of place attachment, specifically how this is formed in relation to significant sports sites. This research is being carried out at Lord's Cricket Ground, London, UK in the form of a case study. She is currently positioned within the Division of Tourism and Leisure at the University of Bedfordshire in England, and currently teaches Sport Events and Tourism Management on the undergraduate and postgraduate tourism and event management degree programmes.

Paul Emery has thirty years of experience in sport management education. As a dedicated and internationally renowned educator, facilitator and manager, he has been awarded institutional and national awards for his innovative and engaging teaching methods. As a co-founder and honorary member of the European Association for Sport Management, Paul has developed significant international experience in sport management course leadership and delivery. He has taught in four continents, and supervised more than 60 research theses to successful completion. Paul has presented and published widely in the area of sport project and major event management.

Warwick Frost is Associate Professor in Tourism at La Trobe University, Melbourne, Australia. He's a gritty opening batsman and an extravagant leg spinner. His honours thesis was in sports history, examining the social and economic implications of first English tour of Australia in 1861–1862. Nowadays, his research interests are in heritage tourism, national parks, events, and tourism and the media. With Jennifer Laing, he is the author of *Books and Travel: Inspiration, Quests and Transformations* (Channel View Publications, 2012), *Commemorative Events: Memory, Identity, Conflict* (Routledge, 2013) and *Explorer Travellers and Adventure Tourism* (Channel View Publications, 2014).

Anthony Kerr has a proven track record in marketing, sponsorship and media relations for a number of sport organisations worldwide and has worked with some of the world's most famous brands. He has postgraduate degrees from the University of Oregon and the University of Massachusetts and is interested in the valuable contribution foreign fans ('satellite supporters') can make to a professional team's bottom line. Anthony is the Course Coordinator for La Trobe University's Bachelor of Business (Sport Management) degree and is heavily involved in the design of its curriculum and currently sits on the board of the Sport Management Association of Australia and New Zealand (SMAANZ).

Robert Maitland is Professor of City Tourism and Director of the Centre for Tourism Research at the University of Westminster, London. His research focuses on the tourist experience of cities, in particular world cities and national capitals, and he chairs the international ATLAS City Tourism and National Capitals Research Group. Current research examines tourism and everyday life, off the beaten track tourism in London and other world cities, and social tourism. He still dreams of opening the batting for Yorkshire.

Contributors xiii

Steve Noakes is Visiting Professor at the Multidimensional Tourism Institute, University of Lapland, Finland. Little cricket is played in Lapland. In the cricketing nation of Australia, he is an Adjunct Professor at the Griffith Institute for Tourism at Griffith University. In Indonesia, he has a long engagement in tourism projects on behalf of the national and provincial governments, and multilateral agencies such as UNWTO, ILO and PATA. He is a part owner of Ecolodges Indonesia and an International Member of the Udayana Cricket Club based at Udayana University, Bali. He has never successfully played the game of cricket.

Joanne Parrett has been teaching leisure related topics for 10 years, primarily at Southampton Solent University. She has extensive management and marketing qualifications, including an MA in Marketing from the University of Luton and a second Masters from De Montfort University, Leicester in the subject of Sport History and Culture. She has contributed sections to the *Encyclopaedia of Sports Management & Marketing* (Swayne *et al.*, 2011, Sage). Outside work interests include Premier League football and Hampshire cricket as the author lives in what many term as the birthplace of English Cricket, Hambledon, Hampshire.

Philip Pearce played his cricket predominantly as an opening batsmen and leg spin bowler. After some experiences as a schoolboy cricketer playing grade level in Adelaide, his move to Oxford provided his best career highlights including a year as captain of his Oxford College. He finished his time in England with a batting average of 49.50. Returning to Australia he played for Flinders University for one season before moving to the tropics. In Queensland he played the short intense adapted version of the game referred to as indoor cricket, completing a final season with his son in 2005. He also researches and writes about tourism and tourist behaviour.

Andrew Rigby was founding director of the Centre for Peace and Reconciliation Studies at Coventry University. He is now Emeritus Professor of Peace Studies.

Ian Talbot is Professor of History at the University of Southampton, where he was head of department from 2009–2012. Educated at Royal Holloway, University of London, he has written extensively on the Partition of India, the colonial Punjab and the history of Pakistan. His recent publications include, *The Independence of India and Pakistan* (Oxford University Press, 2014); *Pakistan: A New History* (Hurst, 2012); with Gurharpal Singh, *The Partition of India* (Cambridge University Press, 2009); *Divided Cities: Partition and Its Aftermath in Lahore and Amritsar 1947–1957* (Oxford University Press, 2006). He is currently Chair of the British Association for South Asian Studies.

Shinder S. Thandi is Principal Lecturer in Economics at Coventry University, UK. He has teaching interests in the areas of development economics, global political economy and Diaspora Studies. He is one of the founders of the Punjab Research Group established in 1984 and has been the founder-editor of the *Journal of Punjab Studies* since 1994. He has published extensively on Indian and Punjabi migration and on different dimensions of Punjabi diaspora and homeland relations. He has co-edited two books: *Punjabi Identity in a Global Context* [with Pritam Singh, OUP, 1999) and *People on the Move: Punjabi Colonial and Post Colonial Migration* [with Ian Talbot, OUP, 2004).

Brian Wheeller holds degrees in Economics, in Applied Economics, in the Economic Impacts of Tourism, in American Studies and his PhD, Critiquing Eco/Ego/Sustainable Tourism, contextualises the debate within the wider arena of tourism planning and management. His interests now embrace the links between travel and tourism with popular culture and the Arts - and their relevance to contemporary tourism thinking: along with humour, image and the visual in tourism and tourism education. He is Visiting Professor of Tourism at NHTV, Breda, the Netherlands and the University of Plymouth, and Honorary Professor at the University of Wales.

Leanne White is a Senior Lecturer in the College of Business at Victoria University in Melbourne, Australia. Her research interests include: national identity, commercial nationalism, popular culture, advertising, destination marketing, events and cultural tourism. Leanne's PhD examined manifestations of official nationalism and commercial nationalism at the Sydney 2000 Olympic Games. She is the author of more than 45 book chapters and refereed journal articles, and co-editor of the Routledge research books: *Wine and Identity: Branding, Heritage, Terroir* (2014), *Dark Tourism and Place Identity: Managing and Interpreting Dark Places* (2013), and *Tourism and National Identities: An International Perspective* (2011).

Alan Wilson is often described as the 'father' of cricket in Indonesia.' In 2009 he was awarded the prestigious Lifetime Service Award by the International Cricket Council, East Asia-Pacific (ICC-EAP) as he 'has been an outstanding long time servant of cricket in Indonesia, and is widely attributed as the man who has made cricket what it is today in Indonesia through his perseverance, commitment and generosity.' He is Chairman of the Indonesia International Rural and Agricultural Development Foundation and founder/Chairman of Ecolodges Indonesia and EcoSafaris Indonesia. He is a self-confessed 'cricket-tragic'.

Acknowledgements

We wish to acknowledge the contributions of our fellow authors in this volume, along with their patience and cooperation over the time taken to complete the manuscript. We hope they find our editorial adjustments acceptable, and errors and mistakes remain our responsibility. We also wish to thank the staff at Channel View for their assistance during the preparation and submission of the manuscript, and in particular Sarah Williams for her enthusiastic and long-suffering support of the project, especially during a depressing period for English cricket in 2013.

We thank our families for their encouragement and assistance and for putting up with the usual problems of frustration and impatience encountered during production of a book.

Tom wishes to thank in particular the Scottish under-19 cricket team (and especially their wicketkeeper, Alex Baum) for providing enthusiasm and distraction during the World Cup in 2014.

Dick would like to thank King Edward's School, Birmingham for teaching him the rudiments of cricket, Bearsden Ski Club for allowing him the opportunity to refine his coarse cricket skills, and Brian Stewart for keeping him from visiting Mount Eden jail by mistake in 2013.

Preface

Tom Baum

> *Well, what is cricket after all,*
> *That so delights the masses?*
> *Six bits of stick, a bat and ball,*
> *And two and twenty asses.*
> The Game of Cricket, Daniel Healey

Cricket is a bit like Marmite to the British or Vegemite to Australians – you either love it with an all-consuming passion or you just don't get it. I certainly don't get Marmite (or Vegemite for that matter) and cannot stand even the thought of that stuff sullying what are otherwise perfectly delicious sandwiches. On the other hand, cricket has been an abiding passion since my days in short pants – a funny expression that, given the number of mature to elderly men in many parts of the world who wear shorts – but certainly not the obvious choice of a playing and spectating pastime for the son of Austrian and German refugees with absolutely no comprehension of the noble game.

Cricket has spawned a fabulous literature which, when set alongside writings about other sports, is frequently also of high literary quality – the names of Neville Cardus, John Arlott and also contemporaries such as Gideon Haigh come to mind. As a youngster, I consumed whatever I could or, rather, whatever books my elder brother bought, both new and dusty second-hand volumes! So I was well versed in the history of the game from its codification as a competitive and international sport as well as the heroes who adorned the pages of the books I read. Writing about cricket and enjoying the life of a nomadic cricket journalist was always one of my unfulfilled dreams. Instead, I found myself writing about tourism as an academic with a reading audience more akin to the County Ground, Derby in April than the Melbourne Cricket Ground on Boxing Day.

The tourism dimensions to international and more parochial forms of cricket come out strongly in the literature and, as will be highlighted elsewhere in this volume, even the language of cricket and its travels has a link to tourism – tourists, hosts, for example. So bringing the two together was always, to me, a logical way to go. Having settled on the notion, I needed the assistance of a far more experienced tourism author than myself and someone equally passionate about cricket as I am. I caught Dick Butler, a self-confessed 'coarse cricketer', after a few glasses of wine at a CAUTHE conference and persuaded him that a project to look at our shared love of cricket through tourism glasses was a viable and, potentially, fun project. On this basis, we jointly approached Sarah Williams of Channel View, another passionate cricket follower, there and then at the conference and she took to the idea with real enthusiasm. So began this journey and without Sarah we certainly would not have reached the end of this particular road.

We invited contributions to our venture from authors worldwide and, given the geographical spread of cricket today – the International Cricket Council has 10 full members, 36 associate members and 60 affiliate members – we were confident of being able to choose contributions that reflected this broad distribution. Despite widespread interest from potential contributors, the business end of delivering real chapters saw them narrowed down to contributions which reflect on cricket in Australia, England, India and New Zealand. So we miss out on vibrant cricketing hotspots elsewhere in the sub-continent and also in Southern Africa and the Caribbean. That is a pity, but what we do include by way of chapters does represent such a diversity of cricketing perspectives that we are confident that a broad and representative spectrum of cricket, travel and tourism is reflected in these pages. Of course, there are missing links here – perhaps it is reflective of our generation of cricket watchers that there is nothing on the 'new' cricket, the Indian Premier League or the Big Bash. Maybe by publishing this volume we will encourage others to address these new cricketing phenomena from a tourism perspective – the Twenty20 superstars, after all, are tourists in every sense, modern hired hands, millionaire mercenaries of sport, whose sworn allegiance to 'their' team in Pune, Hyderabad, Sydney or Perth is for just a few weeks before they jet out to join another band of sloggers, slog-sweepers, reverse-sweepers and the like at the other end of the world.

Reference

Healey, D. (2001) *The Game of Cricket in Bat and Pad*. Choice Books.

Part 1
The Development of Patterns

The first chapter in this section discusses the focus of this volume and the changing face of cricket, both the places in which it is played and the nature of the game itself. These factors have influenced greatly the travel patterns of fans and the competitions which have evolved. From purely local domestic matches between villages and other communities cricket has become international, so much so that new teams join the International Cricket Commission (ICC) on a regular basis and World Cups and other competitions often have to feature seeding and knock-out stages because of the numbers of eligible countries, where before only a handful of teams would be competing. This has resulted in far more people playing the game and many more travelling to watch, including those crossing continents and hemispheres to do so. Participation by the indigenous population has taken place in many countries, building on initial expat involvement which often was dominated either by former English residents or in many places, new residents from the Indian sub-continent. In Australia, involvement by indigenes in cricket began in the middle of the 19th century, and a tour by aboriginal cricketers to England in 1868 was the first international cricket tour by Australians. Before that, the only international travel for cricket had been by England, with a tour to Canada and the United States in 1859 and to Australia in 1861–1862 and 1863–1864. It was not until 1878 that what is regarded as the first representative Australian team visited England. Since then the globalisation of cricket has become complete, with all continents represented at the ICC.

The next chapter traces the origins and the development of the image of cricket, particularly in its place of origin, England, and the way it was played. The day of the gifted amateur is almost past in cricket, with a few exceptions, such as the matches between Oxford and Cambridge Universities, those between a very few other university teams and county XIs, and perhaps even fewer invitational and charity teams such as the Lord's Taverners and traditional village and country house teams. The images that are created by cricket, as Wheeller and Maitland note, are frequently stereotypical of the images of England itself. The game has contributed not only to the social and sporting development of the country but also to its literature and language. The playing of amateur cricket and travelling to watch it have become synonymous with a now vanishing way of life and much more emphasis now exists on the results of matches rather than the way they were played. Nevertheless, as argued in this chapter, cricket remains somewhat different to other sports because of its unique role in shaping society and behaviour, as well as sharing many aspects with tourism.

The present professional game has much higher costs in terms not only of pitches and their surroundings, but also because of the administrative and support teams that accompany and often control the teams of players. International touring test teams in the modern era generally are accompanied by even larger numbers of medical support personnel (therapists, dieticians and nutritionists), selectors, coaches, media spokespersons and logistical staff. The number of games played on a tour frequently includes five-day tests, one-day limited over matches and Twenty20 matches, as well as a number of 'training' and 'courtesy' games at the beginning and end of the tours. The impacts of these changes are discussed in the context of the places that host matches in the second section of the volume.

1 The Changing Boundaries and Geography of Cricket

Richard Butler

> *Oh, take me to a cricket ground,*
> *To hear the cricket's call,*
> *The soothing sentimental sound*
> *As bat belabours ball*
> *The Song of the Pitch*, Daniel Pettiward

Introduction

The advent of live television coverage of sport has often been anticipated to bring about the end or at least a decline in live attendance at sporting events, yet demand for space at such occasions has grown rather than diminished over the last half century for many sports. The Olympic Games, the World Cup in football and rugby, the 'World Series' in baseball, the 'Super Bowl' in American football, the 'classic' horse races, the Ryder Cup in golf and the 'big four' events in tennis and golf, as well as key domestic competitions all see demand for tickets outstrip supply. The locations of some of these events sometimes far from their traditional markets do not seem to deter keen supporters and spectators from travelling long distances and incurring considerable costs to witness first-hand sporting excellence and competition (Earnheardt *et al.*, 2012). Sport tourism has become a recognised and major element in tourism and is responsible for the expenditure of massive funds on the creation of facilities, the holding of events and travelling to those events by spectators, participants and administrators and others (Hinch & Higham, 2004).

In the same vein, cricket is one of the oldest sports and its matches have attracted audiences over at least the past two centuries. For the most part, as with the majority of sports, the largest proportion of spectators has been from within the host country, that is, domestic tourists. In many cases these have been day spectators, travelling only a few miles to a game, whether it be on their local or neighbouring village green, or in a ground in their home town. The traditional backbone of professional cricket has been of a regional nature – county cricket in England, state, province or island matches in other countries – with matches traditionally lasting up to four days and the audience being primarily local with few travelling in support of the visiting team. Over the years, grounds have become more costly to operate and ways have had to be found to increase audiences as well as to extract money from other sources than simply seat sales. The rise of limited over cricket, particularly the Twenty20 format has seen a massive increase in numbers of spectators and expenditure at many matches, stimulated by additional forms of entertainment and offerings from food and beverages to souvenirs in many forms. One form of cricket that has long succeeded in attracting an international audience is test match cricket, initially between England and Australia and now including the 10 countries recognised with test match status by the International Cricket Council (ICC) (Table 1.1). Travelling internationally to watch a test match series involves considerable time and cost as modern day series last for several weeks for the test matches alone, and much longer if the additional matches in limited over formats are included. Long-haul air travel is inevitably involved in most cases as well as additional travel in the host country to the locations of the matches. The financial and time commitments involved are much greater than those for any other sporting event, many of which, like most of those mentioned earlier, involve only one game, or, for a particular country, a maximum of up to seven games, sometimes in the same location.

As with all sports, the nature of cricket (its rules, its rivalries, its fans and its spatial dimensions), is highly dynamic. While cricket has perhaps been viewed as characterising past habits and beliefs more than most sports, it too has evolved. The 'tours' to Australia and other countries by English teams, for example, once involved long journeys by ship, fewer games overall in the visited country, a more gentle itinerary with more courtesy fixtures and a much smaller party of both players and administrators compared to the intensive and more competitive tours of the present day. For players there would almost always be only one tour each year and accompanying supporters from their home country would be extremely few in number and quiet in voice. The travels to the boundaries discussed in this volume involve both the travels of supporters and spectators to games of cricket around the globe in the present day, with an emphasis on international travel, and also on the changing travel of cricket itself, from England to its former colonies and then globally to scores of countries with few direct ties to the motherland. Cricket, as is tourism, is a strong manifestation of changing culture at a national and transnational level. Carter (2003) locates these changes specifically within the context of Northern Ireland and argues that shifting interpretations of 'Britishness' which have contributed to the post-1997 peace process, but also reflect growing multiculturalism, have also impacted on cricket in Northern Ireland, who plays the game and how it is played. Similar themes emerge in Fletcher's (2011) discussion of cricket and cultural/national identity when exploring the loyalties of British Asians, noting their dominant loyalty to teams from the Indian sub-continent which sits alongside support for England in other sports. Clearly, cricket cannot be divorced from the social and cultural context within which the game is played. However, this book makes no claims to provide an authoritative analysis of cricket from a socio-political perspective. Rather, our authors explore two independent socially constructed phenomena, cricket and tourism, and drill down into particular manifestations of their intersection. Our discussion is located within countries where this intersection is clearly evident, dominantly but not exclusively in England, Australia and India. As we show in this chapter, cricket certainly exists much more widely than in just these locations (as, indeed, does tourism) but it is our contention that the intersection with tourism is much more limited and is most effectively illustrated in contexts where it is of social and economic significance rather than a marginal and limited phenomenon. Therefore, we make no claims to representativeness in the range of locations that are included within this book. There is ample and fertile scope for further research to extend the boundaries of this discourse in cricketing, tourism and, indeed, socio-cultural and political senses, but this remains an agenda for the future.

Cricket has been seen and described in many works as the ultimate expression of Englishness, its origin clearly located in England's estates and villages (Wheeller & Maitland, Chapter 2, this volume). From England the game spread widely, most significantly in the 19th century to the British colonies of Australia, New Zealand, the West Indies, South Africa and the Indian sub-continent. As noted elsewhere in this volume (Butler, Chapter 11), it failed to become popular in Canada and the Americas generally, partly for climatic reasons and partly because of the soon-to-be-dominant influence of the United States in many facets of life, including sport (baseball in particular, along with basketball, despite the latter being a Canadian creation). A thriving cricket culture in the United States, particularly in the environs of Philadelphia, was undermined by hostility from the then Imperial Cricket Council which, in 1926, determined that 'the membership of the ICC should comprise, "governing bodies of cricket in countries within the Empire to which cricket teams are sent, or which send teams to England". This definition rather unfortunately excluded the United States, which had regularly received teams from England since 1859 and had dispatched several teams to England' (www.icc-cricket.com/the-icc/about_the_organisation/history.php). In the West Indies, despite the proximity of the United States and the career opportunities there in sport (for example, the number of Dominican Republic baseball players in the top US baseball leagues is out of all proportion to its population), cricket became and has remained extremely popular, primarily in what were the former British West Indies (Jamaica, Barbados, Antigua and Trinidad in particular). In the post-independence era, the rise of the West Indies cricket team to become the most feared team in international competition (due mostly to its superb fast bowlers and some outstanding charismatic batsmen) has epitomised, in a sense, the final throwing off the shackles of colonialism and subservience and the creation of a new image.

In a similar vein, in India it has been argued (Gooptu, 2004) that cricket represents one way in which that country has been able to dispel a feeling of inferiority to the Raj, a movement epitomised in the film *Lagaan*, which has gained cult status in that country and involves a village team in India playing a game of cricket against the British military occupying force and inevitably gaining a hard-earned victory and the removal of the military presence. In India, cricket has become the national sport and its followers in that country are the most numerous anywhere. Cricket is immensely strong in India at the domestic level also, particularly in the Twenty20 format, and crowds for games in the Indian Twenty20 league often outnumber those attending test matches.

It is arguable, therefore, that cricket has morphed from its state as the ultimate expression of Englishness and, by extension, a representation of imperial power and greatness, into what Mehta *et al.* (2009: 694) describe as 'a metaphor for the forces of globalisation and a vehicle for asserting new post-colonial identities'. Scalmer likewise traces the development of international cricket from its origins as a tool of ruling-class formation and control through symbolism of the class struggle to its contemporary commodification, concluding that 'the repackaging of cricket as a form of spectacular entertainment has increasingly stripped it of cultural power' (2007: 431). Underdown also comments on the social reality of this change in noting that 'in the latter part of the twentieth century the game's traditional aristocratic and gentry leaders have been replaced by representatives of the corporate and financial sectors, while at the same time arrangements for the timing and presentation of matches have been increasingly determined by the needs of television, on which so much of the sponsorship of cricket depends' (2006: 48). The seismic cultural shift from bastion of imperial/colonial power and control to instrument of contemporary commercialism that international cricket has experienced perhaps mirrors that in other institutions that owe their origins to the defunct British Empire, notably the Commonwealth and its institutions and activities.

In the 20th century, cricket experienced a resurgence in popularity and has appeared at international levels in more countries than was the case in the 19th century (see Table 1.1). With hindsight, some of that expansion was highly likely, if not inevitable, including, for example, the development of cricket in Pakistan, Sri Lanka and Bangladesh following their emergence as independent sovereign states; they are now well-established as test cricket teams. The mostly British expats in former Rhodesia (now Zimbabwe) created enough interest in cricket that Zimbabwe is now one of the test playing countries (Table 1.1), and the game is present in Kenya and Uganda, also at an international level, although the dominant participant group for a long time was the Asian community in both countries, a situation also found in Canada, Italy and elsewhere. The Masai in Kenya began to participate in cricket in 2007 through the involvement of a group called 'Cricket Without Boundaries' that has been involved in almost 40 projects to introduce cricket to communities in Africa (Atherton, 2012). The Masai team, like others, is involved in fundraising, in their case for education and awareness of HIV/AIDS (www.indiegogo.com/warriorsfilm). Elsewhere, in areas where the British Empire has had a presence, cricket is sometimes still played in what might be described as 'colonial' locations, for example, on the padangs in central Singapore and elsewhere in the Malaysian peninsula and Indonesia (see Noakes & Wilson, Chapter 6, this volume), and in Hong Kong and some

Table 1.1 Test match countries

Country	Date of first test
Australia	1877
England	1877
South Africa	1889
West Indies	1928
New Zealand	1930
India	1932
Pakistan	1952
Sri Lanka	1982
Zimbabwe	1992
Bangladesh	2000

Source: The Times (2012).

of the south Pacific islands, in particular Papua New Guinea, Fiji, Tonga and Samoa. In Papua New Guinea cricket has risen rapidly in appeal and in performance, with the first grass pitch being laid in 2010 and the national team ranked 19th at the time of writing by the ICC (Hobson, 2012).

In Europe, Scotland, Ireland and the Netherlands have international teams at what might be described as the second-tier level as associate members, able to play full one-day international matches against full member countries but, currently, excluded from test cricket. Indeed, the Irish team has enjoyed considerable success and a following on the world stage, including high-profile victories at two recent World Cups (see, for example, Johnston & Siggins, 2007; O'Brien & Siggins, 2011). These achievements were recognised and seized upon by Ryanair, the Irish budget airline, which advertised flights to Ireland 'The Home of Cricket' following the 2011 World Cup. Cricket also has a strong club presence in France and is played in Denmark, Finland, Germany, Greece, Italy and Switzerland, among others. Cricket was introduced to Italy in 1793 with a match in Naples between two teams from the fleet of Lord Nelson, and in 2013 Italy won the European Championship, beating Denmark in the final. Most of the players had overseas origins, including India, Pakistan, South Africa and Australia (Fasola *et al.*, 2013), More recently (2013), the Archbishop of Canterbury, on a visit to Rome, accepted a challenge to the Church of England from the Vatican Cricket Club, the details of the match have yet to be settled. In Germany cricket was played by British army officers in the 1950s adjacent to the Berlin Olympic stadium 'to make a political statement about the racial ideology of the Nazis and the civilising effect of the game' (Boyes, 2011: 45). The present-day occupiers of that pitch (German and also Afghanistan, Australian, British, Indian and Pakistani players), which is the 'cradle of the German cricket team' (Boyes, 2011: 45), are now facing removal from the location on the grounds of the threat to the health and safety of passing pedestrians and have instead been offered part use of a polo field.

The fact that cricket has long left its English rural home and become an international pastime is amusingly illustrated in a letter to *The Times* that records cricket matches between the Geneva Cricket Club and the Paris Cricket Club in the mid-1950s, matches that took place in Paris with the Swiss team fielding no Swiss players and the Paris team fielding no French players! (Rees, 2012). Things have apparently improved since then in that while in 2002 only three members of the French national team were French, in 2012 only three members were not French. This represents a great improvement from 1900 when at the first and only Olympic cricket match, the only teams participating were the French and the English. The French team at that time was mostly made up of British workers involved with constructing the Eiffel Tower, and the English team was the Devon and Somerset Wanderers Club, which was in Paris to watch the Olympics and became the *de facto* British team, winning the only Olympic gold medal for cricket by 158 runs (Sage, 2012).

In a few countries, of which Afghanistan is one, cricket appears to be stronger at the international level than at club or regional level, as witnessed by Afghanistan's recent appearance in international competitions, a rather surprising reversal of the normal development pattern of moving from local to national levels. The success of cricket in Afghanistan and of Afghan cricket generally is vividly recorded in *Out of the Ashes* by Albone (2011), who notes that from a beginning in 1987, Afghan cricket has expanded and improved so much that the national team came incredibly close to qualifying for the 2011 World Cup. Further east, cricket can be found in South Korea, Japan and, most recently, in China, where a Marylebone Cricket Club (MCC) team under former England captain Mike Gatting visited in 2011 to play two matches against the Chinese national side (and a 50-over match in Hong Kong) as part of the MCC's intent to support the development of cricket throughout the world. China became an affiliate member of the ICC in 2004 (*The Times*, 2011) and, given that country's record of the rapid development of players in a variety of sports, the appearance of a strong Chinese national cricket team can be anticipated in the relatively near future.

As we have noted, in other cases the emergence of cricket has been in response to media (particularly television) coverage of the game and the financial rewards available from holding competitions in somewhat surprising locations (Dubai and Abu Dhabi for example). Appropriately, if belatedly, cricket in most, if not all, of those countries mentioned above has permeated the indigenous population to varying degrees (Kidd, 2012). It is perhaps appropriate to note that a team of Aboriginal Australians toured England as early as 1868, before the Ashes competitions began. While some anachronistic clubs still remain in the 19th century in terms of membership and attitudes, cricket generally has shed the paternalism of English dominance. Rather like golf, the rules of cricket have traditionally been decided in the origin country (England for cricket, Scotland in the case of golf, through the Royal and Ancient Club in St Andrews), but power over the game has become increasingly more democratic, and in cricket's case has moved from its traditional home (Lord's and the MCC, as discussed by Cardwell & Ali, Chapter 4, this volume) to India. This reflects in part the income generated by the various forms of the game in the sub-continent (just as the rules of golf in the US and Mexico are now controlled by the US-based PGA). The newly created alternatives to the five-day test match form of cricket (in particular limited over one-day cricket and Twenty20) have undoubtedly helped the spread of cricket to new wickets, requiring less time commitment by both spectators and players (in 1939 an England-South Africa test lasted for ten days) and also allowing for multiple country competitions rather than the one-on-one format of traditional test cricket. Wickets no longer have to be prepared to withstand four or five days of continuous play, and with the introduction of 'drop-in' pitches and floodlighting, games can be scheduled more frequently and can be completed in far less than what would have been a full day's play under traditional conditions. Changes in kit, balls, rules and teams have undoubtedly accounted in part for the rapid rise in popularity of cricket in a growing number of markets, much of this stemming from the impetus provided by Kerry Packer in Australia (Higham & Scott, 2010). Packer was the first to visualise and take advantage of the possibility of linking sport and television at a level not previously experienced, reaping vast financial rewards as a result.

Thus, in the last 500 years cricket has taken on a variety of forms, retaining its original timescale and pinnacle of the five-day test match but widening its offerings to include matches as short as 40 overs, even at the international level, and increasing its market in terms of audience appeal and numbers of countries involved in organised cricket at all levels from club to national and international. With this increased participation and popularity has come an increased interest in following cricket, particularly at the international level. The fourth test in the 2013 series in Australia saw a new record number of spectators (over 91,000) in attendance at the Melbourne Cricket Ground for the first and second days of the match, suggesting that despite doubts about its long-term survival, five-day test cricket can still attract many to the boundary. While attendance at formal sub-national levels (county cricket in England, state level in Australia, for example) may have declined in some countries, overall attendance at professional games has increased enormously, especially in the case of Twenty20 in India. The number of international games and competitions (test series, World Cups) has increased also and so too have the numbers of supporters travelling to such events to support their national or regional team. The rise of the *Barmy Army* and *Swami Army* (see chapters by Emery et al. (Chapter 9) and Baum (Chapter 10), this volume) vividly illustrate this phenomenon and make a strong case for linking cricket and tourism. The increase in the numbers of supporters travelling is mirrored by an increase in the numbers of participants involved; team groups have become larger, supporting staff now regularly outnumber players and international tours have become much more frequent (with attendant problems for players, as Pearce at least (Chapter 7, this volume) has noted). About the only area in which international competition has not existed or expanded for many years has been that between India and Pakistan, reflecting issues arising from the partition of India in 1948. While test matches were played occasionally in the years following partition, they ceased to be held in 1961 and were not resumed until 1978, being suspended again in 1984. Beech *et al.* in Chapter 8 discuss the role of cricket in reconciliation between India and Pakistan, in particular the test series in 2004. Few issues are as important as those involved in this example, and while international cricket is not being played in Pakistan at the present time because of security risks and the potential of violence to players and spectators, matches between India and Pakistan have continued in the interim in competitions in other countries, such as Dubai and England.

The boundaries of cricket have certainly been extended since its inception in the distant past. The 'white flannelled fools' have given way in part to multicoloured warriors of teams with exotic and provocative names, and the class-ridden distinctions between 'gentlemen' and 'players' have long gone in the democratisation of the game. Cricket now presents many different faces to many different audiences and has survived some difficult times to emerge overall stronger and more popular than it has ever been. Most recently, the boundaries have been extended to include the classroom, with the Governor of the Bank of England heading a campaign in schools to use cricket as a teaching tool, particularly in maths (Hopkins, 2011). In the US, one of the most unique cricket teams has emerged from Los Angeles, namely the Compton Cricket Club (www.comptoncricketclub.org). Known first as the LAKrickets, the team has also been called the Compton Homies and the Popz, and has achieved considerable media attention from having 'rapped' at Windsor Castle, and having presented Gerry Adams with a cricket bat to help broker the peace treaty in Northern Ireland in 1999. The team originated in the homeless community in downtown Los Angeles and included former gang members. Their combination of cricket and rap remains somewhat unique but illustrates the widespread and varying appeal of the game. Since their creation this team has toured Australia and Britain, and been active in using cricket to relay a message of peace and respect to others far beyond their home turf.

The chapters which follow address the various themes mentioned above. The historical aspect of cricket represents a dynamic form of heritage, particularly for England and Australia, the oldest of 'foes', through the myths surrounding 'the Ashes'. Cardwell and Ali (Chapter 4), in their review of Lord's and the element of nostalgia which a visit to the 'home of cricket' strengthens, illustrate clearly the ongoing affection for the rivalry over the Ashes and what that rivalry and legacy have come to represent. Lord's is much more than a cricket ground, just as the *Old Course* at St Andrews is much more than a golf course. Each represents, in similar ways, the 'soul' of its sport, and a visit to either site is often described as a once-in-a-lifetime experience and akin to a pilgrimage, its Mecca in terms of almost religious and spiritual feeling. While golfers have the possibility of being able to actually play on their 'sacred ground' at St Andrews, cricketers do not seem to miss such an opportunity, perhaps recognising that to do so would mean they had reached the ultimate level in the sport, and are instead satisfied with observing the relics and the atmosphere of cricket's sanctum. White's discussion of Rupertswood follows a similar theme by exploring the issues involved in preserving cricketing heritage at the birthplace of the Ashes (Chapter 3). Although not as well-known as Lord's, and not being a current venue of first-class cricket, Rupertswood holds a special place as a truly iconic site in the history of cricket and one still visited by many cricket enthusiasts.

One of the issues raised in the discussion of Rupertswood is that of the economic difficulty of maintaining heritage properties and attracting audiences. This is the focus of Parrett's review of the development and redevelopment of the Rose Bowl, the new home of Hampshire County Cricket (Chapter 5). It becomes clear that in the current era four-day county cricket, along with an infrequent test match, even when also supported by Twenty20 matches, is insufficient to maintain economic viability in a purpose-built oval. The Rose Bowl subsequently has gone from being a cricket ground to becoming a year-round leisure facility with additional activities including golf, fitness, training facilities and conference and hotel services incorporated or planned into the complex. Even with such additions, the financial future is not entirely secured. Many other cricket grounds face similar problems, and recent developments implemented and rejected at Lord's and The Oval in particular have created great controversy.

The difficulties of not only surviving financially but also maintaining sufficient interest and commitment in the game are shown vividly by Noakes and Wilson (Chapter 6) in their discussion of the emergence and survival of cricket in Bali, and more broadly in Indonesia generally. What began as an interest of expats, as in the case of cricket in Provence in France and many other areas, grew to create an interest by indigenous players, culminating in the participation of an Indonesian team in international competitions. The particular requirements of formal cricket – the pitch as well as relatively large-sized teams, plus umpires and scorers and player equipment – mean that the commitment is significant and survival is rarely guaranteed. Even where commitment is strong, unless it is broadly based rather than dependent on a few keen devotees, it is likely to wane over time and thus needs continuous reinforcement.

The theme of this volume is the relationship between cricket and travel (tourism) and this is vividly described by Emery *et al.* (Chapter 9) in their review of the 'Armies' of supporters who travel internationally as well as locally to support their national teams. The main armies discussed in Chapter 9 have seen their cohorts grow and benefit from their organisation, by being able to secure advantageous packages of travel, accommodation and tickets to games, as well as mutual support at games and in the attendant travel. Such logistic support was absent for Baum (Chapter 10), who describes his experience of suddenly and rather fortuitously becoming an international cricketing supporter in India, and his interaction both with the *Barmy Army* and with local supporters in brief encounters at the Nagpur 2012 test match between England and India. The travails of travel and organisation in his case are greater than those of the players themselves (with whom he shared his hotel), but the pressures of being an international cricketer are clearly outlined by Pearce (Chapter 7). The players' experiences involve issues of culture shock and culture confusion, learning in the field (figuratively and literally) and motivation. Pearce notes the ways in which some players can handle such problems and how others face great personal difficulty. While his examples are drawn mostly from the writings of Australian players, clearly the problems are universal. In recent years England has lost the services of one of its most successful opening batsmen, Marcus Trescothick, whose personal issues surrounding being unable to stand the stress of being absent from home and family caused him to retire from international cricket prematurely. And most recently (2013), Jonathan Trott departed the test series with Australia because of stress-related problems. Trescothick successfully resumed his county cricketing career but has not returned to the international arena, and time will tell if Trott can recover and overcome the problems of international travel and competition.

Cricket, for all its image of gentility and peacefulness, appears to charge a high price of its participants, especially at the highest levels, with higher than average rates of suicide amongst professional cricketers at relatively early ages. One issue not raised by Pearce but perhaps of relevance is the fact that test cricketers now are considerably younger than their forebears of half a century ago. The current England captain, Cook, is in his 20s, in sharp contrast to players of a generation or more ago, such as Compton, who was recalled to test duties at the age of 50, and the fact that the touring teams at the time of the 'Bodyline' test series had an average age in their 30s rather than their 20s. The pressures of being away from home, performing in different cultures with little time for adjustment and participating in what has become an increasingly competitive job market are very different from the tours of the pre-war era, which involved travel by boat for several days if not weeks, with far fewer matches in a tour spread over a longer time period, and probably only one tour a year, compared to several tours a year for current players. In the days of gentlemen and players, only a few individuals had a job that was dependent on their cricketing ability and performance, and competition was not at the level experienced today, with national, county or state and Twenty20 competition contracts to be won and retained.

The changes between the image of cricket as part of the rural idyll as discussed by Wheeller and Maitland (Chapter 2) and the present-day forms of the game are enormous. Whether cricket is still a part of the essence of Englishness, or even valid for use in the 'Tebbit' test of nationality is questionable. (Lord Tebbit, a former Cabinet minister, suggested that a measure of an immigrant's nationality was which team they would support in a cricket match between England and their original home country.) Cricket matches today have become almost as fervently nationalistic as football matches, with supporters of visiting teams presenting an often loud and very identifiable presence at grounds, and players engaging in 'sledging' rather than polite banter at the wicket. The advent of Twenty20 and the deliberate excitement created at such matches have done little to encourage the retention of tranquility that has traditionally been associated with cricket played on village greens or the lawns of stately homes, as so eloquently described by Wheeller and Maitland.

To survive in the 21st century is difficult for many sports and traditional activities, and cricket perhaps faces a more difficult future than many other sports. The nostalgia which it invokes is both a strength and a weakness. Resistance to change, both in the game itself and at its ovals, has been enormous, as arguments over developments at Lord's and The Oval mentioned above demonstrate clearly. Resistance to changes in the game itself has failed to a large degree as now four forms of professional cricket (test and county/state/province five- and four-day, limited over one-day, and Twenty20) are all well established. Whether all forms will survive is questionable and many have doubted the ability of test cricket or four-day or limited over formats to remain for a long time. To the dismay of many purists (Rees-Mogg, 2011), Twenty20 seems likely to survive for some time, particularly in India where it has become a virtual licence to print money and been responsible in part for the shift in control of cricket to the sub-continent. Inevitably, the amount of money now involved in cricket is causing conflicts similar to those relating to the disappearance of the distinction between gentlemen and players. A recent example being the decision by Sky Sports to deliver its live commentary on the most recent test series between England and India from a studio in England rather than from the Indian cricket grounds where the game was being played. This was in response to a sudden and late demand from the Board of Control for Cricket in India for a fee of £500,000, and resulted in the live television coverage being provided by Star TV from India and the ball-by-ball commentary being overlain in England. Examples of match fixing and cheating relating to the large sums of money now being gambled on games, players and even specific events such as wides or dropped catches, are also seen as evidence of the pernicious influence of the commercialisation of cricket and its financial implications.

Despite the problems mentioned above, 2011 saw the staging of the 2000th test match, appropriately at Lord's, which has held more test matches (122) than any other ground, although the honour of hosting the first test match fell to the Melbourne Cricket Ground in 1877. While it took over 19 years for the first 50 test matches to be held, it took only 11 years for the last 500 matches to be completed, such is the frequency of international cricket today. Whether test cricket will survive another century or more is constantly under debate and is the subject of a film (*Death of a Gentleman*) in production at the time of writing (www.deathofagentlemanfilm.com), which explores the views of players, former players and administrators but fails to achieve a consensus on the likelihood of another 2000 test matches.

With few exceptions, travel to watch cricket is confined to the professional forms of the game. Spectators at amateur cricket matches are few and far between unless celebrities are involved or strong local rivalries exist. Yet large numbers of matches are played in multiple locations at various levels of performance. Near the bottom of the performance table would be the rank amateurs, or 'coarse cricketers'. While cricket is a challenge in any form, to a 'coarse cricketer' (Butler, Chapter 11, this volume) Twenty20 is a form of cricket lying even further from his talents at the game than any other. Scoring runs (let alone scoring them rapidly) is dubious to coarse cricketers, bowling to either take wickets or restrict run-scoring by the opposition is next to impossible, and the standard of fielding and athleticism is far beyond the average coarse cricketer's dreams, let alone execution. Being able to hold up one's end when batting, bowling the occasional relief over and plugging a hole en route to the boundary represents the summit of a coarse cricketer's hopes. Watching test cricket, on television, in one's own country or abroad is much more the reality of many such a person's commitment to the game.

Increasingly, and fortunately for the game, following one's cricket team, at home and abroad, either as an 'army' conscript, on a family holiday or on an academic junket is becoming increasingly popular, perhaps allowing support for the belief that travels to the boundary, wherever it may be, are likely to continue by both players and supporters, whatever the form of cricket being played.

References

Albone, T. (2011) *Out of the Ashes: The Remarkable Rise and Rise of the Afghanistan Cricket Team*. London: Virgin.

Atherton, M. (2012) Anderson's film link helping Aids awareness. *The Times*, 13 December, p. 86.

Boyes, R. (2011) Cricketers are driven off their pitch after 60 years in the shadow of Hitler's stadium. *The Times*, 9 April, p. 45.

Carter, T. (2003) In the spirit of the game? Cricket and changing notions of being British in Northern Ireland. *Journal of the Society for the Anthropology of Europe* 3 (1), 14–26.

Earnheardt, A.C., Haridakis, P.M. and Hugenberg, B.S. (2012) *Sports Fans, Identity and Socialization: Exploring the Fandemonium*. Lanham, MD: Lexington Books.

Fasola, di G., Lombardo, I. and Moscatelli, F. (2013) *Italian Cricket Club*. ADD: Milan.

Fletcher, D. (2011) Identity and divided loyalties amongst British Indians. *International Review of the Sociology of Sport* 47 (5), 612–631.

Gooptu, S. (2004) Cricket or cricket spectacle? Looking beyond cricket to understand Lagaan. *The International Journal of the History of Sport* 21 (3–4), 533–548.

Higham, J. and Cohen, S. (2010) Kerry Packer: World Series Cricket (WSC) and the (R)Evolution of modern sports-related tourism. In R.W. Butler and R. Russell (eds) *Giants of Tourism* (pp. 182–197). Wallinford: CABI.

Hinch, T. and Higham, J. (2004) *Sport Tourism Development* (1st edn). Clevedon: Channel View Publications.

Hobson, R. (2012) Jones ready to rise from the Ashes and help game prosper in his homeland. *The Times*, 27 February, p. 52.

Hopkins, K. (2011) Counting cricket and king. *The Times*, 30 June, p. 49.

Johnston, T. and Siggins, G. (2007) *Raiders of the Caribbean*. Dublin: O'Brien Press.

Kidd, P. (2012) Warriors of the wasteland offer concrete evidence of progress. *The Times*, 25 January.

Mehta, N., Gemmell, J. and Malcolm, D. (2009) 'Bombay sports exchange': Cricket, globalisation and the future. *Sport in Society* 12 (4–5), 694–707.

O'Brien, K. and Siggins, G. (2011) *Six after six: Ireland's Cricket World Cup 2011*. Brickfields Press.

Pettiward, D. (1939) *Truly Rural*. London: Dent.

Rees, G. (2012) Letters to the editor: Paris match. *The Times*, 18 April, p. 22.

Rees-Mogg, W. (2011) For a sport to savour, Twenty20 isn't cricket. *The Times*, 22 July, p. 24.

Sage, A. (2012) Team of (mostly) French cricketers seek to avenge a hundred years of pain. *The Times*, 13 April, p. 36.

Scalmer, S. (2007) Cricket, imperialism and class domination. *WorkingUSA: The Journal of Labor and Society* 10, 431–442.

The Times (2011) Gatting eyes Chinese. *The Times*, 19 April, p. 61.

The Times (2012) 2,000th *Times Sport* marks a great moment in the history of the game. *The Times*, 19 February, pp. 54–55.

Underdown, D. (2006) The history of cricket. *History Compass* 4 (1), 43–53.

2 Looking for Witney Scrotum? Cricket, Tourism and Images of England

Brian Wheeller and Robert Maitland

> *Cricket is an English game,*
> *A game of quiet understatement,*
> *Of gentle summer days,...*
> *And gentle English ways:*
> *Fever-abatment*
> *Under another name.*
>
> *It is not suited to hot-blooded races,*
> *Although we export it to other places...*
> *It might have been our fates*
> *To civilise the whole United States...*
> *But, no.*
> *True cricket is a game*
> *Of gentle English scenes,*
> *For poets dozing on quaint village green*
> *And not the same*
> *As cricket where there's so much dash and din*
> *And people play it so they can* **win**
> *Lovely Cricket*, John Groves

Opening Up[1]

Those in the UK with an ear (as well as an eye) for cricket will be more than familiar with the 'calypso-esque' rhythm of Booker T. and the M.G.'s 'Soul Limbo' (BBC TV cricket's theme music) and, maybe, even 10cc's immortal line 'I don't like cricket, I love it' from the 'Dreadlock Holiday' single. Taken (appropriately) from their 1979 *Bloody Tourists* album it has been re-worked, incorporating the more embracing 'we', for contemporary Sky Sports cricket coverage. Less familiar to cricket fans' audio senses may be Roy Harper's threnody (1975) 'When an Old Cricketer Leaves his Crease'. A friend's brother, exiled in Toronto, 'always plays this when homesick as it is quintessentially English'. Harper, commenting on his work, talks of the track as being one of his highlights – 'My childhood memories of the heroic stature of the footballers and cricketers of the day invoke the sounds that went along with them. Paramount among these was the traditional Northern English brass band, which was a functional social component through all four seasons, being seen and heard in many different contexts. My use of that style of music on "Old Cricketer" is a tribute to those distant memories.'

While on a music theme, although its actual machinations remain mysteriously vague, the name Duckworth Lewis Method is lodged, notoriously, in the minds of most cricketing buffs: the eponymous CD probably not. We refer here to the CD of said name, released in 2009, by the Duckworth Lewis Method group (no relation to the original duo). Well worth a listen to by any self-respecting cricket aficionado with an interest in mind excursions. And mind excursions to the past (which, as L.P. Hartley (2004 [1953]: 1) so memorably put it '...is a foreign country: they do things differently there') are, indeed, where many thoughts of cricket wander.

This chapter suggests that there are links between cricket and travel, but our focus is not simply on travel in a spatial sense, although that is certainly an important element in cricket – tours have been an integral part of the game, for players and spectators, since the 19th century. We are also interested in the links between tourism and cricket through travel in a temporal sense, and the ways in which both cricket and tourism draw on and promote nostalgia, often in ways that link to searches for and reinterpretation of national identities. Numerous books on cricket are within the travel writing genre, in that they frequently incorporate 'a sentimental journey', loosely defined, and usually lament the decline of the game. Lazenby's *Test of Time. Travels in Search of a Cricketing Legend* (2005), in which he retraces the footsteps of his cricketing grandfather's 1897–1898 Ashes tour to Australia, is a classic example – an intriguingly interwoven personal history and travel narrative. As the cover notes 'His tour becomes a cricketing pilgrimage and voyage of discovery...a unique personal history and an evocative portrait of a bygone era' (Lazenby, 2005). The personal touch is fundamental to Simkins' wonderful *The Last Flannelled Fool* (2011), in which he, too, embarks on a journey – simultaneously physical in that he revisits childhood haunts around England while 'undertaking' an exploration via self-reflective introspection through reliving memories. The affectionate cover notes reflect the interplay of cricket and travel. For Marcus Berkmann this is 'One of those rambling, picaresque, unashamedly nostalgic travel books that so enliven a summer afternoon ... funny, crafty and written with extraordinary verve.' While for Graham Boynton 'Michael Simkin's latest ramble around England is supposed to be about cricket but it is much more than that.'

To an extent adopting a similar stance, Travis Elborough (2010) delights in a history of the British love affair with the seaside, where childhood memories are entwined with nostalgia for a vanished age. Reading *Wish You Were Here: England on Sea* evokes whimsical, comfortable, old-fashioned sentiments. So, too, does the *Last Flannelled Fool*. Read in tandem, these two excellent books (with Simkins' and Elborough's common melancholic longings) are the perfect paired combination for those with a love, fascination and appreciation of both cricket and the English seaside.

Nostalgia is bound up with cricket, but also with sport more generally: and with tourism. As Dann and Theobold (1995) say, nostalgia has long been used in tourism development, and draws on dissatisfaction with current – and expected future – social arrangements to look back at times that can be seen as in some way better. But nostalgia is not confined to looking back simply on one's own personal experiences. Fairley and Gammon (2005) point out that nostalgia can be learned, through a process of socialisation – like storytelling – and through learning about past events and the meaning they hold; it is an important part of heritage tourism (Palmer, 1999). Sport experiences, or accounts of them, are rich sources of story and nostalgia. In the third test England played against the West Indies at Old Trafford in 1976, 45-year-old Brian Close, recalled to the England team nine years after his last appearance, unflinchingly took hit after fearsome hit on his unprotected body from the superb fast bowling of Holding, Roberts and Daniel in one of the bravest innings cricket has seen. It is not necessary to have been there to think, nostalgically, that cricketers were grittier and tougher in those times. Nostalgia, myth and storytelling are central to our sense of ourselves; they are some of the means through which national identities are constructed and reconstructed. Sports and national identity have been closely linked since the early 1800s (Frew, 2011), while much tourism revolves around historic symbols and sights that are important in constructing national identity (Palmer, 1999). In times when nations and identities are increasingly fluid, tourism representation is 'a means through which different and contested versions of the national story can be tried out and developed' (Maitland, 2012: 14). We suggest that cricket is a particularly rich source of stories, of travel spatially but also in time to the past – that foreign country – and plays an important role in tourism and tourism representation.

Ed Smith, a former England cricketer who went on to captain Middlesex, argues that 'sport has a rich conceptual framework if only we would open our eyes to it' (Smith, 2008: xiv). In his book *What Sport Tells Us About Life* he reflects on some of the insights he gained in his cricket-playing career and uses them as a basis for thinking about the world at large, covering a wide and eclectic range of topics. Paxman's *Fish, Fishing and the Meaning of Life* (1995) attempts the same for angling. Our approach here is similar but, we hope, more manageable – we want to consider what cricket tells us about tourism, in a specifically English context. As we have already suggested, there are strong links and parallels between the two – after all, Geoffrey Moorhouse, a prolific travel writer, also wrote fine books on cricket, which he once described as 'travel writing in disguise' (quoted in Hamilton, 2010: 291). Like Smith, we hope this will spark new arguments, and provoke disagreement as well as perhaps provide new insights – we offer a discursive discussion rather than drawing on new research and fieldwork. Deploying a possibly idiosyncratic array of cultural references (but with a leaning towards literature) we attempt, by way of illustration, to pursue, and reflect on, some of the obvious, as well as the less tangible, links between cricket and tourism.

My World in Cricket[2]

'…a cricketer always makes a good impression'. So sayeth the shrewd Sunny Farebrother in Powell's (1951: 102) masterpiece of English etiquette and manners, his opus, *A Dance to the Music of Time*. Though Powell was writing about the 1920s – and leaving aside the obvious exceptions of the likes of Butt and Asif, Westfield, the excesses of Flintoff and Pietersen and the tragedy of Cronje – generally, this maxim still holds true today. Indeed, Farebrother's aphorism is probably applicable to both cricketer and cricket alike. After all, certain aspects of cricket (with its positive connotations of wholesome 'play the game, chaps' air of decency) generally retain a flattering image in the public conscience. It is hard, though, to imagine such a positive, glowing endorsement being applied, generically, to 'tourism', still less 'a tourist'. Quite the contrary, in fact, both latter terms being recipients of considerable scorn, derision and loathing. And yet, of course, 'travel' and 'the traveller' escape such odious odium.

Cricket plays an important role in how England is represented – to tourists and to itself. As a sport, as an institution and as a set of cultural practices it has a central role in changing ideas about English national identity and in how the nation sees itself. That means it is also central to tourism – in attracting and setting the expectations of foreign visitors and of the host community. We can see this in how England is marketed as a destination. VisitEngland, the national tourism organisation, promotes the country on its website through three key sporting icons – the FA Cup, Wimbledon, and cricket at Lord's. These seem to have been chosen not because they represent English success in the wider world – the FA Cup is a purely domestic competition, and an Englishman last won the Wimbledon singles title in 1936 – but because they are seen not simply as sporting events, but as a part of England and its history. As Gammon and Ramshaw (2007) say, sport is part of a country's national heritage, part of the nation's fabric, and as such it transcends being simply 'sport' and becomes representative of a people. This seems particularly true of cricket. For Haseler (1996), cricket – notably in the three-, four- or five-day games, and to a lesser extent at league or club level on Saturday and Sunday afternoons – exhibits and encourages a range of supposedly 'sturdy' 'English' qualities: perseverance, patience, team spirit... and, of course, 'fair play'. It is a measure of the extraordinary success of cricket as an English ritual and totem of national character that so much of the terminology of the game has entered into the mainstream of everyday usage: 'sticky wicket', 'close of play', 'stumped me', 'hit for six', 'straight bat', and the like, are all very English phrases (Haseler, 1996: 59).

As Fox (2005: 10) points out, commentators on the decline of English national identity conducting 'post-mortems on Englishness' see a society where breaches of 'traditional rules' like unsporting behaviour in cricket are evidence of decline, and innovations and new cultural norms are to be treated sceptically. These tensions underlie essential debates about the nature of England, different versions of the national story, and how it should be represented as a destination – an old country with royal heritage or a young country – Cool Britannia? These tensions reflect not simply marketing decisions, but contests over the cultural values and identity, and the reinvention, of tradition (Hobsbawm & Ranger, 1983) as societies change. We can see these contests played out in cricket: extended test match series and the county cricket championship or innumerable one-day internationals and Twenty20? Of course all sports have to adapt to a changing world, and sometimes do so with difficulty. But as Hamilton (2010: 285) says:

> no sport so urgently feels the tug of war between modernity and tradition than cricket...in a struggle with itself over whether...(it)...is relevant and really matters...whether it can be tinkered with or improved to compete with more flashy, snazzy sports...But for all the remodelling, cricket still has a cultural nostalgia about it, which contributes to its perpetual charm and inspires devotion.

If we substitute the word 'England' for cricket in this quotation, we have a pretty good summary of contemporary debates about national identity, and about how the nature of England should be represented to visitors and to those who live here. The Marylebone Cricket Club's (MCC) involvement with the financier Allen Stanford stands as a metaphor for attempts at modernisation. In 2008, the MCC signed an agreement with Stanford for a Twenty20 cricket tournament, with total prize money of $20 m. This was publicised by Stanford arriving at Lord's – the 'home of cricket' – in a helicopter in a photo opportunity that featured the prize money, in cash, in a transparent case. Uneasiness about this flashy presentation and the nature of the tournament delayed its progress until it was overtaken by events. Stanford was charged with fraud and is now serving a 110 year sentence in a US prison. This uneasy and in many respects incompetent attempt to engage with a modernity that stands outside cultural traditions can be seen in England more broadly – the engagement with banking and international finance most obviously – but with tourism representation specifically. The Millennium Dome, intended as a symbol to the world of Britain as the then prime minister's 'young country', renewing itself for the 21st century, proved an expensive and embarrassing flop, with pictures of queues and failing transport infrastructure relayed around the world. The surprising success and worldwide acclaim bestowed on the London Olympics has, however, (temporarily?) reversed this trend, the Games apparently a modernising and refreshing representation for potential visitors.

In this respect, on the marketing front it would seem that any exposure is considered good exposure, witness the MCC's eager involvement in the Olympic jamboree of 'show-casing' the UK's tourism potential to the world. John Stephenson, MCC's head of cricket, in response to queries about Lord's being used as an Olympic venue for archery, thought the Games would showcase Lord's to the world: '... this is a once-in-a-lifetime experience. The world of cricket realises it's a unique event. It's a chance for the ground to be exposed to a wider sporting global audience' (in Feekins, 2012: 18), thereby reiterating a familiar VisitEngland sales mantra.

Head On[3]

The struggle between traditional and modern in cricket has other parallels in tourism. We can see attempts to modernise cricket as a process of commoditisation, as the game itself and its culture – what it means and the experience it offers – are changed in order to attract more spectators or, more importantly, to generate higher revenues. Localism has long been a strong element in cricket. Different national sides have been seen to have different approaches and cultures – West Indian and Indian teams having very different strengths, for example. 'There are five major cricketing sub-cultures in the world: the traditional play-up-chaps MCC view; the hard as nails professional version, centred on Yorkshire; the even tougher Australian way; the West Indian, carefree-seeming, but with angry overtones; and the subtle Indian game. These are caricatures, of course, but fair ones. The last four types all exist in opposition to the first' (Engel, in Berkmann, 2011: 4). Within nations, the differences between localities have been at least as strong: for example, the contrast between Surrey and Yorkshire, historically the two most successful sides in the County Championship. Despite regional differences, cricket culture long retained some of the spirit of amateurism. That meant more than fair play – 'it's not cricket' – and included valuing the game for itself, rather than as a business opportunity. For Surrey supporters, cricket remains 'a way of life', drawing on amateur and gentlemanly traditions, and games that were arranged as a series of friendlies rather than in competitive leagues (Stone, 2008). Regional differences are distinct, but that devotion to the game in its own right is shared in Yorkshire, Lancashire and other parts of the north that in the past drew more on the grittier tradition of league cricket and professionalism, and where the game was taken more seriously by players and spectators (Stone, 2008). Crowds were generally knowledgeable and cultures and traditions developed organically and locally. Trying to make cricket racy, as in Twenty20, has meant seeking new, generally less knowledgeable audiences, and overlaying historic, local and organic cultures with imported and commercial practices, such as amplified music accompanying wickets and boundaries, cheerleaders and other entertainment during intervals, along with noisy and excitable public address (PA) commentary. 'Tourists show how game is being degraded' (Berry, 2012) is an apposite headline here.

We might see in this a parallel with tourism developments. It would be going too far to claim a cricket life-cycle comparable to Butler's (1980) acknowledged tourism area life-cycle, yet some elements are mirrored in the game's at times desperate attempts to reinvent itself – the conversion to a mass product, the commodification that results, undermining the original attraction of place or game, control moving from 'the local' to large international corporations, outside of local influence: values eroded by cricket's modernisation. Airing his views on Pietersen, Pringle (2012, S8) asserts 'Like Shakespeare's seven ages of man, cricketers have three phases of their playing life. At first, they play for love and experience, then, as they begin to improve, they play for glory before they spend their dotage chasing the money.' Cricketers have their own life-cycle: so, too, it would seem does cricket itself.

We might equally see points of comparison with McKercher's (2002) typology of cultural tourists. McKercher suggests that cultural tourists can be classified along two dimensions – the centrality of culture to their trip, and the depth of their experience. On this basis, those for whom culture is important and the experience deep – purposeful cultural tourists – would be in a minority, while the others – incidental, casual, sightseeing or serendipitous tourists – would predominate. In cricket we could see a move away from spectators who are there primarily for the game itself, and who are knowledgeable and seeking a deep 'cricket' experience – purposeful cricket watchers – to those for whom the cricket is increasingly incidental – a backdrop to business networking and entertainment (see Butler, Chapter 11, this volume), or for after work drinking with friends, or a generalised kind of sporting entertainment in the short period when there is no football. Much cricket writing – in books, newspapers, blogs and supporters' forums – agonises about change and commercialisation, and the danger that the spirit of cricket will be lost.

But why should cricket – rather than other sports and activities – be seen as of particular importance? Cricket has a particular place in the representation of England to tourists, partly because of its extensive literature, but more because of its place in the landscape and how this is constructed as 'English'. Cricket has prompted far more writing than any other English sport, and according to an *Economist* article, cricket books account for half of all books written on sport (http://moreintelligentlife.com/story/the-man-with-the-largest-collection-of-cricket-books). This cricket writing encompasses a broad range as well as a large volume. The non-fiction most famously includes the *Wisden Cricketers' Almanack*, published annually since 1864, which carefully documents matches (and – of course – tours to, from and within England) as well as autobiography and memoirs by current and former players, and reflections and analysis by commentators, journalists and non-playing enthusiasts. Fictional and semi-autobiographical portrayals of cricket include stories of particular games, usually village cricket (for example A.G. MacDonnell, 1933; Hugh de Selincourt, 1924; Michael Simkins, 2011), and often draw on the idea of a continuing, living English identity reaching back hundreds of years and rooted in the countryside – very much the stuff of much tourism representation. By the end of the 19th century and after a long period of comparative peace at home in England, cricket's traditions could be seen as a more general guide to life – even to war. Sir Henry Newbolt evoked the spirit of cricket as a steadying force in the heat of battle in his famous poem 'Vitaï Lampada'

(1910) which tells of a young man prompted to heroism in battle by his experience of cricket:

> The Gatling's jammed and the Colonel's dead...
> And England's far and honour a name... [but]
> The voice of a schoolboy rallies the ranks
> 'Play up! Play up! and Play the game'

This view did not long survive the first encounter with a powerful enemy and the nightmare of industrialised warfare. On the contrary, cricket is far more often a metaphor for a peace and tranquillity that is longed for in the chaos of war or other trouble (see for example, the work of Siegfried Sassoon (1928, 1930), or Robert Graves (1960 [1929]), both First World War infantry officers). The sheer volume of books that take cricket as their subject, and their explicit concern with England as a place – and hence as a destination – means that they play an important role in constructing the organic image of England. However this is not the only way in which cricket contributes to image making. Novelists, playwrights and screenwriters seem particularly to like cricket, and so it finds its way into their work as metaphor, image and allusion. In his book *Cricket Country*, about cricket and England and published during the Second World War, Edmund Blunden (1944) selected an XI comprising poets and writers that had played or enthusiastically followed cricket; it included Byron, Keats and Gerard Manley Hopkins as well as Sassoon. In 2012 the critic Michael Billington pointed out it would be easy to assemble an XI of contemporary playwrights passionate about the game – his included Samuel Beckett, Harold Pinter, Alan Ayckbourn, Tom Stoppard and David Hare; if film directors were eligible, Sam Mendes could join the team too.

This writing often gives a particular image of England and cricket, with an emphasis on village cricket and its place in the landscape. In a book seeking to identify and celebrate the distinctive and vernacular qualities of England, village cricket is seen as: 'the epitome of Englishness and for most of us a chanced-upon game on the green is hard to pass by. In your mind's eye you remember only untainted summer days, with white flannels against the fading green of the manicured pitch, and the sound of leather on willow' (Clifford & King, 2006: 117). Earlier, Haseler, in his *The English Tribe* (1996: 59) had written 'Of all the icons of theme-park heritage Englishness the most exalted must still be the game of cricket, particularly village cricket. No aspect of Englishness induces such sentimentality as the "leather on willow" images.' He goes on to (quite rightly) claim that 'the game has in reality become a metaphor for the celebration of the English village and rural nostalgia'. (In this light it is perhaps not surprising that the British Pavilion at the Montreal Expo of 1967 included a recording of John Arlott commentating on a test match at Lord's, along with other audio images such as the BBC shipping forecast and a reading of the football scores (Editors' comment).)

The images chosen could have been taken from a promotional tourism brochure or website, as indeed could the familiar, indeed clichéd, language – 'the sound of leather on willow'. That too shows how deeply cricket has penetrated the image of what England is like, and what it is like as a place to visit – peaceful, timeless, perhaps quietly melancholic and ironic. There is continuity here. Returning from fighting in the Spanish Civil War, George Orwell looked out from his train carriage at southern England 'probably the sleekest landscape in the world' and reflected on the country while relishing the peace and continuity it offered. It is not surprising that among the images of England that came into his mind – very much a roll call of tourism images, including men in bowler hats, pigeons in Trafalgar Square, red buses – 'posters telling of cricket matches and Royal weddings' figured prominently (Orwell, 1938: 220–221). He mentioned no other sport, of course.

No Boundaries[4]

Imbued, as it often is, with an intoxicating infusion of sentiment and nostalgia, of 'Englishness', cricket features, symbolically, in a variety of films and television series. On home soil (England's green and pleasant land), cricket matches, creating as they do the requisite ambience, often serve as a backdrop to re-enforce images of a middle England idyll: recurring in *Midsomer Murders*, *The Inspector Lynley Mysteries* and, naturally, *Inspector Morse* – witness the 1989 'Deceived in Flight' episode.

And, of course, in films located abroad cricket is deployed as a device to conjure up thoughts/memories of 'home' – for example in Danny Boyle's *The Beach* and (in a more contemplative way) briefly in John Madden's *Best Exotic Marigold Hotel*, both 'tourist films'. Perhaps the 'best' (most exaggerated? most loved?) cricket screen characters are the two eccentric English buffers Charters and Caldicott, playing supporting roles in Alfred Hitchcock's delightful 1938 classic, *The Lady Vanishes*. As their train speeds across a travelogue trans-European backdrop, the pair are splendid caricatures of blinkered cricket enthusiasts, seemingly oblivious, in equal measure, to both the political intrigue enveloping their fellow passengers within the train and to the splendid scenery outside. Rather, they are single-mindedly transfixed with the/their overriding necessity of returning to England (and, in particular, Lord's) to catch the end of the test match.

More obtuse, reference is made here to a home-made travel film from a similar era. Notable among these 'adventurers' were the wealthy industrialists, the Wrights, who recorded their exploits in some unique, truly memorable film. As evidenced in the recent documentary *Thirties in Colour: Wright around the World* (BBC 4) 2012, colour footage from their world cruise makes for fascinating viewing – quirkily, from a cricketing perspective. Of immediate significance here is material from when their ship *The Stella Polaris* (reputedly, the world's most famous cruise ship) docked in Port Morseby, now Papua New Guinea, in the summer of 1937. A former British colony, it was administered by Australian governor, Hubert Murray who, according to the documentary narration, was determined to limit the impact of Western values on traditional Papuan culture. There was, however, one aspect of British culture that the people were allowed to embrace: cricket. Even more surprisingly, women's cricket took centre stage. And in some unique, revealing footage – the women were, by decree, bare-breasted – Wright filmed Papuan women playing cricket. A remarkable sight. According to one of the contributors, Eric Hirsch, '...there is considerable anthropological value to these images. Although it's been well documented that women were playing cricket after the Second World War, there's been virtually no documentation of this prior to that period... The clip of film offers a very interesting insight into aspects of village life we didn't know much about' (Broadcast BBC 4). Obvious reservations aside, Rachael Heyhoe Flint would, surely, be impressed.

A somewhat (even) less savoury 'imperial' cricketing legacy in far-off lands (geographically; and metaphorically in the realms of personal childhood memories) was the Wolf of Kabul, alias Second Lieutenant Bill Sampson, as featured in *The Hotspur* comic of the early 1960s. Here, the 'sport' materialised in the potent manifestation of a cricket bat, affectionately referred to as 'clicky-ba', and which was wielded with alarming frequency and devastating effect by Chung, his Oriental sidekick, to 'knock the bails-off' any recalcitrant 'native'. Possibly a metaphor for 'the Empire?'

While a game on the sand, organised by Keaty – the very English (*Daily Telegraph* reading, enthusiastic amateur cricket devotee) character – featured in *The Beach*, the film's director (himself hardly an advocate of 'Empire') again deployed cricket, even more symbolically, in his most recent tour de force.

Village green cricket featured (albeit, briefly) in Boyle's chaotic, some might say shambolic, recent Olympic opening ceremony. But then again so did almost everything else remotely considered English/British – as, indeed, did a good deal maybe beyond the pale. The resulting epic, if somewhat baffling, extravaganza had been predicted in a prescient article in which Brown (2012: S19) questioned just what 'of all the marvels in these "Isles of Wonder" are "quintessentially British"'. Well, according to Boyle, cricket seems to be one: its role early on in the ceremony representing 'our green and pleasant land'. But the bucolic bliss is soon besmirched by the 'dark satanic mills'. '...cricketers illustrate the rural idyll before the working class rolls away the grass to beat a more strident rhythm' (White, 2012: 3). Paradise lost. Precious peace and tranquillity swamped by raucous hordes of riff-raff. Pandemonium. Sounds familiar? Rather like the benign travel/traveller sullied by corrosive tourism/mass tourist, then? (Incidentally, Burkart & Medlik (1974), those pillars of early tourism academe, believed that Blake's 'satanic mills' referred to church spires and not the more conventional interpretation like Boyle's). 'The eighteenth century did not deplore the impact of man on the environment (Blake's 'dark satanic mills' refer not to the factories of the Industrial Revolution but to the churches of the Established Church of England.)' (Burkart & Medlik, 1974: 10).)

As Michael Portillo (2012) put it 'the increasing popularity of cricket with the masses would forever change the way it was played'. For 'cricket', read 'travel'. Indeed, in a fascinating cameo in *Great British Railway Journeys* – a television series akin to *Coast* for 'its contribution to tourism' (Wheeller, 2009) – Portillo considers the symbiotic spread of railways and cricket, arguing that the ever-lengthening tentacles of the railway were instrumental in the nationwide spread of cricket. Just as, of course, they were fundamental to the spread of tourism.

> If you look at a map of the expansion of the railway network around England, cricket followed these lines. Trains enabled players to get to more distant places: railways helped transform the game and popularised the sport. The All-England XI that travelled in 1849 used the stage-coach. By 1852 they were using the rail network. Particularly popular in Sheffield, Manchester and other industrial cities in the north, they played as far south as St Ives and as far north as Scotland. By the mid-1800s tens of thousands of Victorians would travel (by rail) across the country to watch a fixture. (Portillo, 2012)

Few institutions smack of Englishness more than the *Daily Telegraph*. True to form, its cricket coverage is extensive. And good. (So, too, some would say its travel section.) The paper's, and many of its readers', dedication to cricket is perhaps best epitomised in the recent publication of *Not in my Day, Sir. Cricket Letters to the Daily Telegraph* (Smith, 2011). If the title alone is not sufficient to set the scene then the book's evocative cover surely does the trick. The view from the open window of a gentleman's study, festooned with cricketing artefacts – an old bat and ball, a copy of *Wisden*, assorted cricketing photos, a picture of W.G. Grace, etc. – oozes nostalgia. The village green, encircled by leafy trees, overlooked by church and vicarage, takes centre stage as the cricketers in their whites play the game. This could be Witney Scrotum, the imaginary home village of Peter Tinniswood's (1981) crusty, cricket-obsessed Brigadier. 'For more than eighty years, the *Telegraph*'s Letters page has offered an august forum for discussion of all manner of subjects, but none has been as durable as cricket. Be it the Bodyline controversy, the d'Oliveira and Packer affairs, or the sticky question of players chewing gum out in the middle, *Telegraph* readers have never been short of an opinion or several, wryly or even cholerically expressed. By turns acerbic, witty, opinionated and hilarious, they are always to the point, silly or otherwise' reads the inside flap.

Cricket, and cricket letters to the paper, are to the fore in a recent *Telegraph* Obituary for Major John Forte, a former British vice-consul in Corfu 'who resurrected cricket on the island' (Anon., 2012). In 1959 Forte wrote a letter to the *Telegraph* appealing to all 'lovers of the game' to send any discarded cricketing paraphernalia to the island. Within a few months 50 bats and 350 balls had been donated by Telegraph readers. From then on cricket in Corfu went from strength to strength and it was largely due to the development of the game on the island (Corfu has 11 of the 14 clubs in the country) that Greece was admitted to the International Cricket Council in 1995.

Around the same time, 'Forte's knowledge and love of the island led to the publication of a number of highly successful travel guides which helped to open it up to tourism. *Corfu: Venus of the Isles* (1963) ran into six editions' (Anon., 2012). Shades of Moorhouse here, as Forte wrote on cricket, too – see his *Play's The Thing* which traces the history of cricket on the island. Corfu – cricket and tourism, hand in glove.

Recently, in the *Telegraph* – a cricketing paper, if ever there was one – Bremner (2012: 5) selected his choices for 'Britain's best 5 cricket grounds' all, apparently, worth a visit in their own right. For Kent's ground at Canterbury he suggests 'Visit during Festival Week, when the place is overrun with military bands and bustling beer tents', while Arundel Castle Cricket Ground is recommended as 'a great stop on a family day out in the Sussex countryside'.

In the same paper's *Sunday Telegraph* travel section's 'My kind of town' series 'celebrities' extol the virtues of their favourite town/city destination. Broadcaster Chris Tarrant goes for Sydney, but cautions 'Avoid talking loudly about cricket in any bar, because the locals will turn on you...and quote every game when Australia have beaten England.' So tread carefully, otherwise an inauspicious, inappropriate comment can provoke a rapid deterioration from conversation to heated argument as to the merits of 'Bodyline', even 'Gallipoli' (Berkman, 2011). And possible unfortunate recourse to 'clicky-ba'.

Worth the Wait[5]

Cricket is part of the image of England as a tourism destination. It also shares some elements of tourism as an experience. Unlike most other sports, cricket requires comparatively long periods away from home, for both players and keen supporters. Orwell, reviewing Blunden's book in 1944, was worried that the 'increasing hurry and urbanisation of a life' would make the game less popular (Orwell, 2002: 587). Before the advent of Twenty20, a day – a day visit – was the minimum that would be required for a professional cricket match. Test matches last five days, and county matches four. And, like tourism, cricket is absorbing and different from everyday routine. A day at the cricket can include breakfast, morning coffee, lunch and tea – preferably with cake. It will probably include drinking, which may lead some spectators to be vocal and raucous, but not to be violent. On some days at some matches, spectators will turn up in fancy dress (see Emery *et al.*, Chapter 9, this volume, regarding *The Barmy Army*). During the English season of 2011, following England's Ashes victory in Australia, a life-size photograph of the English team was displayed, with the head of the captain, Andrew Strauss, cut out. Fans could insert their own head and be photographed as part of the victorious team – a seaside attraction and cricket coming together. This all adds to the sense in which to be 'at the cricket' in England is to be in another world, to have in that sense a touristic experience. In the immediate aftermath of one of England's 2011 riots, which had seen the death of three young British Asian men in Birmingham as they tried to protect their property, cricket correspondent David Hopps was reporting on the test match between England and India beginning in the same city. He noted that among the diverse crowd, spectators had no sense that it was inappropriate for the match to go ahead. 'The riots were one thing, the test match quite another. They felt themselves moving between unconnected worlds... supporters of England and India descended together upon Edgbaston, with barely a police officer in sight' (Hopps, 2011). He felt that the idea of cricket as a retreat from the harsher realities of the world had never been more apt.

On the experience theme, cricket serves as a conduit for 'displaced' friends getting together on the international stage: Greek friends, now living in Australia, travel to Thailand to frequent the annual Chiang Mai Cricket Sixes, re-acquainting themselves with friendships sealed, long ago, on Ios in the 1980s.

Basically we are the Ios Malakas, a bunch of people who met on the party island of Ios in the eighties. Some of the people who show up we haven't seen for years or are friends of friends and some have known each other for years... there is always an excuse to party even though most of us are on the wrong side of 50 and in various shapes of disrepair. The cricket is rather incidental to us but most teams including ourselves are very competitive when on the field... there are a few functions throughout the week but many free nights. The first night is great when the 32 odd teams come together for the opening night party.

Similar stories are to be found elsewhere. The 'experience' is the thing. Incidentally, for some, it would seem 'the' experience is everything – witness the couple caught, at 3pm, having sex on the pitch at Three Bridges Cricket Club, Crawley. Fortunately, not on a match day (Anon., 2010). Bowling a maiden over, indeed.

Like much of tourism, much of cricket can be seen as a search for time out in a pleasanter place. Cricket enthusiasts maintain a fantasy of cricket and what it means as an idealisation and difference from the rest of life. There is sentimentality here, no doubt, but also deliberation and a consciousness about what they are doing. In the same way, would-be travellers may wish to maintain their image and fantasy of a place they have not visited, and avoid having it disturbed (Cherifi, 2012). In England, tourism and cricket can never be far apart. In Julian Barnes' novel *England, England* (1998), about a plan to turn the Isle of Wight into a theme park that includes everything that a visit to England should offer, the businessman behind the plan commissions a marketing survey to discover what potential tourists from around the world see as quintessentially English. In the list of 50 attractions that results, it is no surprise that cricket is listed in the top 10 – below Robin Hood but above the White Cliffs of Dover.

Just as travel begets tourism (and off the beaten path becomes, sequentially, off the beaten track, then inevitably, off the beaten-trek) so too with cricket, itself not immune from a similar process of assimilation as established cricketing 'destinations' give way to (or, rather, are supplemented by) off the beaten creases. The familiar becomes blasé as writers delight in tales of cricketing feats in ever more unorthodox places. Not content with the success of their *Tales from Far Pavilions* (1985), the cover of their 'follow on' sequel *Beyond the Far Pavilions* (1987) states 'Messrs Cooper and Synge have here assembled a yet more remarkable collection of strange and delightful tales of cricket played at exotic and unlikely venues – from Finland to the Falklands and from Tipperary to Korea.' Shades of Turner and Ashs' *Pleasure*

Peripheries (1975)? Recommendations on the back cover include one from the *Yorkshire Post*: 'the ideal book to turn to for home thoughts from abroad' (www.Yorkshirepost.co.uk). Whether Robert Browning or Clifford T. Ward, these very words from beyond the boundary, the evocative 'home thoughts from abroad', resonate with a certain English psyche, conjuring up, as they do, misty-eyed, H.V. Morton's (2006 [1927]) images of 'home'. And from (an English) cricketing sensitivity and perspective it is probably the pastoral idyll, the village and amateur cricket – or, maybe, professional cricket of a long-ago lost world – that these 'home thoughts' hanker for. At least it is for those of us of a certain vintage.

Notes

(1) *Opening Up: My Autobiography*, Michael Atherton, 2003.
(2) *My World in Cricket*, Stuart Broad, 2012.
(3) *Head On: Botham – The Autobiography*, Sir Ian Botham, 2008.
(4) *No Boundaries: Passion and Pain On and Off the Pitch*, Ronnie Irani, 2009.
(5) *Worth the Wait: An Autobiography*. Darren Lehmann, 2005.

References

Anon. (2010) Couple caught having sex on cricket field. *Daily Telegraph*, 24 September, p. 3.
Anon. (2012) *Daily Telegraph*, 14 September (accessed online 1 April 2014).
Atherton, M. (2003) *Opening Up: My Autobiography*. London: Coronet.
Barnes, J. (1998) *England, England*. London: Jonathon Cape.
Berry, S. (2012) Tourists show how game is being degraded. *Daily Telegraph*, 20 July, p. S12.
Billington, M. (2012) 'Michael Billington on the link between cricket and the theatre'. The Guardian Theatre Blog 27.05.2012. http://www.theguardian.com/culture/2012/may/27/michael-billington-cricket-theatre-link (accessed 31 March 2012).
Blunden, E. (1944) *Cricket Country*. London: Collins.
Botham, I. (2008) *Head On: Botham – The Autobiography*. London: Ebury Press.
Bremner, R. (2012) Britain's best cricket grounds. *Sunday Telegraph Seven*, 8 July 2012, p. 5.
Broad, S. (2012) *My World in Cricket*. London: Simon and Schuster.
Brown, O. (2012) Is Boyle's epic leaning too far to the left? *Daily Telegraph*, 26 July, p. S19.
Burkart, J. and Medlik, S. (1974) *Tourism. Past, Present, Future*. London: Heinemann.
Butler, R.W. (1980) The concept of a tourist area cycle of evolution and implications for management of resources. *The Canadian Geographer* XXIV (1), 5–12.
Cherifi, B. (2012) *Imagining a Country Never Visited: Images of London Held by Czech Nonvisitors*. Seminar presentation, University of Westminster.
Clifford, S. and King, A. (2006) *England in Particular*. London: Hodder and Stoughton.
Cooper, L. and Synge, A. (1985) *Tales from Far Pavilions*. London: Cornerstone.
Cooper, L. and Synge, A. (1987) *Beyond the Far Pavilions*. London: Arrow.
Dann, G.M.S. and Theobold, W.F. (1995) Tourism – The nostalgia industry of the future. In W.F. Theobold (ed.) *Global Tourism – The Next Decade* (pp. 29–43). Wallingford: CABI.

De Selincourt, H. (1924) *The Cricket Match*. London: Rupert Hart Davies.
Elborough, T. (2010) *Wish You Were Here: England on Sea*. London: Sceptre.
Fairley, S. and Gammon, S. (2005) Something lived, something learned: Nostalgia's expanding role in sport tourism. *Sport in Society* 8 (2), 182–197.
Feekins, S. (2012) Olympics set for Lord's takeover tomorrow. *Observer*, 1 July, p. 18.
Fox, K. (2005) *Watching the English*. London: Hodder and Stoughton.
Frew, E. (2011) Location and landscape: Small scale sporting events and national identity. In E. Frew and L. White (eds) *Tourism and National Identities* (pp. 136–148). Abingdon: Routledge.
Gammon, S. and Ramshaw, G. (eds) (2007) *Heritage, Sport and Tourism: Sporting Pasts – Tourist Futures*. London: Routledge.
Graves, R. (1960) *Goodbye to All That*. London: Penguin (Originally published 1929).
Groves, J. (1999) *Lovely Cricket in The Learning Curve of Love*. Penzance: United Writers Publications.
Hamilton, D. (2010) *A Last English Summer*. London: Quercus.
Harper, R. (1975) *'When an Old Cricketer Leaves his Crease' HQ*. London: Harvest Records.
Hartley, L.P. (2004) *The Go-Between*. London: Penguin (Originally published 1953).
Haseler, S. (1996) *The English Tribe*. London: Macmillan.
Hirsch, E. (2012) Broadcast BBC 4 23.07.2008. Executive producer David Okuefuna. See http://www.bbc.co.uk/programmes/b00cp456 (accessed 1 April 2014).
Hobsbawm, E. and Ranger, T. (1983) *The Invention of Tradition*. Cambridge: Cambridge University Press.
Hopps, D. (2011) Class on display at Edgbaston provides relief from England underclass. *The Guardian*, 10 August.
Irani, R. (2009) *No Boundaries: Passion and Pain On and Off the Pitch*. London: John Blake Publishing.
Lazenby, J. (2005) *Test of Time. Travels in Search of a Cricketing Legend*. London: Murray.
Lehmann, D. (2005) *Worth the Wait: An Autobiography*. London: Methuen.
MacDonnell, A.G. (1933) *England Their England*. London: Macmillan.
Maitland, R. (2012) 'Capitalness is contingent': Tourism and national capitals in a globalised world. *Current Issues in Tourism* 15 (1–2), 3–17.
McKercher, B. (2002) Towards a classification of cultural tourists. *International Journal of Tourism Research* 4, 29–38.
Morton, H.V. (2006) *In Search of England*. London: Methuen (Originally published 1927).
Newbolt, H. (1910) 'VitaiLampada' in *Collected Poems 1897–1907*. Edinburgh: Thomas Nelson.
Orwell, G. (1938) *Homage to Catalonia*. London: Secker and Warburg.
Orwell, G. (2002) *Essays*. London: Everyman Library.
Palmer, C. (1999) Tourism and the symbols of identity. *Tourism Management* 20, 313–321.
Paxman, J. (1995) *Fish, Fishing and the Meaning of Life*. London: Penguin.
Portillo, M. (2012) *Great British Railway Journeys*. BBC 2, 17 July.
Powell, A. (1951) *A Question of Upbringing*. London: Fontana.
Pringle, D. (2012) This looks a case of astonishing arrogance. *Daily Telegraph*, 16 July, p. S8.
Sassoon, S.L. (1928) *Memoirs of a Fox Hunting Man*. London: Faber.
Sassoon, S.L. (1930) *Memoirs of an Infantry Officer*. London: Faber and Faber.
Simkins, M. (2011) *The Last Flannelled Fool*. London: Ebury House.
Smith, E. (2008) *What Sport Tells Us About Life*. London: Viking.
Smith, M. (2011) *Not in My Day, Sir. Cricket Letters to the Daily Telegraph*. London: Aurum Press.

Stone, D. (2008) Cricket's regional identities: The development of cricket and identity in Yorkshire and Surrey. *Sport in Society* 11 (5), 501–516.
Tarrant, C. (2012) My kind of town. *Sunday Telegraph*, 8 July, p. T11.
Tinniswood, P. (1981) *Tales from a Long Room*. London: Arrow.
Turner, L. and Ash, J. (1975) *The Golden Hordes: International Tourism and the Pleasure Periphery*. London: Constable.
Wheeller, B. (2009) Tourism and the arts. In J. Tribe (ed.) *Philosophical Issues in Tourism* (pp. 191–208). Bristol: Channel View Publications.
White, J. (2012) Opening ceremony. *Daily Telegraph*, 28 July.

Part 2
The Homes of Cricket

The chapters in the first section discussed the spread of cricket from its rural English origins to its present pattern of existence, which is truly global. The following four chapters discuss the places at which the game is played and the problems which they face. Cricket, while it may still retain an element of its English or British colonial past, with all the test playing countries once being a part of the British Empire, is now, like most major sports, clearly international and professional and subject to the whims and desires of those controlling the purse strings. The timing and location of matches and series, including test match series, are influenced heavily by the media and by anticipated gate and advertising receipts. In England in particular, the allocation of test matches to grounds has become a crucial element in the financial success or failure of specific ovals, given that there are now more grounds designated for test cricket than matches to be played, particularly with Lord's and The Oval always hosting such matches in any full tours.

The chapter on Rupertswood and Sunbury illustrates the nature of 'courtesy' or 'friendly' tour matches, as this location was a regular stop on all test tours by England to Australia, and holds a special place in cricket lore as the birthplace of the Ashes. The changing nature and travel patterns of cricket, its players and supporters are illustrated here by the fact that the once obligatory match is no longer played there, overtaken by the financial and logistical considerations that now rule international cricket, and it has been relegated to a role as a historical icon in the story of cricket.

Of all the cricket grounds in the world, Lord's, the home of the Marylebone Cricket Club (MCC) in central London is the most iconic. Like the clubhouse of the Royal and Ancient Golf Club in St Andrews, it is not only the spiritual home of cricket but also the seat of the body (MCC) responsible for maintaining and updating the rules of the game. The MCC was established in 1787 and created the first set of laws of cricket the following year. The club moved to Lord's in 1814. It has traditionally been the setting for the opening game of the English county cricket championship, which takes the form of a match between the MCC and whichever was the previous year's champion. Since 2010, however, again reflecting the changes in the organisation and location of cricket, this match has been played under floodlights in Abu Dhabi. Lord's still remains a major tourist attraction for cricket devotees as Cardwell and Ali illustrate. The ground has seen major investment over the last decade, including floodlights, new pitches and stands, and has gained an impressive list of sponsors. Its appeal remains, however, in the history and traditions of the game preserved in its exhibits, including the Ashes urn, which attract large numbers of tourists even when no match is being played.

The Rose Bowl also reflects the issues plaguing cricketing and other sporting venues in the modern era. Like golf courses, the ovals themselves can become outdated through new developments of bats, balls, floodlighting, and the technique and performance of the players and require extending, and in some cases re-orienting. The costs of such renovations or replacements are generally higher than can be recouped from attendance at regular county or state/provincial games, and new stadia become increasingly dependent on international competitions, matches such as tests and limited over games between touring sides and host countries, and also local Twenty20 matches. Even then, those travelling to the boundaries of such ovals are generally insufficient in numbers and, as Parrett shows, other facilities have become essential for the survival of renovated or new stadia. Cricket has, in many cases, become one of rather than 'the' attraction at these grounds and in some cases, Eden Park in Auckland is one example, along with several test grounds in Australia, shares the playing surface with other sports, such as rugby, a situation not envisaged in the 19th or the first half of the 20th century.

In contrast to the preceding chapters, Noakes and Wilson describe the evolution of cricket in Bali, along with comparisons to more lively cricket and sports tourism in general. A very different pattern of development of the game emerges, and the absence of tradition and differences to the host culture and climate explain the continuous struggle to keep the game alive in Indonesia. The contribution of visitors, permanent and temporary, is significant, and the limited number of teams and pitches makes travel for and to cricket both necessary and difficult. Cricket can be seen as one of several sports in Indonesia which may gain a tourist audience and prove of value to the country as a source of foreign exchange, thus its relative significance as a generator of funds may be far greater than in cricket's more established and traditional settings. It can serve too as a hopefully positive influence on national culture and develop and encourage international links through participation with its neighbours.

3 Rupertswood and Sunbury: Commemorating Cricket and the Birthplace of 'the Ashes'

Leanne White

> *Yes cricket will live till the trumpet trumpets*
> *For the wide pavilioned sky.*
> *And time, the umpire, lays low the stumps*
> *As his scythe goes sweeping by...*
> *Yes, cricket's a glorious game, say we*
> *And cricket will live in eternity.*
> *A Glorious Game Say We,* William Douglas-Home

Introduction

This chapter examines tourism advertising and promotional material in the historic town of Sunbury in Victoria, Australia. In particular, Rupertswood Mansion, which is known as the 'Birthplace of the Ashes' (one of the world's most sought-after sporting trophies), will be explored. The chapter ties in with some of the themes of this book, including: early travels of cricket teams and their supporters; cricket, tourism and Empire; packaging cricket tours in the modern era; and the economic and socio-cultural impact of cricket's travelling support. The chapter will closely examine numerous signs and symbols surrounding the historic mansion and the town.

It has been widely reported that the Ashes began as something of a joke with a mock obituary published in *The Sporting Times* in 1882 after Australia defeated England at The Oval. It was announced that English cricket had 'died' and that the body should be cremated and the remains taken to Australia. When the English cricket team visited the 50-room Rupertswood

Mansion a few months later (one of the largest homes in Victoria at the time), the team captain was presented with a tiny terracotta urn containing some ashes (supposedly of the bails from the last test stumps). While there has been some controversy surrounding the origin of the Ashes, it is now generally accepted that the urn came into being after a social game of cricket at Rupertswood in Sunbury (Munns, 1994: 7).

This chapter will closely analyse the significance of this building in cricketing history and the surrounding town. The cricket and tourism nexus will be explored through the dual theoretical frameworks of nationalism and destination marketing. This chapter examines links between tourism, tradition and national identity at one of Australia's most fascinating buildings.

Heritage, Nationalism, Tourism and Sport

Heritage

Gammon has argued that heritage has the ability to 'guide and cement national identities' (2007: 1). When exploring our past, we are delving deeper into our own heritage and also that of the nation. Underlying this suggestion is the proposition that heritage is a 'cultural and social process' that is 'ultimately intangible' (Smith, 2006: 307). With this in mind, this chapter also aims to demystify the ways in which the often intangible concept of heritage is imagined, and will examine a particular cricket match at Rupertswood in 1882 to make that case. By examining the events that took place in Sunbury on Christmas Eve in 1882, we can rethink our understanding and awareness of cricket's long heritage and tradition 'in our everyday lives' (Waterton, 2010: 206).

For the tourist visiting Rupertswood or visiting some of the historic tourist attractions in Sunbury, heritage becomes somehow embodied and personified by the experience and images of past residents and visitors of the mansion and impressive surrounds. If we understand heritage as a process that constructs meaning about the past, then the construction of cricket heritage at Rupertswood is illustrative of this process. It is, essentially, a construction of cricket heritage based upon stories, memories, reports and photographs that have been organised, documented and passed down by committed family and volunteers. Contrary to popular notions of heritage that situate it as 'object-based', this example offers a new interpretation of heritage that builds on the work of Smith, Waterton, Gammon and others.

Nationalism

The term 'nation' encompasses more extensive thinking than simply the borders of a particular country. Theorists of nationalism have acknowledged that the term can incorporate political, social, cultural, historical, economic, linguistic and religious factors. While numerous theorists have analysed the term 'nationalism', Benedict Anderson's ground-breaking 1983 work (revised in 1991) *Imagined Communities: Reflections on the Origin and Spread of Nationalism* has reconceptualised the way scholars have come to think about nationalism and national identity. Anderson popularly conceptualised the nation as an 'imagined political community'. He argued, 'It is *imagined* because members of even the smallest nation will never know most of their fellow-members, meet them, or even hear of them, yet in the minds of each lives the image of their communion' (Anderson, 1991: 6). Anderson contends that official nationalism is the 'willed merger of nation and dynastic empire' and argues that the concept came about in response to popular nationalism that emerged in Europe from the 1820s (Anderson, 1991: 86). He explains that official nationalism emanates 'from the state' and has as its primary feature a focus on 'serving the interests of the state first and foremost' (Anderson, 1991: 159).

The three forms of nationalism that are relevant to the issues examined in this chapter are: official nationalism, popular nationalism and commercial nationalism. First, official nationalism is the civic, formal and ceremonial nationalism such as the Australian federal government's planning of the Bicentennial celebrations in 1988 or the Centenary of Federation commemoration in 2001. The national anthem, flag and official symbols are part of official nationalism. For example, Australia Day commemorative ceremonies, often organised by federal, state or local governments, come under the category of official nationalism. Official nationalism is the dominant pool of nationalism that primarily emerges from the nation-state. Both popular and commercial nationalism fall under the larger umbrella of official nationalism. The concept of popular nationalism, introduced by Russel Ward (1966) and others, includes nationalist messages and images depicted in popular culture such as Australian film, television drama, popular songs and sport. Finally, commercial nationalism refers to consumer-related uses of these national symbols, images and icons. Commercial nationalism is the material, everyday nationalism represented by organisations, products and services such as Qantas, Vegemite and Aussie Home Loans. For many years, the phenomenon of commercial nationalism has been evidenced in advertising slogans that occasionally develop into popular jingles such as *Aussie Kids are Weet-Bix Kids*, *I'm as Australian as Ampol* and *Football, Meat Pies, Kangaroos and Holden Cars*. While popular and commercial nationalism generally play a subservient role to official nationalism, these forms of nationalism occasionally overlap. An example of all three forms of nationalism intersecting in Australian culture would be former Prime Minister John Howard's admitting to being a 'cricket-tragic', the widespread popularity of the Australian cricket team (particularly after the convincing 2006–2007 Ashes victory), and the selling of green and gold merchandise to cricket fans so that they can overtly show their support for Australia and the team (see Noakes *et al.*, regarding branding in sports, Chapter 6, this volume).

Tourism

Recent studies in tourism have considered the role of heritage attractions in helping create a national identity (see, for example, Palmer, 2005; Pretes, 2003). Pretes notes that tourists receive messages sent to them by the creators of the sites they visit, and these sites of significance, presented as aspects of a national heritage, help to shape a common national identity, or 'imagined community' among a diverse population. He also argues that a shared identity is often an official goal of countries comprised of many different cultures where there exists a common urge to create a national identity to overcome diversity and difference within the nation-state. He adds that monuments in particular represent something shared by all citizens, helping to 'popularize a hegemonic nationalist message of inclusion' (Pretes, 2003: 127). Another perspective on diversity is offered by Spillman (1997) who argues that in a diverse country, diversity itself can become an aspect of national identity.

Rojek has argued that 'most tourists feel they have not fully absorbed a sight until they stand before it, see it, and take a photograph to record the moment' (1997: 58). If tourism sites can help create a common identity or imagined community, can photographs taken at these destinations help to develop a better understanding of the place visited? Morgan *et al.* have argued that travel for the purpose of leisure is 'a highly involving experience, extensively planned, excitedly anticipated and fondly remembered' (2004: 4). The photographs that capture the highlights of the travel occasion constitute a vital element of both remembering the event and sharing the experience with others. As such, a number of key photographs will form part of the analysis undertaken in this chapter.

Sport

Australia is often described as a sport-loving nation, where sport has had a substantial influence on the shaping of Australian society (Stoddart, 1988) with Veal and Lynch (2001: 286) describing sport as being one of the key social forms through which the 'values of the British Empire were cemented into the Australian culture via activities such as horse racing, cricket, tennis and fox hunting'. In modern-day Australia one of the most popular sports is racing, which may reflect colonial times when early white settlers were heavy gamblers and even gambled on the proverbial 'two flies crawling up a wall' – betting on which one would reach the top first (Veal & Lynch, 2001: 55).

Televised sport has been a powerful magnet for viewers for many years. Media magnate Rupert Murdoch states that sport overpowers film and everything else in the entertainment industry. This observation is entirely correct in the case of a major cricket event such as the Ashes. At a major event such as this, the industries of tourism, sport and the media are intimately connected and all contribute to the overall experience that is consumed by the visitor to the venues and (in a different way) the television viewer. As Gemmell (2008: x) argues, as cricket evolves on a global scale 'it has become increasingly associated with national identity'. At this event the people of Australia and England are able to successfully unite around the common theme of unity, sport, and 'their' cricket team in particular. This iconic game and contest to win a small, seemingly insignificant urn has helped create key archival images that will continue to shape the individual nations and their sense of identity into the future.

In recent years, the number and range of events occurring around the world have increased substantially. This has led researchers to investigate various aspects of events. Jago and Shaw (1998) note that most of this research has focused primarily on the impacts and outcomes of special events. Other benefits of events have been identified as an extension of the tourist season and enhancement of community pride (Getz, 1997). The direct connection between one of cricket's most significant events and the town of Sunbury has fostered community pride and increased tourism to the region.

Australia's Proud Cricketing Heritage

As well as being the most successful team in the history of the Cricket World Cup, Australia has the honour of being the 'most successful Test-playing nation of the past 130 years' (Derriman, 2006: 117). The attitude of the seemingly invincible Australians might be best reflected by the tattoo on Michael Clarke's left arm – 'Carpe Diem', or seize the day.

The green and gold (with red gloves) boxing kangaroo flag became popular with Australia's success at the 1983 America's Cup yacht race. Hutchinson (2002: 72) explains that since 1983, the flag has become 'a kind of unofficial Australian sporting flag – but was officially endorsed for waving at the

Sydney Olympics'. As explained by Cashman (2001), spectators supporting Australia at major sporting matches wave almost as many boxing kangaroo flags as the national flag, and test matches are no exception. Cashman also argues that it is likely that 'sport is contributing to the current debate on flag reform' (2001: 9).

The current Australian flag became the nation's official flag in 1954. Almost in defiance against the 'mother country' England, many Australian sporting teams choose to wear green and gold rather than the red, white and blue of the nation's flag. Although for test matches, the traditional white kit remains. Horne (1981: 67) has claimed that it was in the 1960s that a discourse emerged in Australia about severing constitutional links with Britain, changing anthems and flags, examining the symbolism of stamps and currency, and generally re-assessing the images projected by Australia in many forms of national symbolism. Horne asserted that Australia experienced a genuine 'cultural awakening' which essentially consisted of Australian participation in the arts and entertainment, and in works produced by intellectuals. It was an acceptance that there was nothing embarrassing in being an Australian and that our country's themes and legends were as valid as any others. Unfortunately Australia has yet to officially endorse a flag with its own unique identity (as opposed to projecting the image of an English colony). The union flag of Great Britain has been associated with Australia since Captain James Cook first flew it in 1770. However, on the sporting field, the fresher images of green and gold are as close as the country currently gets to projecting a distinctive Australian identity.

The question of what constitutes the Australian national character has been explored in both academic and popular literature since European settlement of Australia, using historical, cultural and sociological frameworks such as exploration, settlement, migration and war service (Pearse, 2006) and via the people, traits, images and experiences (Hogan, 2009). Purdie and Wilss (2007) suggest that the genesis of an Australian national identity dates back to the time of early white settlement where influences on the developing culture at the time were the British or Anglo-Saxon heritage and the harsh conditions due to terrain and climate. Thus, physical toughness, 'mateship' and the ability to withstand hardship were foundational in the development of an Australian identity. The way in which 'the Ashes' came into being at Rupertswood and Australia's proud test cricket heritage with England (where the current scorecard is Australia 123, England 100, Matches Drawn 87) are vital elements of the Australian concept of mateship. While England is considered the home of cricket, their overall form (particularly against test rival Australia) has for many years embarrassed English cricket fans (2013 being no exception, Editors' note).

Sunbury: The Town and Outer Suburb

The town of Sunbury is located 33 kilometres north-west of Melbourne. As the town is located only 10 minutes from Melbourne Airport, it is considered by some to be part of Melbourne's vast suburban sprawl. When entering the town of Sunbury, the visitor is welcomed with a large sign proudly declaring that the town is the 'Birthplace of the Ashes' (see Figure 3.1). The signs were erected in 1994 and were placed at various entrances to the town and at the front gates of Rupertswood. The Hume and Hovell expedition passed through the area in 1824, and Sunbury is now part of the metropolitan area known as the city of Hume. The town was first settled by Europeans George Evans, Samuel Jackson and William Jackson in 1836 and is named after Sunbury-on-Thames in England. In the 1850s, Sunbury was a town where those heading to the gold diggings in Central Victoria would stop and rest.

The Gunug-Willam-Balluk indigenous population were the original inhabitants of the area. They were a clan of the Woiwurrung people and named the area Korrakorracup. The 'Official Visitor Guide' of the nearby Daylesford and Macedon Ranges Regional Tourism Board acknowledges the original inhabitants of the land with the following statement: 'The region has been a

Figure 3.1 Sunbury is branded the 'Birthplace of the Ashes'

gathering place for thousands of years. A sacred place for aboriginal nations since time began' (Daylesford and Macedon Ranges Tourism, 2011: 3).

Sunbury has a rich and intriguing history. Victoria's oldest homestead, Emu Bottom, was built by George Evans in 1836. An impressive bluestone Railway Viaduct with five large arches was built in 1859 and can be seen from a number of vantage points in the area. In 1865 an industrial school was built on Sheoak Hill (now known as Jackson's Hill) in Sunbury to educate and house orphaned children. Due to the high rate of deaths caused largely by poor nutrition and cold conditions, the school quickly developed the nickname 'Sunbury Slaughterhouse' and was closed in 1879. The building was used as a psychiatric hospital and training centre for the intellectually disabled until it was closed in 1992. From 1994 until 2009, the buildings were used by Victoria University.

Sunbury is the closest wine region to the city of Melbourne and cool climate wines have been produced in the area since the 1860s. The winery that produced the world's best Shiraz in 2008 (Witchmount) is also located nearby. Many of the older wineries, including Goona Warra and Craiglee (built in 1858 and 1866 respectively), feature significant bluestone buildings. A food and wine festival is held in the region annually. Sunbury is also known for the Woodstock-like Sunbury Pop Festival which was held in the area on four occasions in the early 1970s. Just a short distance from

Figure 3.2 The Rupertswood display at the Sunbury Visitor Centre

Melbourne Airport at Woodlands Historic Park can be found 'Living Legends' where some of Australia's celebrated retired racehorses are housed, including: Saintly, Rojan Josh, Might and Power, Paris Lane, Better Loosen Up, Fields of Omagh, Doriemus and Brew.

In 2011, a survey by airline Virgin Blue rated Sunbury number six on a list of the top 10 places to visit in the world. The first five destinations on Virgin's list were: Brazil; The Pilbara in Western Australia; Tallinn, Estonia; Canada; and Istanbul in Turkey. The key attractions which helped make Sunbury a popular destination included wineries, closeness to the city and rich history. As mentioned above, Sunbury is marketed as being the 'Birthplace of the Ashes' and the town's information centre features a display with the scoreboard of the first test match at The Oval in 1882, some photographs and cricket memorabilia (see Figure 3.2).

Rupertswood: The Birthplace of the Ashes

Construction of the grand Italianate mansion named 'Rupertswood' began in 1874 with the laying of a three-ton bluestone foundation. The event was marked with a half-day holiday for school children and 1200 residents from surrounding areas were invited to take part in the festivities. A significant feature of the 50-room Italianate building is the striking tower, which is 100 feet tall. Well-known architect George Browne was chosen to design the building, while William Sangster was selected to landscape the impressive gardens (Clarke, 1995: 77). An underground fernery was also created and the large stained glass windows at the mansion are considered to be some of the finest in the world. Rupertswood was the country home of the Clarke family. The Clarkes' main residence (Cliveden) was located just a short distance from the Melbourne Cricket Ground on Wellington Parade in East Melbourne. It was built in 1886 and featured 100 rooms. Cliveden was demolished in 1968 to make way for the Hilton Hotel.

The Clarke family had first settled in the Sunbury region in 1837. In 1850, William John Turner Clarke (known colloquially as 'Big Clarke') obtained a vast expanse of land in the area – more than 62,000 acres. The Clarke property effectively incorporated a large part of Melbourne's northern and western surrounds from what is now Campbellfield in the north to Williamstown in the south-west and across to Sunbury in the north-west. Australia's first millionaire, Big Clarke, died in 1874. By the time of his death, the Clarke estate was worth almost £2.5 million, with freehold land in Victoria, Tasmania, South Australia and New Zealand. His memorial at the Melbourne Cemetery resembles the country mansion he would not live to see. His first son (also named William) was given the responsibility of running much of the family empire.

William John Clarke, the eldest son of Big Clarke, inherited the properties in Victoria. After the birth of four children, his first wife (Mary) died as a result of being thrown from a carriage. In 1873, William later married again, and he and his wife Janet started planning the Sunbury mansion, which would be named after eldest son, Rupert.

Both William and Janet Clarke were actively engaged in Melbourne's social scene and a number of philanthropic ventures. Between 1880 and 1886, Clarke was President of the Melbourne Cricket Club. He was also a member of the Victorian Legislative Council, and was honoured as Australia's first Baronet in 1882. Being a generous and sociable man, Clarke invited the English cricket team to stay with them when they were in Victoria. Many grand balls, hunt meetings and other social and sporting events were regularly held at Rupertswood. The property even had a private railway siding to accommodate Melbourne's elite who either travelled by train or horse and carriage in the pre-motor era. Rupertswood was a focal point for high society in Victoria and entertained in such a manner which was second only to Government House. In keeping with the proud national sentiment of the time, the Clarke family also had a large ornamental lake built on the property in the shape of the Australian landmass.

The idea about burning ashes had been placed in the minds of many when journalist Reginald Brooks published a mock obituary in *The Sporting Times* on 2 September 1882. The notice lamented the death of English cricket. The important words of the notice appeared in the final line which read, 'NB – The body will be cremated and the Ashes taken to Australia.' At the time the notice appeared, a heated debate was taking place in English society about the practice of cremation. Soon after, the English cricket team travelled to Australia, and English Captain Ivo Bligh jokingly reported that he was coming to claim those ashes. The Australian team captain William Murdoch had also made reference to the mythical ashes at a dinner speech and mentioned placing them in a suitable urn.

On Christmas Eve in 1882, a social cricket match was held between the English team and some Rupertswood staff. Although no one appeared to be keeping score, the more experienced English team was generally thought to have won the match and Janet Clarke, Florence Morphy (music teacher to the Clarke children), and a couple of other women humorously decided to burn what is believed to have been a bail and placed the Ashes in a small terracotta urn which had held perfume. Today's forensic technology would now be able to ascertain exactly what was burnt but the ongoing mystery seems better suited to the cricket world. The burning possibly took place in one of Rupertswood's many fireplaces. A small sticker which reads 'the Ashes' and a witty verse were also glued onto the urn and presented to Bligh at dinner that evening. The urn and its important contents were later placed in a hand-made embroidered velvet bag. Showing his gratitude, Bligh presented William and Janet Clarke with a silver tray (Hilton, 2006: 136).

A romance between the English captain and Florence Morphy had developed during Bligh's visits to Rupertswood. The couple married in Sunbury in 1884, and took the Ashes back to England when they returned there in 1888. In 1900, Ivo Bligh became the eighth Earl of Darnley and the urn was a fond souvenir of Lord and Lady Darnley's memories of their early relationship and Sunbury. The larger cricket world eventually came to know of the Darnley Urn when Florence donated it to the Marylebone Cricket Club after Ivo's death in 1927. As the actual Darnley urn is too fragile to travel, a large Waterford crystal trophy was commissioned in 1998 and is now presented to the winning captain every two years. When visiting Rupertswood today, the visitor will find the cricket memorabilia in the first room on the left, known as 'The Smoking Room' (see Figure 3.3).

Rupertswood was sold to H.V. McKay, a millionaire industrialist known for inventing the Sunshine Harvester, in 1922. After McKay's death in 1926,

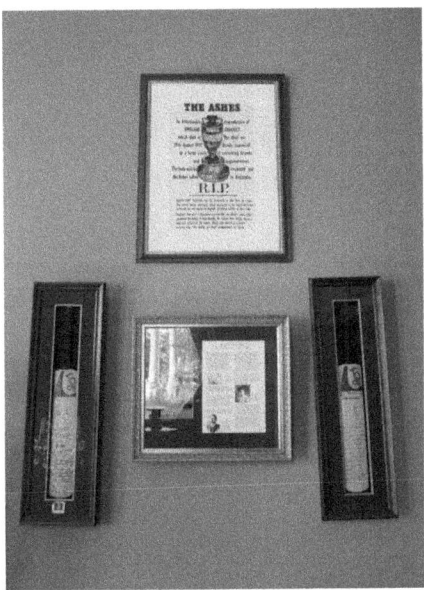

Figure 3.3 Some of the Ashes information and memorabilia displayed in 'The Smoking Room'

the mansion was owned briefly by pastoralist William Naughton, then sold to the Roman Catholic Salesian Order. The mansion and surrounding buildings and property, including the grand ballroom which is now used as a chapel, was occupied by the school for many years. Salesian College still operates out of some of the Rupertswood buildings and the busy school car park is found next to the historic cricket ground where the famous match once took place.

As mentioned earlier, Sunbury was re-branded as the 'Birthplace of the Ashes' in 1994. Soon after, it was decided that a re-enactment of the famous cricket match at Rupertswood should take place. The North Melbourne Cricket Club organised a commemorative match on 18 January 1995 and a plaque was later unveiled at the site where the original cricket match had taken place just over 112 years earlier on 24 December 1882 (see Figure 3.4).

Rupertswood charges a general admission price of $5.00. However, in order to undertake the maintenance to the mansion, the organisation relies on state government funding and raising revenue by other means. Consequently, a range of programmes are marketed to maximise visitation and encourage visitors to pay more. Rupertswood offers a variety of services including: accommodation, degustation dinners, Mother's Day luncheons,

Figure 3.4 A plaque commemorating the Ashes re-enactment in 1995

mid-Winter Christmas dinners, a Christmas Day lunch, a New Year's Eve black tie dinner dance, traditional high teas, cocktail parties, rock and roll nights, conferences and weddings. Room types include eight rooms in the Servants' Wing, the Master Room, the King's Room (as the Duke of York – later King George V stayed in the room), and the H.V. McKay Suite (now the mansion's wedding suite).

And, like any well-planned tourist attraction, the modest souvenir cabinet is positioned in the foyer. The mansion sells a number of souvenirs for tourists to savour the Rupertswood experience such as: plates, soap, candles, books, replica 'Ashes' urns, miniature cricket bats, greeting cards, postcards, spoons, glasses, mugs and wine.

Conclusion

Sunbury's vision to be a world tourist destination may be laughable to some but could also be well on the way to being achieved. Rupertswood and Sunbury have achieved a good deal of brand recognition among its target audience – predominantly cricket fans and those interested in history. Further integrating the various logos with the actual visitor experience at the venue should further strengthen public recognition. When visiting the iconic mansion, the only encounters with the brand logo were found at the main entrance (among other signs), and on the soap and greeting cards found on the shelves of the souvenir cabinet shown above. Signs around the property varied enormously in design, colour, size and font.

This chapter has examined the branding and marketing of Rupertswood and Sunbury in 2011 and 2012. With its various logos, the Hume Shire has embarked on a relatively solid marketing campaign that appears focused and reasonably consistent. However, when one visits the Rupertswood mansion and walks around the old Clarke property and witnesses the run-down state of the building, and the multiple types of signs and communication messages, the branding is much less obvious and to a large extent, virtually non-existent. Despite this, the enduring cricketing story of 'the Ashes' holds an important place in the heritage, culture and identity of Sunbury, and for the wider cricketing community – particularly in Australia and England. This chapter has attempted to reveal how intangible and tangible cricket heritage is experienced and imagined by business operators, locals and tourists in Sunbury.

Cricket heritage is a key component of Australia's national identity. When visiting Rupertswood and Sunbury, the heritage experience is integrated into the tourist gaze through visitors' overall experience of the area. The heritage moment can be savoured by partaking in activities such as: visiting

The Smokers' Room, enjoying afternoon tea or a meal in the Clarke Dining Room, attending a wedding, staying in the rooms where the Ashes were originally placed into that seemingly insignificant perfume container, purchasing a souvenir of Rupertswood, and of course capturing some of these memories with the all-important photographs which we now readily share with friends via social media.

The cricket heritage of Rupertswood is a microcosm of the early colonial rivalry between Australia and England which continues to be played out every two years. Sunbury's success as a tourist destination owes much to the legacy of the Clarke family who had the foresight to host significant sporting and cultural events. It seems likely that cricket heritage will continue to be a strength for the region and its identity, and Rupertswood's contribution to that tradition is only likely to become stronger in the coming years.

References

Anderson, B. (1991) *Imagined Communities: Reflections on the Origins and Spread of Nationalism* (revised edn). London: Verso.

Cashman, R. (2001) Introduction. In R. Cashman, J. O'Hara and A. Honey (eds) *Sport, Federation, Nation* (pp. 1–13). Petersham: Walla Walla Press (in conjunction with the Centre for Olympic Studies), University of New South Wales.

Clarke, M. (1995) *Clarke of Rupertswood 1831–1897: The Life and Times of William John Clarke First Baronet of Rupertswood*. Melbourne: Australian Scholarly Publishing.

Daylesford and Macedon Ranges Tourism. (2011) *Daylesford and the Macedon Ranges Official Visitor Guide*. Daylesford: Designscope.

Derriman, P. (2006) Landmarks. In M. Ray (ed.) *Long Shadows: 100 Years of Australian Cricket* (pp. 116–141). Milsons Point: Random House.

Douglas-Home, W. (1954) A glorious game say we. In *Half Term Report*. London: Longmans.

Gammon, S. (2007) Introduction: Sport, heritage and the English. An opportunity missed? In S. Gammon and G. Ramshaw (eds) *Heritage, Sport and Tourism: Sporting Pasts – Tourist Futures* (pp. 1–8). Oxon: Routledge.

Gemmell, J. (2008) Introduction: Cricket, race and the 2007 World Cup. In J. Gemmell and B. Majumdar (eds) *Cricket, Race and the 2007 World Cup* (pp. x–xix). London: Routledge.

Getz, D. (1997) *Event Management and Event Tourism*. New York: Cognizant Communication Corporation.

Hilton, C. (2006) *The Birth of the Ashes: The Amazing Story of the First Ashes Test*. Derby: Breedon Books Publishing.

Hogan, J. (2009) *Gender, Race and National Identity; Nations of Flesh and Blood*. New York: Routledge.

Horne, D. (1981) National identity in the period of the new nationalism. In *Nationalism and Class in Australia: 1920–1980*. Brisbane: Australian Studies Centre, University of Queensland.

Hutchinson, G. (2002) *True Blue*. Camberwell: Viking.

Jago, L. and Shaw, R. (1998) Special events: A conceptual and definitional framework. *Festival Management and Event Tourism* 5 (1–2), 21–32.

Morgan, N., Pritchard, A. and Pride, R. (2004) *Destination Branding: Creating the Unique Destination Proposition*. Oxford: Elsevier.
Munns, J. (1994) *Beyond Reasonable Doubt: The Birthplace of the Ashes*. Melbourne: McPherson's Printing Group.
Palmer, C. (2005) An ethnography of Englishness: Experiencing identity through tourism. *Annals of Tourism Research* 32 (1), 7–27.
Pearse, A. (2006) (Re)constructing Port Arthur and Thredbo: Tourist site tragedies and myths of national character. *Media International Australia Incorporating Culture and Policy* 120, 51–62.
Pretes, M. (2003) Tourism and nationalism. *Annals of Tourism Research* 30 (1), 125–142.
Purdie, N. and Wilss, L. (2007) Australian national identity: Young peoples' conceptions of what it means to be Australian. *National Identities* 9 (1), 67–82.
Rojek, C. (1997) Indexing, dragging, and social construction. In C. Rojek and J. Urry (eds) *Touring Cultures: Transformations of Travel and Theory* (pp. 52–74). London: Routledge.
Smith, L. (2006) *The Uses of Heritage*. Oxon: Routledge.
Spillman, L. (1997) *Nation and Commemoration: Creating National Identities in the United States and Australia*. New York: Cambridge University Press.
Stoddart, B. (1988) The hidden influence of sport. In V. Burgmann and J. Lee (eds) *Constructing a Culture: A People's History of Australia since 1788* (pp. 124–135). Melbourne: McPhee Gribble.
Veal, A.J. and Lynch, P. (2001) *Australian Leisure*. Frenchs Forest: Pearson Education.
Ward, R. (1966) *The Australian Legend*. Melbourne: Oxford University Press.
Waterton, E. (2010) *Politics, Policy and the Discourses of Heritage in Britain*. Basingstoke, Hampshire: Palgrave Macmillan.

4 Nostalgia at the Boundary: A Study at Lord's Cricket Ground

Denise Cardwell and Nazia Ali

> *Ascot is royal*
> *but Lord's is ah divine*
> *Donkey Drops*
> Chris Sparkes

Introduction

Lord's Cricket Ground, also referred to as Lord's, in London (England, United Kingdom) is an internationally recognised iconic site and landmark in the world of cricket. The historical roads of English cricket and the British colonial growth of the tradition of cricket to the colonies lead back to Lord's. This chapter examines the prevailing nostalgic importance of Lord's Cricket Ground to Australian cricket fans embarking upon a journey to the 'Home of Cricket'. The aim of the chapter is to understand how significant events – the Ashes – in cricket over the past years have reinforced the nostalgic value of Lord's Cricket Ground among Australian fans (see also Chapter 3 by White, this volume), especially during the Ashes test series at Lord's in July 2001 and July 2009 – played on English soil. The symbolic reference to Lord's Cricket Ground as 'The Home of Cricket' recognises the nostalgic symbolism of a place, which is entwined with history and sporting memories. The chapter sets out the theoretical and conceptual frameworks, which originate from the term nostalgia and lead further to the review of sport and cricket in the context of nostalgia. An overview of Lord's Cricket Ground is given, which explores the marker of Lord's as the 'home of cricket' and traces the history of Lord's. To comprehend the bond between Australian cricket and Lord's Cricket Ground the Australian presence at Lord's and the colonial legacy is inspected. This leads into the discussion of methodological issues associated with the fieldwork relevant to this chapter, in particular outlining the two phases of data collection: (i) stage one – the distribution of questionnaires; and (ii) stage two – textualisation of documentary sources. The qualitative and quantitative data were thematically analysed to interpret nostalgia at the boundaries in view of the past (for example, tradition/history), conations to 'home', the giving-and-taking of the Ashes, and residues of memories and emotions. This chapter contributes to the current literature on nostalgia in the field of sport tourism studies/management and in particular understanding nostalgic encounters and experiences at cricket grounds where little research to-date can be found. The work, in addition, builds on Cashman's (1984) observations that 'cricket takes place, as all cricket works attest, both within and beyond the boundary' (cited in Hutchins, 1996: 1) by drawing attention to the intangible importance of the boundary at Lord's Cricket Ground for Australian cricket sport tourists. Hutchins (1996: 1) adds to Cashman's (1984) statement by suggesting that the 'boundary between players and the crowd is too often interpreted as a boundary inside which the game is impervious to the crowd's influence'. In relation to Hutchins' (1996) argument, this chapter illustrates the never-ending or ever-lasting influence of Lord's boundary during and beyond a game of cricket.

Theoretical and Conceptual Issues: Nostalgia, Sport and Cricket

Nostalgia

Nostalgia stems from the Greek words 'nostos', translated as 'returning home', and 'algos', meaning 'pain, suffering, or grief' (Hofer, 1688 and Daniels, 1985 cited in Havlena & Holak, 1991; Legg, 2005; Wildschut *et al.*, 2006). Fairley (2003: 287–288) defined nostalgia as:

> a preference (general liking, positive attitude or favorable affect) towards objects (people, places, experiences, or things) from when one was younger or from times about which one has learned vicariously, perhaps through socialization or the media.

This brings to the forefront the 'bittersweet' nature of nostalgic reflections (Havlena & Holak, 1991; Wildschut *et al.*, 2006; Goulding, 1999), which are influenced by the past and aroused by the present or 'presentness of the present' in geographical spaces and places (Legg, 2005: 106). To comprehend the relationship between the past and present-day nostalgia, Davis' (1979) seminal text *Yearning for Yesterday: A Sociology of Nostalgia* attempts to bridge the yesterday with the today. Davis (1979: vii) asserts that the sociology of nostalgia 'is concerned with tracking down the sources of nostalgic experience in group life and determining what general relevance and meaning nostalgia has for our present life'. These nostalgic connections to the past or yester-year are central in this chapter as a means to interpreting the collective emotional and cognitive value of cricket to fans and/or spectators in a certain place. The work is underpinned by the socio-psychological theory of nostalgia and the associated concept of 'imagined (sport) geographies'. Sport places as nostalgically mediated landscapes give rise to 'imaginative sport geographies' as they are dependent upon the nostalgic recollections of the spectator (Bale, 2003). Moreover, in the context of the nostalgic element of place, Riley (1992) states that when the physical landscapes are familiar with a group of people these symbolic places become a source of shared memories and emotions, which bond people together. Imagined geographies reflect what Norberg-Schulz (1980) refers to as 'genius loci' – the unique spirit of place – and suggests that people experience something beyond the physical or sensory properties of places and can feel attachment to a spirit of a place. This interpretation can be extended to understanding the nostalgic symbolic value of Lord's Cricket Ground as the 'Home of Cricket' for colonies (for example, Australia) where historical and nationalistic ties with English cricket are prevalent.

Sport and nostalgia

The intention here is not to present a transdisciplinary review of definitions of sport-oriented nostalgia but to identify a fitting explanation of the theory which can be applied to sporting grounds or places. The location of place, which in this instance is Lord's Cricket Ground in London has a significant link to the past as it continues to reside in the nostalgic consciousness of cricket fans, across the world, today. It is not uncommon for sporting 'homes' and places to warrant a symbolic value reflective of the past, which serves to nourish the nostalgic minds and collective memories of sport fans in the present (Snyder, 1991). According to Fairley (2003: 288) 'nostalgia and memory are inextricably linked'. This framed in the context of sport can lead to the study of identity, sport-related consumption and tourism. Sport in its wider context is a 'fertile ground for nostalgia' because sporting events fuelled by media reports foster the collective and individual recollections of past in the present (Ramshaw, 2005: 2). As Snyder (1991: 229) notes in his study on the importance of nostalgia at the Sports Halls of Fame and Museums in America:

> [...] the attraction may also be based on the contrasts and incongruity between past and present. This juxtaposition of the past with the present creates the context for feelings of nostalgia.

This association between sport and nostalgia has been noted by several other researchers (Gibson, 1998; Hutchins, 2000; Bale, 2003; Fairley, 2003; Ramshaw, 2005; Ramshaw & Gammon, 2005; Bennett et al., 2007). Gibson (1998) announces the concept 'nostalgia sport tourism', which is recognised as a form of behaviour, associated with sport tourism, influenced by the desire to visit or pay homage to a significant stadium or venue reflective of a particular (sport) event. Ramshaw and Gammon (2005) build upon Gibson's (1998) interpretations of 'nostalgia sport tourism' by linking the concept to (sport) tangible and intangible heritage. Moreover, they assert that one of 'nostalgia sport tourism's' shortcomings is that nostalgia situates heritage in view of visitor attraction rather than considering heritage in the context of tourist perception or motivation (Ramshaw & Gammon, 2005). In this chapter, therefore, the nostalgic worth of Lord's Cricket Ground is appreciated on the one hand as a heritage site for Australian (and other) visitors and on the other hand as motivating the desire to search and engage with, what Ramshaw and Gammon (2005: 234–235) categorise as, 'intangible sport heritage' (for example, rituals, traditions, chants, memories and nostalgia).

Cricket and nostalgia

This chapter focuses upon nostalgia, shadowed by colonial and postcolonial sport heritage in cricket, which is infused by intangibles such as emotions, traditions, memories and imaginaries. The relationship between cricket and nostalgia in this chapter, therefore, directs attention to the imagined geographies of nationalism or what Anderson (1983) refers to as 'imagined communities of nationality'. For Hutchins (2000), following his analysis of Australia's legendary batsman Don Bradman and Australian cricket in the context of nostalgia, the functional importance of nostalgia as retrieval and retreat was noted. According to Hutchins (2000: 38):

> Nostalgia gives purpose and meaning to the present. It can work to retrieve and maintain the character and integrity of traditional practices and values in the development of contemporary viewpoints without

creating a static, reactionary and jaundiced mindset that insists on retreat from the uncertainties of the present and future.

The nostalgic value of cricket for Australians is deep-rooted in matters of nationalism and independence, hence the consolidated status of Australian cricket as a 'national sport' (Stewart, 2003) or 'cultural practice' in Australia (Stoddart, 2008). In particular, the Australian national collective-esteem is most vulnerable when Australia comes face-to-face with the old colonisers – England, especially during the Ashes test matches (whether home or away) (Stewart, 2003). Thus, cricket is more than a competitive game, in and beyond the boundary another 'game' is at play: an 'escape from coloniality and the expression of identity' (Stoddart, 2008: 1678). However, whereas India has managed to server all linkages with the colonial past (Majumdar, 2007: 88), this chapter explores Australia's perceived nostalgia to Lord's Cricket Ground, due to colonial linkages which cannot be broken, such as with the Ashes urn and consequently the associated Ashes test matches. As Bradbury (2008: 10) clearly notes:

> The significance of Australia and England test matches is neatly encapsulated in the words of Frank Tyson: The sporting world would not be the same without the compelling struggle for supremacy between England and Australia. Romance and drama – and high skill: those are the ingredients that have made the fight for the Ashes a matter of passion as a sport. It is with something approaching religious heights that an Ashes series is contested – and watched.

Lord's Cricket Ground: Background to 'The Home of Cricket'

Lord's: 'Home' of cricket

Lord's Cricket Ground in London, England is commonly referred to and recognised as the 'home' of cricket. This reference to Lord's as 'The Home of Cricket' was first coined by Lord Harris in 1921, subsequently creating a worldwide identity for this London-based cricket ground. In sport the term 'home' is used in different contexts and it is not unusual for sport venues to be labelled as 'home', not only relating to a team's or individual's 'home' ground, but a 'spiritual' home of a sport – the site that is recognised as the birthplace or significant centre of that sport, that over time has created an aura of tradition (Hinch & Higham, 2004: 7). The 'spiritual' importance of

Lord's was further reinforced by the Australian Prime Minister Sir Robert Menzies during the 1950s and 1960s in his reference to Lord's as 'the cathedral of cricket' (Stoddart, 2008). The status of Lord's Cricket Ground as the 'home' of cricket draws attention to the general emotive and nostalgic value attached to 'home' as a 'locus of our memories' (Tuan, 1974: 93), and the attachment to 'home' can become so powerful that it is perceived to be 'an irreplaceable centre of significance' (Relph, 1976: 39). Besides being an actual physical location, 'home' can be seen as a place of collective and individual construction, that is, an act of imagining (George, 1996), a narrative of identity (Sarup, 1996), and a project of unification (Waetjen, 1999). Subsequently, embedded within the concept of home are cognitive nostalgic constructions, which fulfil the need to locate one's sport 'home', to permit a sense of unification with one's yester-year in the today. The following quote, the introduction to Heald's (1990: 10) edited book, reflects the nostalgic myth and identity that has developed for Lord's Cricket Ground over the past 250 years:

> Some places are more than just places and one of these is Lord's. A cricket ground for a true cricket lover is never just a cricket ground, but some are more prosaic than others and there are some that do not lift the soul. It would be a curmudgeonly cricketing person, however, who did not feel some *frisson* of excitement at the idea of the Mecca of cricket, that still spacious oasis of green and wrought iron, linseed oil and Blanco, which lounges in glorious anachronism among the high rise flats, the private hospitals and the tourist hotels of London's St John's Wood. Even someone alien to cricket would surely sense that Lord's is special.

A history of Lord's Cricket Ground

Lord's Cricket Ground had two previous locations prior to its current one in Regents Park, London, England, and it may have been the early history of the ground which laid the foundations of the formation of its exclusivity. Cricket, as far back as 1723, had the support of royalty. Frederick Louis, Prince of Wales, encouraged other nobility to follow his lead (Harris & Ashley-Cooper, 1914). A forerunner to the Marylebone Cricket Club (MCC), The White Conduit Club was set up by this nobility in 1782 and assisted in the revising of the Laws of Cricket, and is fondly remembered by cricketers as 'the acorn from which sprang the gigantic oak known as the M.C.C' (Harris & Ashley-Cooper, 1914). Thomas Lord himself befriended these gentlemen 'of means', in particular the Earl of Winchilsea, and was encouraged, with backing, to make a private ground for their use. So 'Lord's' took residence in Dorset Fields, acquired from Lord Dorset on a 21-year lease, and by May 1787 it was ready for use. It was about this time that the Earl of Winchilsea, whilst making improvements to the game of cricket, was considered to be the instigator in the formation of the MCC. The link with nobility remained, therefore, as did the exclusivity embedded within the club, as most of the early members were all from public schools, wealthy and with positions and titles (Harris & Ashley-Cooper, 1914). After a brief move to a site near Regent's Park, the current site was eventually acquired and was ready to hold its first match in 1814.

The Case of Australia, Lord's Cricket Ground and the Ashes

The Australian presence at Lord's Cricket Ground

To exemplify nostalgia at the boundary of Lord's Cricket Ground this chapter focuses on Australian cricket fans and spectators during the Ashes test matches played in England in July 2001 and July 2009. This further draws attention to Australia's (nostalgic) relationship with Lord's, which is the steward, or the 'home', of the Ashes urn, which is displayed in the resident MCC Museum. Since 1882, various arguments over who should keep the Ashes urn and to whom the urn was originally given, have caused debates and controversy for followers and officials of the game of cricket. This has further reinforced the myth and symbolism attached to the Ashes and subsequently to Lord's Cricket Ground among Australian cricket enthusiasts (Osmond, 2006). According to Forsyth (1977), the only test matches that matter to Australians are the ones between themselves and England, not only on the field but also off the cricket ground. It can be argued such emotions are further stirred by the Ashes test matches on English soil and in particular at the 'Home of Cricket' – Lord's – a 'passionate rivalry' (Stewart, 2003). Thus, the more controversy the better to breed excitement and anticipation into the next game (Andrewes, 2000), which is the ultimate 'duelling in cricket' (Forsyth, 1977: 6). One of the most publicised episodes during one of these duels was the 'Bodyline' controversy of 1932–1933; the repeated use of fast, short deliveries by the England team to try to overcome Australian Don Bradman's excellent batting. Radio broadcasts at the time brought Australian society together as one, and led to newspapers confirming that 'cricket was a game...bound up with tradition, empire, codes of conduct, honour and manliness...' (Andrewes, 2000: 100). Winning in England, therefore, became the 'ultimate achievement'

(Cashman, 1992: 130) and international matches were a 'powerful symbol of the ambiguous relationship between Australia and England' (Stewart, 2003: 44).

The colonial legacy at Lord's Cricket Ground

As the main focus of this chapter is upon the Ashes test series in July 2001 and July 2009, the reference to the colonial relationship between England and Australia is inescapable. Australia won the Ashes test by a 4-1 win in 2001, and in 2009 England reclaimed the Ashes from the Australians after winning 2-1. The Ashes test matches played during July 2001 and July 2009 have been selected because Lord's Cricket Ground hosted the Ashes on English soil, which contains remnants of the 'bittersweet' (nostalgic) colonial legacy – both on and off the field for both England and Australia. It is not surprising then that Australian cricketers considered the importance of trashing the mother country at cricket a priority (Cashman, 1992; Stewart, 2003; Stoddart, 2008). Generally, within the British Empire sport was used to instil colonialist and nationalistic ideas in the colonies, with cricket in particular making a unique contribution within the Empire (Holt, 1990). According to Cashman (1998), cricket was associated with colonial nostalgia, reinforced by artistic illustrations depicting grounds with a bucolic English setting. Colonies embraced the game with enthusiasm and fervour as sport was used 'to build cultural bridges' (Holt, 1990: 212), especially for the earlier settlers to Australia from England. These earlier settlers from England to Australia quickly established a class structure within the 'New Country' and considered themselves to be of 'middle class' status as opposed to their working-class Welsh and Irish counterparts (Cashman, 1992). To this end, cricket in Australia also became a middle-class sport, very much in keeping with the class-defining structure within the game in England. Australians have just not felt the need to break their ties to the motherland by embracing other sports such as baseball (an American sport), and cricket was seen as the link between England and colonial Australia (Cashman, 1998).

Research Population and Methodological Issues

The research for this chapter was carried out in two stages, using both primary and secondary data. Stage one involved both quantitative and qualitative data which were obtained by random sampling of a cross section of visitors to Lord's Cricket Ground. Data were collected using questionnaires during October 2004 to January 2005. The questionnaire data presented in this chapter are specifically from responses obtained from Australian tourists visiting the museum at Lord's Cricket Ground because Australian cricket fans are the main focus in this chapter. Stage two involved qualitative data retrieved from documentary sources in March 2012, and involved analysing comments made by Australian tourists in the visitor books held in the museum at Lord's Cricket Ground. The assumption was that Australians were likely to visit Lord's Cricket Ground before, during or after the Ashes cricket matches, the second of five tests, played between the 19 and 22 July 2001 and 16 and 20 July 2009.

Stage one – questionnaire design and sample

This study took place at the MCC Museum which houses 140 years' worth of cricketing artefacts within the grounds of Lord's Cricket Ground and investigated the effect of the museum exhibits on the visitor. Quantitative and qualitative data were obtained from the results of a questionnaire that was designed with both open and closed questions, including Likert attitude scales (Oppenheim, 2003) to determine the extent, if any, of nostalgia experienced. To give the respondents the opportunity to express themselves about their visits open questions were used (Gratton & Jones, 2004); this would provide a further indication as to whether nostalgia had been experienced. Likert scales were used to provide a more accurate measurement of feelings experienced by the respondents than just yes or no answers: 'the reliability of Likert Scales tends to be good' (Oppenheim, 2003: 200). The original data collection came from visitors who comprised many nationalities, for example, New Zealanders, Indians, Sri Lankans, South Africans, Australians and British. From these, 19 questionnaires were completed by Australian visitors. Stage one of the data collection phase was conducted after the museum visits, so that the visitor was not looking for a nostalgic moment and to minimise the risk of influencing nostalgically skewed data. Davis (1979: 29) elaborates on this by commenting that '...to become too conscious of the mechanism of nostalgia is to endanger the ability to experience it'.

Questions were mostly related to the museum visit and tried to establish whether nostalgia had been experienced whilst looking at the exhibits and whether the visitor enjoyed the visit, as nostalgia is synonymous with positive feelings and pleasant memories. More specifically, some questions used were to establish whether visitors felt they had a nostalgic encounter whilst looking at the exhibits and were looking for the type of nostalgia experienced by establishing whether it was personal, collective or related to a time before the visitor was born. The Likert attitude scales used were designed using phrases taken from the literature, to establish the degree of nostalgia (if any) experienced, and whether the answers agreed with previous questions. The quantifiable data was analysed using the Statistical Package for the Social Sciences (SPSS) computer program. The categories for evaluations referred to in this chapter are: (i) looked back on a time with special affection; (ii) comparison of past with life today; (iii) remembering a pleasant time from the past; (iv) yearning to return to a particular moment in time; (v) left feeling warm and contented inside; (vi) talk to other visitors about the past; and (vii) sharing the same memories with other visitors.

Stage two – documentary sources

Research carried out in 2012 concentrated on the visitor books on display in the MCC Museum at Lord's Cricket Ground before, during, and just after the Ashes test matches of 2001 and 2009. According to Creswell (2003: 187), documentary sources give the researcher access to the actual words and language of participants and are an 'unobtrusive source of information'. Unlike some documentary sources, visitor books in particular have no issues of authenticity attached to them (Platt, 1981) and are a source of 'numerous individual comments' (Macdonald, 2005: 123). Some of these individual comments are sometimes a response to previous written comments and have been considered, according to Reid (2005: 8 cited in Macdonald, 2005), 'as a kind of virtual public sphere, something like an internet message board'. According to Walliman (2011), the analysis of secondary data, and according to Macdonald (2005) specifically the analysis of visitor books, is no different from the analysis of any other kinds of texts and qualitative research data. This source of visitor experience may be the only written evidence of a person's visit to Lord's Cricket Ground and what has been written in the visitor book is an emotional as well as a presumably valid and reliable source of the visitor's feelings about the site. The validity and reliability of comments presented in the visitor books is further reinforced by applying the principles of data triangulation in this research, which entailed combining the findings from documentary sources with the questionnaire method. The application of data triangulation is noted by Macdonald (2005: 123):

> Where visitor books are used in combination with other sources and methods, it may be possible to compare the responses made in visitor books with those produced in other contexts, and in this way to possibly

gain more insight into socio-demographic or other features of those making certain kinds of entries.

The researchers (Cardwell and Ali) read through the visitor books for the years 2001 and 2009 when the Ashes test series was hosted in England. In particular the focus was upon specific dates: before (5 July 2001–18 July 2001, and 8 July 2009–15 July 2009), during (19 July 2001–22 July 2001, and 16 July 2009–20 July 2009), and after (23 July 2001–27 August 2001, and 21 July 2009–24 August 2009). The Ashes fixtures at Lord's Cricket Ground were the occasions when Australian tourists and cricket fans were likely to be on-site; with the assumption they were either touring the museum and/or watching the Ashes test matches at Lord's. Tables 4.1 and 4.2 present the Ashes test match fixtures by date, venue/location and winning team for the years 2001 and 2009, respectively. Australian tourists in the visitor books were identified by location (for example, cities, states, territories and towns) and for ethical purposes the names of visitors were not recorded; therefore, in this chapter comments are accompanied by the

Table 4.1 The Ashes 2001 – England v. Australia

Test match	Dates	Venue/location	Winning team
One	5–8 July 2001	Edgbaston: Birmingham	Australia
Two	19–22 July 2001	Lord's: London	Australia
Three	2–4 August 2001	Trent Bridge: Nottingham	Australia
Four	16–20 August 2001	Headingley: Leeds	England
Five	23–27 August 2001	The Oval: London	Australia

Source: ESPN Cricinfo (2012).

Table 4.2 The Ashes 2009 – England v. Australia

Test match	Dates	Venue/location	Winning team
One	8 July–12 July 2009	SWALEC: Cardiff	Match drawn
Two	16 July–20 July 2009	Lord's: London	England
Three	30 July–3 August 2009	Edgbaston: Birmingham	Match drawn
Four	7 August–11 August 2009	Headingley: Leeds	Australia
Five	20 August–24 August 2009	The Brit Oval: London	England

Source: npower (2011).

visitor's location or place of residence in Australia and the date of the statement. For the purpose of this second stage of data collection the comments in the visitor books were classified and integrated into themes and based upon the contextual structure of this chapter. The textual interpretation comprised the following themes: tradition/history; home; nostalgia; the Ashes; and emotions.

The Nostalgic Boundary at Lord's Cricket Ground

The emergent findings from the research draw attention to several elements of nostalgia reviewed as theoretical and conceptual constructs earlier in this chapter. For matters of data triangulation the quantitative SPSS categories of evaluation created for the analysis of questionnaire data were subjected to a thematic analysis, which closely reflected the themes used in the interpretation of comments in the visitor books. Table 4.3 presents alignment of the categories of evaluation with related themes of analysis. The qualitative data presented in this part of the chapter refer to narratives collected from open questions in the questionnaire during stage one of the study and comments retrieved from the visitor books in stage two of the inquiry. The nostalgic boundary at Lord's Cricket Ground is discussed in view of before, during and after the Ashes test matches at Lord's, with much of the data extracted from the visitor books and the use of questionnaire responses to reinforce the comments presented.

Table 4.3 Thematic analysis of questionnaire SPSS categories of evaluation

SPSS categories of evaluation	Theme	Associated visitor book theme
(i) Looked back on a time with special affection.	Emotions	Emotions
(ii) Comparison of past with life today.	Tradition/history	Tradition/history
(iii) Remembering a pleasant time from the past.	Memories	Nostalgia
(iv) Yearning to return to a particular moment in time.	Nostalgia	Nostalgia
(v) Left feeling warm and contented inside.	Emotions	Emotions
(vi) Talk to other visitors about the past.	Nostalgia	Nostalgia
(vii) Sharing the same memories with other visitors.	Memories	Nostalgia

Lord's Cricket Ground and the aroma of nostalgia: 'The air is thick with nostalgia'[1]

In both the quantitative and qualitative data collected, direct reference to the concept of nostalgia was limited; however, associated motivational concepts such as tradition and history, emotions and imagined geographies defined by notions of 'home', which mediated the nostalgic encounter with Lord's Cricket Ground, exemplified the nostalgia experienced. Thus, the research brings to light the intangible nostalgic sport tourism motivations, which according to Ramshaw and Gammon (2005: 229) are 'hidden' beneath the umbrella concept of nostalgia. Questionnaire data revealed that approximately half of the respondents questioned agreed that Lord's Cricket Ground featured as a memorable place in their life because it reminded them of a pleasant time from the past and stirred memories of past tour matches and Ashes tests. Consequently, there was a yearning to return to a particular moment in time, a yester-year associated with Lord's. One questionnaire informant stated that being at Lord's gave rise to 'a feeling of nostalgia. A time back to my youth.' The findings support Gibson's (1998) observations that the search for authenticity in sport tourism experiences drives the nostalgic desire to visit a prominent place. For those with no nostalgic connection with Lord's Cricket Ground and no memory of Australia's cricket personalities and moments there was a sense of frustration, as one participant stated: 'disappointed I am too young and missed some memorable cricket moments'.

For the majority of Australian cricket supporters nostalgia extended beyond the self or individual to the collective, thus a collective sense of nostalgia, or what Davis (1979) calls 'collective nostalgia', emerged through the unification of memories with other Australian cricket fans. The questionnaire data indicated that collective nostalgia associated with sharing of memories was a result of talking to other visitors about the past and sharing the same cricket memories with other Australian tourists. Although, the focus is not upon group travel in sport tourism, the manifestation of collective nostalgia in sport memory and identity can foster a sense of comradeship, which contains the remnants of the cultural heritage of sport (Fairley, 2003). The only direct acknowledgement of the actual feeling of nostalgia is given in the following visitor comments after the Ashes test match at Lord's in 2001:

Chock a block full of nostalgia (South Australia, 13 August 2001).

Great nostalgia (Melbourne, 25 September 2001).

Tradition and history at Lord's Cricket Ground: 'A great tribute to cricket gone by'[2]

Lord's Cricket Ground plays a significant role in Australian cricket history and as traditional resonance it reinforces the nostalgic connections to the 'Home of Cricket'. Tradition and history are prerequisites to understanding the past and retain their transitionary character through one's life journey and are sustained through 'nostalgia-evoking events' associated with people and places (Holak & Havlena, 1992: 385), in this case Lord's Cricket Ground and the Ashes. The association with cricket at Lord's was utilised as a milestone in one's life, as a means to compare the past with life today, as questionnaire data revealed. However, it is unclear exactly which notable life events and happenings were aligned with cricket. The intangible heritage of Lord's, which is further sustained by the Ashes urn, narrates the legendary tradition and history of cricket in the present day. The comments in the visitor books written by Australian cricket fans clearly indicate the traditional and historical nostalgic significance of Lord's before, during and after the Ashes test matches in 2001 and 2009 in England:

Before the Ashes:
   Historical tradition (Melbourne, 3 July 2001)
   The stuff legends are made of (Melbourne, 9 July 2001)
   Tradition of cricket makes a life story (New South Wales, 9 July 2001)
   Enjoyed the history (Northern Territory, 7 July 2009)

During the Ashes:
   This is history (Queensland, 22 July 2001)

After the Ashes:
   Tradition (Sydney, 7 August 2001)
   Keep up the great tradition (Queensland, 15 August 2001)
   It just wouldn't be cricket without a visit to Lord's (New South Wales, 15 September 2001)

'I'm home!'[3]: Coming 'home' to the 'Home of Cricket'

The qualitative data illuminated the 'home' dimension of nostalgia, with Lord's Cricket Ground being the nostalgic 'home' of cricket, which houses the Ashes urn. Lord's was 'home' to the cricketing stories of tradition and Australian history, which was caught in the dynamics of sport and nationalism. Bradbury (2008) also points out the bond between Lord's, the great sporting institution, and the tradition of cricket, and Australia functioned to bridge the cultural gap between the 'mother country' and the 'loyal dominion'. The 1930s Australian cricketer Bill O'Reilly, when embarking on a tour in England, claimed he was 'going home' (Bradbury, 2008: 8). As one participant questioned stated in the questionnaire: 'I really came here today for my father and brothers. I grew up with cricket in Australia, my father and brothers played for many years and would expect me to visit here, after all it is the home of cricket.' For Australian cricket enthusiasts, coming to Lord's was about coming 'home' to the origins of cricket and the imagined 'home', which announced the presence of Australia on English soil. There was one insertion in the 2001 visitor book from an Australian expatriate living in Pennsylvania (US) which captured the value of Lord's in locating 'home' by stating 'makes me homesick for Australia'. Homesickness is equated to nostalgia because of its close associations with yearning for yester-year and the longing to return home (Wildschut *et al.*, 2006). When the Swiss Johannes Hofer (1688/1934) first introduced the concept nostalgia as a neurological disease, he observed the constant thinking of 'home' as a symptom of nostalgia (cited in Wildschut *et al.*, 2006). The following visitor comments taken from the 2001 and 2009 visitor books highlight the location of Lord's Cricket Ground as 'home' in the minds of Australians:

Before the Ashes:
    At last, here where it all began (Western Australia, 17 July 2001).
    Birthplace of the Ashes (Victoria, 7 July 2009).
    I feel at home with my feet up (Melbourne, 27 August 2001).

During the Ashes:
    Great feeling at the home of cricket (South Australia, 18 July 2009).
    Home! (Melbourne, 21 July 2009).

After the Ashes:
    Good to be back at the home of cricket (Australia, 24 September 2001).
    Home of Glenn McGrath (New South Wales, 23 July 2009).
    Happy to have made it to the home of cricket (Victoria, 20 August 2009).

It has been recognised that some sport attractions and sites of sport have special meanings for visitors and can generate deep attachments (Hinch & Higham, 2004), which is depicted in references to Lord's as 'home' by

Australian (cricket) sport tourists. Of relevance to imagined geographies of 'home' is Low's (1992) suggestion that place attachment can occur for mythical places that have never been experienced, and these places are imbued with special meaning within a culture through storytelling or place naming. These narratives may become embedded in the history of places and Robertson and Richards (2003) believe that landscapes can be viewed as a palimpsest, that history can be seen through the layers that have built up around a place.

However, for some Australian cricket fans, Lord's as the 'home' of the Ashes urn featured as a rather controversial and bittersweet reminder of the colonial and imperial ownership powers of the game, and the endless rivalry between Australia and England during the Ashes. The cricket test matches with England were a stark reminder for Australia of the British colonial gaze and to win against England was a mechanism for Australians to 'prove themselves in the eyes of the British' (Kaufman & Patterson, 2005: 101). In the visitor books the angst of the Ashes urn residing in the MCC Museum at Lord's is aired in the following comments:

> ...but what are the Ashes here for? (New South Wales, 29 August 2001)
>
> Thanks for the memories kept – give us back the urn (Western Australia, 30 August 2001)
>
> Bring home the Ashes (Sydney, 5 July 2009)

The emotive value of Lord's Cricket Ground: 'Can now die a happy man'[4]

The journey to Lord's Cricket Ground was an emotionally overwhelming and moving encounter for Australian cricket fans and enthusiasts alike. Generally, there is a 'shared love of cricket' between competing nations, which fuels the emotions of cricket lovers both on and off the field (Stoddart, 2008) and cricket is 'treated [...] as being more than just a game' (Hutchins, 1996: 3). The theme tune 'we don't like cricket, we love it', from the song 'Dreadlock Holiday' (1978) by the English rock band 10cc is played before and after the advertising intervals during the broadcasting of cricket test matches on the Sky Sports satellite/digital channel. Moreover, an emotion such as love is synonymous of nostalgia because according to Wildschut *et al.* (2006: 989) 'like love, nostalgia bolsters social bonds', which is also evident in the works of Davis (1979), Holak and Havlena (1992), and Fairley (2003). The analysis of the questionnaire data revealed that many Australians at Lord's agreed that they looked back on a time, reflected in cricket, with special affection. The majority of comments in the visitor books (2001 and 2009) – before, during and after the Ashes test games – from Australian (cricket) tourists were skewed towards the dynamic relationship between Lord's, cricket and themselves. Prominent sport venues have the ability to extract emotions from spectators, and the stadium plays a pivotal role in transforming the passive spectator into an emotional being, which further nourishes collective emotions – as is the case at Lord's Cricket Ground for Australian audiences. As Jaireth (1996, cited in Hutchins, 1996: 1) states:

> Mass spectacles have the capacity to trigger collective emotions, to persuade an individual to become one with a group, to be loyal to a team, a group and a nation. Modern stadiums, the hosts of modern sports spectacles, are some of those sites where... contrary to normal theatrical conventions, the spectators do not remain passive observers but turn into actors.

To physically be at Lord's Cricket Ground was evidence of transforming the once imagined or dreamed experience into a reality. The affective nature of this achievement is depicted in the following visitor book statements:

Before the Ashes:
 Had always wanted to come to Lords (New South Wales, 11 July 2001)
 Experience of a lifetime (Brisbane, 16 July 2001)
 Absolutely brilliant, left me gasping for air (New South Wales, 17 July 2001)

During the Ashes:
 Lifelong dream (New South Wales, 14 July 2009)
 Dream come true (South Australia, 17 July 2009)
 A dream come true after 30 years (Sydney, 18 July 2009)

After the Ashes:
 A boyhood fantasy (New South Wales, 23 July 2001)
 Am thrilled to be here (Adelaide, 11 September 2001)
 Words can't describe (Melbourne, 17 September 2001)
 Can't believe I'm here (Victoria, 5 August 2009)
 I finally made it here, what an honour!!! I love this place (Perth, 10 October 2011)

Conclusions

Lord's Cricket Ground was of strong nostalgic importance to Australian cricket fans, enthusiasts, visitors, tourists and spectators journeying to England to watch the Ashes in 2001 and 2009. The colonial encounter with Lord's Cricket Ground has become a long-lasting affair for Australian cricket fans and has been at the heart of the battle for the Ashes. The nostalgia is both of a tangible and an intangible nature because the geography of nostalgia is a manifestation of physical proximity of being (the tangible) and affective imaginary of being (the intangible). These nostalgic (politicised) landscapes or boundaries at Lord's Cricket Ground are entanglements of the past (for example, tradition/history), conations to 'home', the giving-and-taking of the Ashes, and residues of memories and emotions. Thus nostalgia at and beyond the boundary of Lord's Cricket Ground is an amalgamation of the aforementioned encounters and experiences of Australians as supporters of their national team (Australia) and as ambassadors for their nations. For Australians the Ashes test matches present an opportunity to pay homage to Lord's – the 'home'/'cathedral' of cricket. Lord's Cricket Ground, the Ashes test matches and the Ashes urn are symbolic nostalgic reminders of the duality of the boundary, which marks the bittersweet cricket relations of passion and rivalry between Australia and its mother country, England. Nevertheless, Lord's continues to play a significant role in the lives of Australians, for whom cricket bears a nostalgic value, which is not limited to the Ashes as highlighted by the findings before and after the Ashes test matches.

As an endnote to this chapter it is worth directing attention to impending implications concerning the future of Lord's Cricket Ground as the 'Home of Cricket' and of its continued nostalgic value to nations such as Australia. The movement of the International Cricket Council (ICC), and subsequently its administrative powers, from Lord's in London to Dubai in the United Arab Emirates could possibly undermine the symbolic and imaginary presence of Lord's as the 'Home of Cricket'. Rumford (2007) refers to this relocation of the ICC to Dubai and the diminishing of the 'traditional' test cricketing format for the more favoured marketable and revenue-generating one-day international matches as a project of the *'post-Westernization'* of world cricket (perhaps reflected even more strongly in the Twenty20 format). Moreover, according to Rumford (2007), this move signifies for the game of cricket the shifting of colonial/Western powers to post-colonial/Eastern 'superpowers'. This presents opportunities for future research into the changing dynamics of nostalgia beyond the boundary of Lord's Cricket Ground following the relocation of the ICC to a 'new' home. Other possible directions for future research are to study the nostalgic attachments of England with Lord's Cricket Ground in view of the Ashes, as England also enters into battle with Australians to win the Ashes. This would entail interpreting the comments of England cricket fans in the visitor books to understand the nostalgic boundary at Lord's Cricket Ground from the exporters of cricket to the colonies and in extending research agendas to other colonies with no links to the Ashes, such as India, Pakistan and South Africa, to comprehend the interrelationship between cricket, nostalgia and Lord's Cricket Ground.

Acknowledgements

The authors would like to thank Dr Sally Everett (University of Bedfordshire, Head of Division of Tourism and Leisure) for her continued support during the writing of this chapter and the time given to us for the associated fieldwork activities and writing of this chapter. We are both grateful to Mr Neil Robinson, Research Officer, at the Lord's Cricket Ground for the use of the library facilities and access to the visitor books for the purpose of this chapter.

Notes

(1) A recent comment by an Australian cricket fan taken from the 2011 visitor book (New South Wales, 18 September 2011).
(2) A recent comment by an Australian cricket fan taken from the 2011 visitor book (Melbourne, 20 September 2011).
(3) A comment by an Australian cricket fan taken from the 2001 visitor book (New South Wales, 17 July 2001).
(4) A comment by an Australian cricket fan taken from the 2001 visitor book (New South Wales, 23 July 2001).

References

Anderson, B. (1983) *Imagined Communities*. London: Verso.
Andrewes, F. (2000) 'They play in your home': Cricket, media and modernity in pre-war Australia. In J.A. Mangan and J. Nauright (eds) *Past and Present* (pp. 93–109). London: Frank Cass.
Bale, J. (2003) *Sports Geography*. London: Routledge.
Bennett, R., Ali-Choudhury, R. and Mousley, W. (2007) Television viewers' motivations to follow the 2005 Ashes test series: Implications for the re-branding of English cricket. *Journal of Product and Brand Management* 16 (1), 23–37.
Bradbury, C. (2008) Sport and imperialism: The bonds of empire between the mother country and a loyal dominion (online). New South Wales: The Kings School/Premier's Westfield History Scholarship. See www.det.nsw.edu.au/media/downloads/deta wscholar/scholarships/yr08/june/cbradbury.doc (accessed 21 March 2012).

Cashman, R. (1992) Symbols of imperial unity: Anglo-Australian cricketers: 1877–1900. In J.A. Mangan (ed.) *The Cultural Bond: Sport Empire, Society* (pp. 128–141). London: Frank Cass & Co.
Cashman, R. (1998) 'Australia'. In B. Stoddart, B. and K.A.P. Sandiford (eds) *The Imperial Game* (pp. 34–54). Manchester: Manchester University Press.
Creswell, J.W. (2003) *Research Design* (2nd edn). Thousand Oaks: Sage.
Davis, F. (1979) *Yearning for Yesterday: A Sociology of Nostalgia*. New York: The Free Press.
ESPN Cricinfo (2012) The Ashes 2001/results (online), ESPN EMEA. See www.espncricinfo.com/ci/engine/series/60708.html (accessed 12 April 2012).
Fairley, S. (2003) In search of relived social experience: Group-based nostalgia sport tourism. *Journal of Sport Management* 17, 284–304.
Forsyth, C. (1977) *Pitched Battles*. Victoria, Australia: Widescope International Publishers.
George, R.M. (1996) *The Politics of Home*. Cambridge: Cambridge University Press.
Gibson, H. (1998) Sport tourism: A critical analysis of research. *Sport Management Review* 1, 45–76.
Goulding, C. (1999) Heritage, nostalgia, and the 'grey' consumer. *Journal of Marketing Practice: Applied Marketing Science* 5 (6/7/8), 177–199.
Gratton, C. and Jones, I. (2004) *Research Methods for Sport Studies*. London: Routledge.
Lord Harris (1921) *A Few Short Runs*. London: John Murray.
Lord Harris and Ashley-Cooper, F.S. (1914) *Lords and the MCC*. London: The London & Counties Press Association Ltd.
Havlena, W.J. and Holak, S.L. (1991) 'The good old days': Observations on nostalgia and its role in consumer behaviour. *Advances in Consumer Research* 18, 323–329 (online). See www.acrwebsite.org/volumes/display.asp?id=7180 (accessed 22 March 2012).
Holak, S.L. and Havlena, W.J. (1992) 'Nostalgia: An exploratory study of themes and emotions in the Nostalgic experience. *Advances in Consumer Research*, 19, 380–387.
Heald, T. (ed.) (1990) *My Lord's, A Celebration of the World's Greatest Cricket Ground*. London: Willow Books Harper Collins.
Hinch, T. and Higham, J. (2004) *Sport Tourism Development*. Clevedon: Channel View Publications.
Holt, R. (1990) *Sport and the British*. Oxford: Clarendon Press.
Hutchins, C. (1996) It's just not cricket: The making of the Australian cricket crowd 1877–1979. BA (Hons) thesis (online), University of Adelaide, Australia. See http://digital.library.adelaide.edu.au/theses/09AR/09arh974.pdf (accessed 14 April 2012).
Hutchins, B. (2000) The uses of nostalgia: An analysis of Don Bradman and Australian cricket. *Social Alternatives* 19 (2), 35–39.
Kaufman, J. and Patterson, O. (2005) Cross-national cultural diffusion: The global spread of cricket. *American Sociological Review* 70, 82–110.
Legg, S. (2005) Memory and nostalgia. *Cultural Geographies* 11, 99–107.
Low, S.M. (1992) Symbolic ties that bind, place attachment in the plaza. In I. Altman and S. Low (eds) *Place Attachment* (pp. 165–185). New York: Plenum Press.
Macdonald, S. (2005) Accessing audiences: Visiting visitor books. *Museum and Society* 3 (3), 119–136.
Majumdar, B. (2007) Nationalistic romance to post-colonial sport: Cricket in 2006 India. *Sport in Society* 10 (1), 88–100.
Norberg-Schutz, C. (1980) *Genius Loci, Towards a Phenomenology of Architecture*. New York: Rizzoli.

npower (2011) npower Ashes test series 2009 (online), npower's cricket website. See http://cricket.npower.com/web/npower_ashes_test_series_fixtures/index.htm (accessed 12 April 2012).

Oppenheim, A.N. (2003) *Questionnaire Design, Interviewing and Attitude Measurement*. London: Continuum.

Osmond, R. (2006) *The Battle for the Ashes: A Cricket Timeline History*. Cambridge: Worth Press.

Platt, J. (1981) Evidence and proof in documentary research: 1. *Sociological Review* 29 (1), 31–52.

Ramshaw, G. (2005) Nostalgia, heritage, and imaginative sports geographies: Sport and cultural landscapes'. Paper presented at *The Forum UNESCO University and Heritage 10th International Seminar 'Cultural Landscapes in the 21st Century'*, 11–16 April, Newcastle upon Tyne, UK.

Ramshaw, G. and Gammon, S. (2005) More than just nostalgia? Exploring the heritage/sport tourism nexus. *Journal of Sport Tourism* 10 (4), 229–241.

Relph, E. (1976) *Place and Placelessness*. London: Pion.

Riley, R.B. (1992) Attachment of the ordinary landscape. In I. Altman and S.M. Low (eds) *Place Attachment* (pp. 13–35). New York: Plenum Press.

Robertson, I. and Richards, P. (eds) (2003) *Studying Cultural Landscapes*. London: Hodder Arnold.

Rumford, C. (2007) More than a game: Globalisation and the post-westernization of world cricket. *Global Networks* 7 (2), 202–214.

Sarup, M. (1996) *Identity, Culture and the Postmodern World*. Edinburgh: Edinburgh University Press.

Stewart, B. (2003) The crisis of confidence in Australian first-class cricket in the 1950s: Causes and consequences. *Sporting Traditions* 20 (1), 43–62.

Sparkes, C. (2000) *Donkey Drops Sheffield*. In press.

Stoddart, B. (2008) The centrality of cricket in Indo-Australian relations: India, Australia and the 'cricket imaginary'. *The International Journal of the History of Sport* 25 (12), 1671–1685.

Snyder, E.E. (1991) Sociology of nostalgia: Sport halls of fame and museums in America. *Sociology of Sport Journal* 8, 228–238.

Tuan, Yi-Fu (1974) *Topophilia*. New Jersey: Prentice-Hall Inc.

Waetjen, T. (1999) The 'home' in homeland: Gender, national space, and Inkatho's politics of ethnicity. *Ethnic and Racial Studies* 22 (4), 653–678.

Walliman, N. (2011) *Your Research Project* (3rd edn). London: Sage.

Wildschut, T., Sedikides, C., Arndt, J. and Routledge, C. (2006) Nostalgia: Content, triggers, functions. *Journal of Personality and Social Psychology* 91 (5), 975–993.

5 Development of the Rose Bowl as a Venue for Cricket and Other Events

Joanne Parrett

> *Do you remember Brentwood*
> *Where Essex used to play*
> *On a sporting wicket*
> *Every year in May?...*
>
> *They do not play in Brentwood now.*
> *The umpires in their long white coats, and players*
> *All have gone.*
> *Uneconomic, so they cried*
> *Much too small...*
> *...So Brentwood died.*
> *Brentwood*, D.A. Williams

Introduction

Our mission at the Rose Bowl is to create the region's finest leisure village, producing excellent sports and leisure facilities for the entire community all day, every day. (*Southern Daily Echo*, 2001 – Graham Walker, chief executive, Rose Bowl plc)

The purpose of this chapter is to look at the economic impact of the development of the Rose Bowl, how it came into existence as the home of Hampshire County Cricket (HCCC), and also how the venue has become more than just a home for cricket.

In recent years there have been a number of studies focusing on the economic impacts of the development of sports venues (Gratton & Henry, 2005);

however, most of these are not based on cricket stadiums (rather mostly football), but they should still be considered. We have also seen the increased importance of the role that sport plays in *urban economies* (Bale & Moen, 1995; Gratton, 1998) and the growing importance of the service sector in the development of new sports venues. Much has been written about the cost and benefits of the development of a new stadium, particularly relating to stadium development in the United States as for example Baade and Dye (1988a), who look at the economic rationale for pubic subsidisation of sports stadiums, and more recently, Williams (1997), who discusses consumer services and the economic development of stadiums). Before looking into the Rose Bowl in depth, I feel it is appropriate to consider Gratton and Henry's (2005) core arguments for investment of funds in the development of a sports stadium like the Rose Bowl, as such aspects appear not have been considered before when discussing the development of cricket stadiums.

First, the reality today is that sports teams like HCCC (Gannaway, 1990; Wynne-Thomas, 1998), and the events that are run from its stadium at the Rose Bowl, are in fact 'business investments both for the organisation that sponsor them and for the communities which help host the events' (Gratton & Henry, 2005: 15). When the Rose Bowl was originally developed, there was no investment from the Local Council (Eastleigh Borough Council) in terms of public money, but we shall see later in this chapter how this had to change to ease the financial concerns of the club (Renshaw, 2001). Communities surrounding a venue like the Rose Bowl attract visitors from outside the area, who in essence are providing 'an infusion of new wealth into the community' (Gibson, 2005: 59). While the Rose Bowl organisation can obviously assess the financial success or failure of an event, the community surrounding the Rose Bowl needs to assess the benefits in the broader public interest, such as transport issues (Jones, 2001).

Second, a professional sports club like HCCC is 'likely to attract a significant amount of media coverage for the area in which it is located' (Gratton & Henry, 2005: 17). The issue of media coverage started in advance of the move to the new stadium at West End, with the hope of it becoming a test match venue, meaning that the media could play an important role in the life of the Rose Bowl.

Third, Gratton and Henry (2005: 19) go on to talk about an 'enhanced community image', as it was evident that there had been increased exposure of the development of the Rose Bowl, and this could be seen as an opportunity to change the image of cricket, placing it in a wider context, and changing people's perceptions of what the purpose of a new cricket stadium could be for the area. What the stadium today is trying to do is to be service-oriented, i.e. catering for consumer needs, whether they are pure sports spectators or spectators of other events being held at the stadium.

Fourth, Gratton and Henry (2005: 19) discuss the 'notion that a sports facility will stimulate additional development' and therefore this would contribute to the local area in terms of increased visibility and an enhanced image from the investment made and in turn may provide additional revenue for the local council. Over time the Rose Bowl has seen an upgrading of its facilities as a result of demand for the services currently offered by the stadium, in the hope it would generate more income for the stadium.

Finally, Gratton and Henry (2005: 20) discuss 'psychic value', relating to the benefits accrued by local residents who support their team, as a successful event or team like HCCC could mean that the locals 'grow in confidence and have a sense of pride in what has been achieved' (2005: 20). However, what will become evident is that local residents are more concerned about the impact that the development of the Rose Bowl will have on local communities from a negative point of view.

The Rose Bowl clearly represents a state of the art cricket ground, being designed by Sir Michael Hopkins, who designed the Mound Stand at Lord's. The ground is like a circular amphitheatre with a three-storey pavilion of which its canopied roof is the main feature. It has been home to HCCC since its construction in 2000. The ground has evolved in a short space of time into a leading leisure venue in the county, with seating for 10,000, having no obstructed views, and floodlights enabling matches to continue after dark. However, the development of the Rose Bowl has not been easy, resulting in many issues that have had to be addressed (Allen, 2007).

The Process of Redevelopment

The planning process of the move from the existing ground at Northlands Road in Southampton began early in 1988 when two committee members wrote to the club's 6000 members. This resulted in the establishment of a feasibility study and a search for land adjacent to the M27. By the summer of 1988 a site had been located in West End (eastern edge of the city), some 40 acres in size, which was owned by Queens College, Oxford. Queens College offered the land on a 999-year lease and in October 1988 Eastleigh Borough Council granted outline planning permission for the main and nursery ground. By 1990 when the first edition of the Hampshire Members Newsletter was issued it informed members 'The new County Ground planned for West End will take Hampshire Cricket into the 21st century with more space and modern facilities, a target date for first class cricket at the new headquarters is 1995' (1990: n.p.). During 1994/1995 two important events occurred; the lease of the land was signed (October 1994) and in January 1995 the club submitted a 50-page application for lottery funding. This year also saw the launch of the 'Centenary 95 Appeal' to raise funds. In August 1996 an announcement was made that the National Lottery Sports Fund had made an award for the project of £7,176,728 – the largest award in the southern area of England.

By 1996 the process towards the creation of the new ground was moving slowly, and in an article written in the *Daily Telegraph* by Mark Nicholas (past Hampshire cricketer) it was mentioned that 'the ground has been there since 1884 and was falling apart' (www.rosebowlplc.com). The bulldozers finally moved in on the Southampton County Ground in October 2000 and in line with what members and spectators had known for many years, namely that the building and facilities were not suitable for a sporting venue, they were easily demolished.

By 2000/2001, the financial position of Hampshire cricket had become very difficult. Brian Ford (chairman) resigned in October 2000 and the new chairman, Rod Bransgrove reviewed all aspects of the new development in advance of the 2001 annual general meeting (AGM). In March 2001 the *Southern Daily Echo* had a dramatic headline – 'Change or Die! Hampshire cry', 'Hampshire CCC members know they will not only be voting for a piece of history at the AGM but to stop the club becoming history' (n.p.). The club, which was suffering from financial concerns, had asked its members to vote on converting the club from being a members' club to the first privately owned company in cricket. At the 2001 Annual General Meeting, Rod Bransgrove (Chairman) noted 'our club will be the first to respond to the changing environment in this way but certainly won't be the last' and went on to announce to the members that his vision was to create one of the best stadiums in the world (Minutes HCCC, 2001: n.p.). Later in the year the *Southern Daily Echo* had an interview with the new chief executive (Graham Walker) who is quoted in saying 'Our mission at the Rose Bowl is to create the region's finest leisure village, producing excellent sports and leisure facilities for the entire community all day, every day and creating one of the best cricket stadiums in the world' (2001: n.p.). It was decided that a privately owned company would be more suitable to run the complex business that the club would become rather than a committee on a part-time basis. The final cost of the Rose Bowl when the county started playing was estimated to be £24m, of which £5m was still needed in 2001.

The Rose Bowl, even in its early years, has already staged a number of high profile international cricket matches and the way the ground has been constructed means that the seating can be expanded to 20,000 when necessary. However the problem of traffic in the area when such large audience matches are being played has caused many issues with the local community that need to be addressed. Eventually a second access road was built and the issues over traffic congestion resolved. Primarily the Rose Bowl is a cricket venue, but in order to maximise income from the stadium its use has expanded into being a concert venue, with a number of high profile artists performing (between 2005 and 2008) to sell-out crowds, including Oasis, Blue, Neil Diamond, The Who and R.E.M. According to the Rose Bowl website there were no planned concerts in 2012 (http://www.atmevents.co.uk/cricke_rose_bowl.php).

In November 2006, the English Cricket Board awarded the Rose Bowl provisional Category A accredited status. A Rose Bowl press release also announced a £45m development plan to turn the ground into the 'best cricket and entertainment venues in the world' (http://www.atmevents.co.uk/cricke_rose_bowl.php).

By early 2008, Rose Bowl plc. had made a financial loss and at the time of writing the company had yet to record a profit since cricket began at the West End site in 2001. The reality was that the income generated is heavily dependant on major matches such as Tests, and in 2008 the Rose Bowl had only one international match according to Hampshire chairman Rod Bransgrove (BBC Sport, February 2008). He then went on to say that 'other aspects of the business continue to improve and we are striving for the current trading year to produce breakeven results'. By April 2008, Hampshire had been granted planning permission to begin the previously announced £45m redevelopment of the Rose Bowl, planned to increase capacity by 5000 (BBC Sport, April 2008). Plans included the construction of two new stands, a 175-bedroom hotel and the expansion of the golf course to 18 holes. The Rose Bowl plc managing director Glen Delve stated 'it allows us to move to the next stage in the development of this fabulous stadium, a facility which will bring enormous economic, social, sporting and community benefits to Eastleigh and South Hampshire in general' (Southern Daily Echo, October 2007: n.p.).

In April 2008, the BBC Sport website stated that Hampshire's Rose Bowl would host a test match for the first time when England faced Sri Lanka in 2011 (BBC Sport website, 2008). Rod Bransgrove stated in an interview at the time 'we fully intend to be a permanent fixture on the test match calendar from 2011 onwards' and that the 'allocation of matches demonstrates that with the £45 m development, turning the ground into the first ever model test match ground, we are now one of the major sports and entertainment venues in the country' (BBC Sports, 2008), making clear that the venue had turned a corner in terms of its potential for income generation.

By 2009, Eastleigh Borough Council (EBC) – (Full Council, Rose Bowl Update, n.p.), recorded that 'the Rose Bowl is a high quality sports and entertainment complex recognised as being one of the finest in the country, providing a real asset to the Council and they recognise the contribution it can play in regeneration, community facilities and the reputation of the area'. EBC had previously approved the investment of £32m in the development of the hotel and additional conference facilities, which it had hoped to be completed in time for the start of the 2011 cricket season. However an application for a judicial review had been made by three major local hoteliers who had hoped to see the decision overturned by the courts, which was to delay the major building work of this development (new hotel facility).

In 2010, the first stage of the redevelopment was realised as two new stands were completed around the ground, increasing capacity to 25,000. It was intended that the development would include the building of a 175-bed, four-star hotel and 75 hospitality boxes overlooking the ground. Also during this year, readers of *All Out Cricket* magazine voted the Rose Bowl 'Best International Ground' in an independent survey of fans around the country and the 'Most Improved Ground' (www.alloutcricket.com).

Related Facilities

As with many modern sports facilities, the Rose Bowl now accommodates a range of additional services and facilities, most related directly or indirectly to its primary cricketing function.

The venue itself is located in the heart of southern England with motorway and air links nearby. The Rose Bowl has a range of flexible spaces and offers an impressive setting for a variety of events. This venue is capable of accommodating a wide range of events and activities throughout the year from small board meetings for 10 people to full-day conferences for 200, with opportunities for an intimate dinner for 20 or a banquet for 300 guests. In total there are seven meeting rooms with a maximum capacity of 250 in theatre style and 10 breakout rooms. The range of events that can be organised include: activity days, awards dinners, breakfast meetings, Christmas parties, company fun days, conferences, corporate hospitality, dinner dances, gala dinners, product launches, teambuilding, training courses and weddings.

The Rose Bowl offers a number of different ways to entertain corporate guests and the venue offers three types of hospitality – domestic, CB40 and county championship hospitality. Looking at these in more detail reveals the following typical offering. A domestic match following a Twenty20 format, for example, would have a typical itinerary that started at 5 pm and finished at nearly 11 pm. An alternative would be CB40, which is List A cricket (usually 40 or 50 overs per side) and for this type of cricket the hospitality would be either a full evening or a Sunday afternoon, with the usual hospitality offerings. The final type of hospitality is the traditional form of cricket – county championship, which would have a full day of hospitality from 9.30 am to nearly 7 pm.

At the highest (test) level of cricket, the 2012 season, which saw England playing one-day internationals against the West Indies and South Africa, had corporate hospitality (offered by other companies) available in two suites – the Robin Smith Suite and the Shane Warne Suite. The Robin Smith Suite is situated in the main pavilion and the hospitality includes reserved seating on the roof terrace located between the players' dressing rooms, giving the opportunity to meet competing players. The Shane Warne Suite is located in the new West Stand, with excellent views of the ground.

The new development also contains an indoor cricket school that offers a large training facility located on the first floor of the main Pavilion primarily used as a six-lane full cricket venue, with different nets offering varying batting conditions. It is also used to host a number of indoor competitions and is used on match days as an extension to the Rose Bowl's corporate hospitality facilities to host trade exhibitions. This part of the Rose Bowl is offered to the general public for hire and has been used for various different sporting activities, and has a viewing balcony for spectators to watch the action.

A personal training company – Catalyst PT Ltd – is located at the Rose Bowl, offering a state of the art fitness suite featuring high-quality cardiovascular and resistance equipment. Hampshire Cricket members get a free consultation and a first session at the facility. Also based on-site and attached to Catalyst PT Ltd, are the Hedge End Podiatry and Chiropody Clinic. A variety of services are offered including treatment of a range of foot problems, and analysis of foot and lower limb pain analysis. Another business is also located within Catalyst: Julia's Saloon. This is a beauty salon run by a professional beauty therapist offering a variety of beauty treatments. The land on which the tennis/fitness centre is located is owned by the council and leased to the Esporta Group on a 99-year lease (EBC – Rose Bowl Update 2009: n.p.).

The Rose Bowl Country Golf Club was established in 1999, the course offers interesting holes for all abilities. It embraces the traditions of a golf club and the course is available to both members and visitors. A golf professional can be booked for lessons and a wide range of golfing products are available in the pro shop.

As part of the redevelopment of the Rose Bowl, a 175-bedroom, four-star hotel is planned and will be located at the northern end of the ground. The hotel is to offer restaurants, bars and a function room facing onto the pitch as well as a Spar Leisure Club and gym for treatments and relaxation. It is also expected that this hotel will accommodate the club house for the Rose Bowl's 18-hole, par 71 course, including a terrace with views across the 18th green. A high-quality main restaurant will offer cuisine for 150 diners outside, with views across the countryside surrounding the Rose Bowl. The hotel is a key addition to the Rose Bowl's conference and exhibition facilities and forms part of the overall leisure venue (Source – Rose Bowl plc).

Redevelopment Issues

During 2011, the Rose Bowl was at the centre of a number of stories in newspapers concerning its poor financial position. The *Guardian* Newspaper (2011: 49) detailed the fact that the Rose Bowl had 'become the notable loser in the ECB's allocation of major international matches' (Haralabakis, 2005), reflecting the fact that Hampshire had missed out on staging Ashes tests in 2013 and 2015. Unfortunately the Rose Bowl was only awarded one test in 2014, seven one-day internationals between 2011 and 2016 and two Twenty20 internationals, which represents a lost opportunity in terms of income for the venue, something which will be difficult to achieve by other means.

The Rose Bowl has grown out of the ECB's system of competitive tendering, which basically shook up the established order of test grounds, and saw the rise in prominence of new venues like Chester-le-Street, Cardiff and the Hampshire ground at Southampton. This policy of using English international matches as the major driver in financial terms for the game has been often criticised as being a short term measure and the argument made that a highly visible Twenty20 tournament using national players would be needed for financial solvency for many grounds. The first test match at the Rose Bowl, held earlier in 2011, suffered from bad weather which resulted in only moderate attendances and did not make a profit.

By December 2011, after four months of negotiation, the 999-year lease of the ground was sold to EBC for £6.5 m, thus providing funding for the development of the 175-room Hilton Hotel that is due to be built on the site. Hampshire CCC will rent the stadium back for £420,000 a year and the investment means that the hotel and golf course developments can be started. In a statement made by EBC, leader of the council Keith House said, 'the decision is good news for our residents and for the local economy, it will give the Council significant rental income that will help protect frontline services and keep the council tax down'. … (and that it was anticipated that it would) … 'bring around £55 m spending a year to the local economy and create around 500 local jobs and protect and develop a world class sporting venue' (EBC Press Release, 2011: n.p.).

Interestingly, looking at the report by Professor Stephen Wanhill on the *Economic Impact of the Rose Bowl Resort Complex*, the author notes that 'the object is to re-launch the flagship Rose Bowl attraction as a sports tourism resort complex through the addition of a four star Hilton Hotel, Spa and Championship golf course built around the Rose Bowl, building on the regions strong communication links and the international brand that is Hilton' (Wanhill, 2011: 2). The TRI consulting report cited in Wanhill (2011) suggested that 'the long term effect is to create additional demand through developing a resort cluster that will generate a high visibility for the area and so attract more visitors for conferences, sporting and other events' (2010: 22). The views expressed in this statement are far removed from the ethos of the original HCCC, and it is difficult to appreciate how the new way of thinking actually relates to the creation of a new home for Hampshire Cricket.

The reality today is that for a stadium to be successful it has to evolve into something offering more than an arena for one sport. The old home of Hampshire County Cricket Club was becoming uncomfortable, unwelcoming, and visually falling apart, and as a result potential spectators preferred to watch the matches from the comfort of home using improved TV coverage. The club did its best to regenerate the venue at the original Northlands Road location to its best ability but it simply was not big enough to generate sufficient income to enable it to compete with newer more efficient and more attractive leisure venues (a fate which befell Brentwood as noted in the Epigraph: Editors' note).

By the end of the 1980s there had been a number of disastrous events in stadiums in the UK and elsewhere, including fires in wooden stands, overcrowding such as that which caused the disaster at the Sheffield Hillsborough stadium and inadequate entrances and exits causing additional injuries and deaths during emergency exits. These catastrophes resulted in 1990 in the government of the day introducing new safety measures that were required to be adopted by UK stadiums. As a consequence, facilities at stadiums were made more accessible, safe and comfortable and started to draw a more diverse range of spectators. It was seen as an opportunity to introduce business activities in stadiums, such as sponsored teams, museums, guided tours, hospitality boxes and restaurants. This meant there was a new approach in managing such a facility which was now regarded as a 'public area not just a sports arena and open 7 days a week' (www.worldstadiums.com).

The solution for HCCC was the Rose Bowl, which is a commercial stadium that has the opportunity to exploit the potential of a more varied clientele than just sports fans and also include other events like concerts, weddings and business events as part of the offerings and operations of the facility. The Rose Bowl today incorporates various aspects of marketing and communication from corporate boxes and conference rooms that can be converted into sponsors' lounges; also, the stadium has been developed to transmit television broadcasting to a wider audience. The Rose Bowl now has the opportunity to draw on many users all year round and to turn the area in which it is located into a 'catalyst for neighbourhood development' (www.worldstadiums.com). But there still remain issues of access that have had to be addressed by the local council.

In many respects the Rose Bowl has become an 'icon' as a cricket stadium structure, it is a unique facility in the UK in terms of what it can offer to both the community and to the spectator, something that will no doubt be copied by other professional cricket clubs worldwide. Looking at the future of stadiums, the modern ones (like the Rose Bowl) have now become 'centres of attraction', which does bring into question the issues of 'economic and environmental sustainability, (and) the reality is can it be balanced without jeopardizing their sports nature and architectural qualities' (www.worldstadiums.com).

Whatever happens in the future to the Rose Bowl, whether it is in terms of investment from other parties or the next stage in its development, each step will be an other evolution in terms of the history of HCCC and reflect how cricket grounds, like those of many other sports, have had to look beyond the boundaries of the pitch to survive.

References

Allen, D. (2007) *Hampshire County Cricket Club 1946–2006 – Entertain or Perish*. Stroud: Phillimore.
Baade, R. and Dye, R. (1988) An analysis of the economic rationale for the public subsidisation of sports stadiums. *Annuals of Regional Science* 22 (2), 37–47.
Bale, J. and Moen, O. (1995) *The Stadium and the City*. Keele: Keele University Press.
Eastleigh Borough Council (2011) *Press Release*. 16 December. See: www.eastleigh.gov.uk.
Gannaway, N. (1990) *A History of Cricket in Hampshire*. Eastleigh: Hampshire Books.
Gibson, H. (2005) Understanding sport tourism experiences. In J. Higham (ed.) *Sport Tourism Destinations: Issues, Opportunities and Analysis* (pp. 57–73). London: Elsevier.
Gratton, C. (1998) The economic importance of modern sport. *Culture of Sport and Society* 1 (1), 101–117.
Gratton, C. and Henry, P. (2005) *Sport in the City – The Role of Sport in Economic and Social Regeneration*. London: Routledge.
Haralabakis, M. (2005) Three years in the lists of shame: In the margin children with learning difficulties until they are assessed. *The Times*, 17 February, p. 15.
Jones, C. (2001) A level playing field? Sports stadiums infrastructure and urban development in the UK. *Environmental Planning* 33 (5), 845–861.

Renshaw, A. (2001) *The Road to The Rosebowl*. Hampshire Handbooks. See http://hampshirecrickethistory.wordpress.com/

Saunders, S. (1997) *Cricket in Hampshire – A Biography*. Eastleigh: Green Tree Press.

TRI Hospitality Consulting (2010) *Rose Bowl Plc: Proposed Hilton Hotel*. Hampshire, London: The Rose Bowl.

Wanhill, S. (2011) *The Economic Impact of the Rose Bowl Resort Complex*. Eastleigh: Eastleigh Borough Council.

Williams, D.A. (1984) Brentwood. *Journal of the Cricket Society* 12 (1), 11–12.

Williams, C. (1997) *Consumer Services and Economic Development*. London: Routledge.

Wynne-Thomas, P. (1998) *The History of Hampshire County Cricket Club*. Hove: Guild Publishing.

Daily Telegraph, 1996 (date unknown).
Guardian Newspaper, 16 December 2011.

Hampshire Cricket Society Newsletter, 13 October 2000.
Hampshire Members Newsletter, February 1990.
Hampshire Members Newsletter, September 1998.
Hampshire Members Newsletter, February 2001.
Southern Daily Echo, various dates from 1937 onwards.
Times Newspaper, various dates.

City Archivists Office, Southampton.
Hampshire County record Office, Winchester.

Websites

http://www.atmevents.co.uk/cricke_rose_bowl.php (accessed 20 December 2011).
http://wwww.worldstadiums.com/stadium_menu/architecture/historic_stadiums.shtml (accessed 15 February 2012).
http://www.news.bbc.co.uk (accessed 15 February 2012).

6 Cricket: Biology and Bali

Steve Noakes and Alan Wilson

*For the only thing that is not good is that this game originates
from Europeans
Salute King William's Town,*
Anonymous translated by ThiyiweBafanoKhumalo

Introduction

A scholarly search for 'cricket' in 'Indonesia' will most usually present detailed information on the high protein, 123 species of cricket (Brata & Saepudin, 2012), such as the *Pteronemobiustaprobanesis* or 'lawn ground cricket' (Masaki, 1979), the 'litter cricket' also known by its scientific name of *Lebinthusmiripara* (Otte, 1992) and the 'house cricket', *Achetadomesticus*, found within this biodiverse South East Asia nation-state archipelago. Biology catalogues on the taxonomy of crickets in the natural world illustrate their place in the *Animala* Kingdom. They belong to the Phylum of *Artropoda* and the Class of *Insecta* (Bisby et al., 2009). Male crickets use the strength of their chirping to establish dominance over other males. In the case of Indonesia, it appears that research on crickets has been, to date, in the realm of biology.

Centuries of European imperial domination led the development of global trade networks with port cities as hubs throughout Asia and influenced contemporary political and social cultures, including recreation and sporting pursuits (Jones & Shaw, 2006). As a game of European origins, cricket was not played in any structured fashion by the colonial rulers from the Dutch East India Company (*De Vereenigde Oost-Indische Compagnie* or VOC) and the government of Holland during their three and a half centuries of domination in what is now known as the independent Republic of Indonesia. The Dutch colonial period came to an end with the Japanese invasion during the Second World War and the subsequent success of the independence movement to resist Netherlands attempts to re-establish its rule.

In the previous century, for a short period from 1811–1816, Sir Thomas Stamford Raffles of the British East India Company served as Lieutenant-Governor of Java, based in Batavia (Jakarta), but there is no evidence of this Englishman introducing the game of cricket to Indonesia. Nevertheless, 18 years after he founded the settlement of Singapore in 1819, cricket was being played at Padang on the island port (Singapore Cricket Club, 2011).

Cricket Indonesia claim references can be found on cricket being played in Indonesia as far back as the 1880s. They report the mention of a cricket game played '…between the Batavia Cricket Club and a visiting circus eleven in Jakarta (the visiting circus team opted to play in full clown regalia and lost the match)' (Cricket Indonesia, 2014).

While the Indonesian people's cultural, social and political background leads to different perceptions of sport from the Western concept (Lutan, 2005), there is evidence that sport has been an integral part of the nation's post-colonial transformation into what is now the world's largest primarily Muslim faith democracy. As an independent sovereign nation, Indonesia is still a young country, not coming into existence as a self-governing Republic until the middle of the 20th century.

Cricket is less than two decades old in terms of its legally formal and more strategically planned organisation in Indonesia. Dependent on the source of the information, current take-up figures for the game vary. For example, Cricket Indonesia reports that there are now 16 cricket centre locations covering 16 provinces from Banda Aceh in the west to Papua in the east, with some 40,000 Indonesian school children now introduced to cricket as well as over 20 senior men's teams, 167 junior boys teams, 15 junior girls teams, 11 cricket grounds and around 10,000 new children being introduced to cricket every year. However, Wilson (personal communication, 2012) states: 'The figures are grossly exaggerated for political purposes both to the International Cricket Council and Government of Indonesia. Children in 16 provinces have certainly been exposed through the Ultra Milk sponsored programme in 2009; however sustaining these numbers has not occurred. The current actual numbers of Indonesians actively playing the game in four provinces could not be more than 500.'

Cricket's emerging contribution to generating a new visitor market segment and spectator or active engagement activities for visitors to Indonesia, provides a fertile ground for new academic enquiry in the field of sports-induced tourism, broadening the appeal of leading destinations such as Bali and other popular destinations within Indonesia.

This chapter will discuss sport within the social and political history and context of Indonesia. It also addresses tourism development and performance in Indonesia and particularly in Bali given its status as the highest profile tourism destination within the country and a focal point of initiatives to introduce the game of cricket to the Indonesian people. It provides key stakeholder commentary of the origins of Cricket Bali as the pioneer for cricket development in Indonesia, Cricket Indonesia, and the Udayana Cricket Club based at Bali's oldest and largest university, Udayana.

Sport in the Social and Political History and Context of Indonesia

While research into the thousands of years of *homo erectus*, *homo sapiens* and, more recently *homo floresiensis* remains an inexact science, there is, nevertheless, evidence of a long and extensive history of human activity throughout the Indonesian archipelago (Bartstra, 1982; Broadfield *et al.*, 2001). Modern Indonesian history from around 1300 AD, when the Islamisation of the thousands of islands now known as Indonesia began (Ricklefs, 2001), documents periods of religious and cultural infusion, colonial dominance, major trading ports, involvement in world wars, internal revolutions and nation building.

Indonesians have also had a long association with Westerners. For some four centuries Portuguese, Dutch, Spanish (not renowned cricket playing nations) and British (the 'home' of cricket since the 16th century) traders influenced the islands with the Dutch gaining control of the largest island, Java, through the Dutch East Indies Company (VOC) – until it was dissolved in 1799. During the period of French domination over the Netherlands from 1795–1813 (Wintle, 2000), the Dutch government established the Dutch East Indies as a nationalised colony. During the Napoleonic Wars a successful British invasion of Java in 1811 saw the island remain under British control until the 1814 Treaty of Paris restored control back to the Dutch, where it remained until the Japanese invasion in 1942. The defeat of the Japanese saw the Dutch attempt to regain control after the Second World War, but after bloody struggles a republic was declared on 17 August 1945 (Vickers, 2013). Five years later, on 17 August 1950, the constitutional structure of the revolutionary years was formerly swept away and the Republic of Indonesia, with a unitary constitution, was formed (Ricklefs, 2001) and Indonesia became a member of the United Nations.

The sports and games inherited from the Dutch colonialists such as korfball and kasti were abolished from physical education programmes in schools post-independence. However, their pre-Second World War support for football (soccer) and badminton endured. Sport was identified by the new post-Second World War leaders for its potential to support the nationalist movement, and in 1946 the Indonesian Sports Association (*Persatuan Olahraga Republik Indonesia* – POTI) was formed (Adams, 2002).

Sport was used for nation building and regional political engagement as evidenced by the construction of a national sports stadium under the leadership of Indonesia's first President, Sukarno. Its initial aim was to host the Asian Games in 1962 and the Third World version of the Olympics, the Games of the New Emerging Forces or GANEFO, in 1963 (Pauker, 1964). Partly funded with a loan from the Soviet Union, the Gelora Bung Karno Stadium (*Stadion Gelora Bung Karnoor* or its official name of Gelora Bung Karno Main Stadium – *Stadion Utama Gelora Bung Karno*) also provided the capital city of Jakarta with a catalyst for major urban development during the first half of the 1960s, including boulevards, statues and memorials.

Tourism Development and Performance in Indonesia, Particularly in Bali

While the early development stages were hampered during the 1970s by internal policy barriers, currency appreciation induced by an oil boom and high costs compared to neighbouring destinations, by 1980 Indonesia received 562,000 international visitors (ILO, 2013). Thirty years later, Indonesia welcomed 7 million international visitors in 2010. By 2014, the Ministry of Tourism and Creative Economics aimed to double that figure, targeting 14 million arrivals. As global tourism demand has now exceeded one billion arrivals and the Indonesian domestic tourism market continues to develop, the nation's share of the global tourism market and new opportunities to service the rapidly growing middle class and pool of potential domestic tourists are expected to ensure tourism remains a key strategic sector within the national development agenda (UNWTO, 2014).

The expansion of the Ngurah Rai International Airport in 1969 to accept direct international flights heralded the start of large-scale tourism development in Bali. The government of Indonesia (GOI) had established the Directorate General of Tourism (*Direktorat Genderal Parawisata*) and supported the development of a Regional Plan for Bali in 1969 and the Strategy of Development in 1972 (Picard, 1990). In June 1974 the World Bank (Project ID P003738) approved its first tourism project in Indonesia to develop a master plan for tourism in Bali and enable infrastructure to promote tourism on the island, particularly on the 310 ha tourism estate at Nusa Dua.

Foreign visitors travelling to Bali grew at around 12–15% per annum, from 34,147 in 1971 to 1,306,316 in 1997. A decade later, in 2007, annual foreign tourist arrivals into Bali reached 1,664,854, rapidly increasing to 2,229,945 in 2009 despite the global financial crisis experienced during this period (Bali Tourism Board, 2012). In the five decades to 2010, Bali's population growth reached 118.5%, increasing from 1.78 million in 1961 to 3.89 million in 2010, then up to 4.22 million in 2012 (Jakarta Post, 2012).

Originally built in 1931 in the village of Tuban, in 2013, major expansions and improvements were completed at the State-operated Bali Ngurah Rai International Airport. This is the only airport in Bali and also known as Denpasar International Airport, now with annual passenger handling capacity of 25 million people, expected to cope with expected increase in tourist numbers (Airport Technology, 2014).

Cricket in Indonesia

Indonesians, as well as dedicated expatriate citizens from nations such as the UK, India, South Africa, Australia, New Zealand and others, now actively engage in organised cricket competitions around the country, but mainly in the Bali and Jakarta areas. In 2000, with the help and support of Andrew Eades, the first national cricket organisation, the Indonesian Cricket Foundation (ICF), was established by marrying the only two cricket playing areas in the country, namely, Jakarta (represented by James Arthur of the Jakarta Cricket Association – JCA) and Bali (represented by Tetty Firmstone, Ray Elliott and Alan Wilson of the Bali International Cricket Club – BICC). The International Cricket Council (ICC) recognised the ICF immediately as the country's main cricketing body and in 2001 organised for Indonesia to formally join the ICC as an affiliate member in the ICC East Asia Pacific region in 2001. The chairman of the ICF was shared between Bali and Jakarta with Alan Wilson and James Arthur as the first two individuals jointly sharing the position.

Areas where the ICC has assisted to develop cricket within Indonesia include:

(i) The ICC has enabled the ICF to tap into grants available to affiliate members, thereby creating some facilities (nets, upgrading an oval, equipment, underground irrigation system) to be built at the Bukit oval, Udayana University, giving Bali its first proper cricket oval.

(ii) The ICC has supported an aggressive training programme for local cricketers, resulting in the following persons having received ICC Level 1 Training from the ICC (initially from Tim Anderson) over the period 2001–2002: Soni Hawoe, Zachariah Awang, Melvin Ndoen, Wayan

Suwandi, Agus Anom Abadi, Yeri Rosnongna, Osseh Hendrik Laka and Umbu Frengke Shony. All of these persons were based in Bali and largely initially funded by Udayana Kingfisher Ecolodge located at Udayana University. The Timorese component of this group was trained by an Australian veterinarian, Bruce Christie, based in Kupang over the period 1993–1996.

(iii) The ICC EAP (with leading contributions from Tim Anderson – who moved on to become Director of Global Development ICC, Dubai, and Mathew Kennedy – who became a senior executive of Tennis Australia in Melbourne) were very supportive of the ICF concept of funding salaries of Indonesians as cricket trainers so they could directly train in local Bali schools, which commenced in 2002. Much-needed accommodation support came from Udayana Kingfisher Ecolodge.

(iv) The ICC supported the holding of training camps in Bali so that a national side could be established to begin competing in the international arena. This support had immediate results and Indonesia participated in its first ICC EAP tournament in Perth, Australia in 2002 with seven Indonesian nationals plus seven expatriates who passed the residency requirements.

(v) The ICC gave significant assistance to all the expenses of tours involving ICC-organised tournaments. Since 2002 the ICC has paid for Indonesian adult, under 19 and under 15 teams to play tournaments all over the Pacific region including Japan, Australia, New Zealand, Vanuatu, Papua New Guinea and Samoa.

(vi) The ICC funded the first General Manager (Prakash Vijaykumar) in 2008, whose role was to develop the game of cricket in Indonesia.

(vii) The ICC assisted the attendance of Indonesian delegates to workshops held by Cricket Australia (CA) in Melbourne every two years.

(viii) The ICC enabled specially chosen Indonesian trainers and players to attend the advanced CA cricket training facilities (initially in Adelaide and subsequently in Brisbane).

The ICF is now known as Cricket Indonesia (CI). It oversees the organised game of cricket throughout the country as the peak national coordinating body for the game. From 2006 onwards, a keen interest in the development programme emanated from Jakarta, resulting in future control being placed in the hands of the JCA, in particular the Indian community. Sahin Gopalan became Chairman of ICF, Prakash Vijaykumar became the first General Manager, the name was changed to CI, serious sponsors were obtained enabling the game to rapidly develop in over 12 provinces, and national teams participated in ICC EAP tournaments in New Zealand, Vanuatu,

Samoa and Papua New Guinea. Indonesia itself held its first ICC EAP tournament in 2009.

In 2010, under pressure from the Government of Indonesia, a government backed cricket organisation – Persatuan Cricket Indonesia (PCI) – was formed to take the game forward; hopefully with inputs of government funding. The ICC thus now recognises the PCI alone as their partner in Indonesia. This relationship is not at present strong and will require nurturing if the ICC is to continue to play a significant role in cricket development in the country. The latter is seen as essential. The role of CI is still important to represent the private sector and clubs in the country and to liaise with PCI.

Initially, the CI strategy was to use the services of the ICC to assist in upgrading the governance structures of the organisation, train key Indonesians to be professional coaches and target primary schools as the prime development area. Nine Indonesians received ICC training up to Level 1 coaching and umpiring both in Australia and Indonesia and four of these have spread the game over a 2000 km area in four provinces from a Cricket Development Centre based at Udayana University Bali. A secondary strategy to develop cricket tours aimed to develop brother-sister relationships; for example, Top Enders (Darwin) with Udayana Cricket Club (Jimbaran, Bali) and Zamigos (Holland) with Red Ants (Gianyar Bali) have been successfully implemented. The country has six league structures; national, local clubs, regency, under 19, under 15 and primary school. There are also three international events, two cricket training centres, two women's teams, a range of cricket grounds and a residential cricket club in Bali in the grounds of Udayana University.

The JCA (*Perkempuluan Jakarta Cricket*) consists of clubs in and around the nation's capital. Most of the players are expatriates, although one team, the KMV Tigers, mainly attracts Indonesian players. The association conducts the annual JCA League over the southern summer season from August to April and the Jakarta International Sixes tournament in the last week of October each year, attracting teams from Singapore, Malaysia, Hong Kong and Thailand. Each July they also host an annual Twenty20 tournament. The gala end-of-season JCA Annual Dinner and Awards nights celebrate team and individual player achievements and over the years have attracted leading cricketing guest speakers such as Fred Truman, Richard Hadlee, Vivian Richards, Ian Botham, Kapil Dev, Max Walker, Geoff Lawson, Sunil Gavaskar, Dean Jones, Keith Stackpole, Greg Matthews, Rodney Hogg, Zaheer Abbas, Ken Rutherford, Alan Wilkins, Syed Kirmani, Tom Moody and Geoff Marsh (Jakarta Cricket Association, 2012). The JCA continues to support the interests of expatriate cricket but makes little effort to train Indonesians in the game. The development of Indonesian players in the

Jakarta area has been pioneered by Indonesian trainers (Yeri Rosongna, Melven Ndoen and Fernandes Nato) supplied from Bali from around 2007 in the regencies of Bogor and Banten. These efforts have resulted in the Papatong CC (initiated by a Dutchman Taco Bottema), the Banten CC (pioneered by Melven Ndoen) and the University of Indonesia CC (pioneered by Yeri Rosongna).

Cricket in Bali

In 1993 there was not a single Indonesian who played regular organised cricket in Indonesia. The BICC, which was legalised into a foundation in 1994, commenced teaching a few Indonesians (including the club barman) the game of cricket in 1995 during their social cricket games every Sunday. At the same time, an Australian veterinarian (Bruce Christie) commenced teaching some young Indonesians cricket in Kupang (West Timor). The latter group (six persons) came to Bali to work for another veterinarian (Alan Wilson) when Bruce Christie returned to Australia in 1997. These Timorese integrated into the small Bali cricket scene, including marrying local girls. Bali became the embryonic centre of cricket development in the Indonesian people; this attracted the attention of Andrew Eades of the ICC, East Asia Pacific region.

From 2001–2006, cricket experienced a 'golden era' of rapid development in Indonesia and the base of the game where local Indonesian people played was Bali. Bali played a key role in selecting Indonesian players on the national team, supplying all seven Indonesians in the first adult international ICC EAP tournament in Perth in 2002 (resulting in a win against South Korea) and again in 2004, where they won an international against Japan but lost to Tonga, Samoa and Fiji. An under 15 team (almost all from the small village of Jimbaran in Bali) participated in an under 15 ICC East Asia Pacific tournament in Melbourne in 2005 where this team beat Fiji, Japan, Samoa and Tonga to clearly demonstrate the potential of Indonesians to play the game.

The impetus to create an all Indonesian national team stalled in 2006 when CI was formed and the administration of the national game moved to Jakarta. The national team, comprised a mixture of Indonesians and Indians (who fulfilled the ICC residency requirements); however, their international performance did not improve. The ICC give a high (40%+) rating to the performance of national teams in their overall country ratings. BICC was dissolved in 2010; and now Cricket Bali represents clubs (mainly the Udayana Cricket Club (UCC)) headed by Nyoman Dedi. PCI has a presence in the local government which answers to Jakarta.

Udayana Cricket Club

The UCC was established in 2003 in the belief that local clubs were needed to foster the game privately and Indonesians needed experience in club management. It became the first (and is still the only) residential cricket club managed by Indonesians in Indonesia. The role of the ICC is acknowledged as UCC used the Indonesian ICC trainers (for example, Soni Hawoe, an ICC trainer, was the first UCC president). Also, Charlie Burke (then staff member of ICC EAP) became a founder member and there were 20 other founder members from Indonesia, Australia, India, Holland and the UK. The club facilities include an oval (owned by Udayana University) only 1 km from the club house located at Udayana Kingfisher Ecolodge, which is residential with a restaurant and a bar. The governing committee has had a president, secretary, treasurer and captain. In 2010, the positions of chairman and manager were added, so the president became an important figurehead.

Governance of the club has improved over the years, annual general meetings are held annually in January, and in 2010 a constitution was developed with the help of Brent Palfreyman of Cricket Tasmania. Also in 2010, the signals of a new management approach were becoming apparent with a more rigorous members register established for over 139 members and membership cards incorporating the club's new corporate branding and logo design. By 2012, with some 200 members, the club had four teams: an under 15, an under 19, an adult and a veterans. The latter two play in the Bali League. The club also has four employees, a grounds man based at the Bukit oval, two trainers (both ICC Level 2 certified) and a manager (ICC Level 2 certified and ICC Umpire certified).

A Typical Bali Cricket Season

Cricket is played at the UCC throughout the year, although it is curtailed during the wet season. Activities can be divided into social and official.

(1) Social
    (i) These include social games every Saturday and Sunday morning beginning at 9.30 am (excluding public holidays).
    (ii) Friendly games with other clubs or visiting teams (the number of overs played is decided by the captains). During the last few years, the UCC has played against teams from the Marylebone Cricket Club (MCC), the Madras Sports Club, the Cricketers Club of New

South Wales, the Top Enders, the Shanghai Hot Dogs and a number of teams from Jakarta. The club is attempting to encourage 'cricket tourism' as a means of strengthening its financial and technical capabilities. In recent years, UCC appointed a club in Sri Lanka to become its agent in that country.

(2) Official
 (i) Every Saturday afternoon there is official training at the nets at the Bukit oval attended by manager and trainers.
 (ii) The trainers now have training programmes in eight elementary and four secondary local schools in the Nusa Dua and Kuta Selatan areas. It is hoped that good players will be identified and become members to play in the under 15 and under 19 teams.
 (iii) The adult and veterans teams play in the Bali League (currently having five teams) which is played during April–September, with each team playing each other three times. This league commenced in 2001 and is played annually.
 (iv) The club now hosts the Bali International Sixes Tournament (BIST) over the Easter weekend every year. The 16th BIST took place 6–8 April, 2012.
 (v) In 2012, an 11-a-side Twenty20 tournament took place, organised from Perth and involving teams from Australia, Indonesia and Singapore.
 (vi) The national sports body, the PCI, offers support with training camps and assists players to participate in ICC EAP tournaments. The UCC has played a dynamic role in the development of Indonesian national under 15, under 19 and adult squads. For example, the whole of the 2005 under 15 squad (except two players) who played in the ICC EAP tournament in Melbourne came from the club. UCC players have played for Indonesia in all ICC tournaments from 2002 until 2011 in Australia, New Zealand, Vanuatu, Japan, Samoa and Papua New Guinea.

Extending from Bali

With the support of UCC, the Flores Cricket Association (FCA) was formed in 2004 with a base at the Labuan Bajo Tourist Training School. While the association developed without an ICC trained coach, since 2004 it has held an international hard ball 11-a-side Twenty20 tournament, which is the first of its kind in Indonesia. In 2006 a formal cricket club, the Komodo Cricket Club, was established with a club house at the Bajo Komodo Ecolodge, also part of Ecolodges Indonesia. This has provided a base for national and international players to play cricket and enjoy a great holiday viewing Komodo dragons or going diving and snorkelling. The development of cricket in Kabupaten West Manggerai on the western side of the island of Flores followed the CI 10-point training programme and this was given a boost by the Ultra Milk under 15 junior development programme in 2008 and 2009. The FCA has spread the game 120 km inland to Ruteng where two secondary schools have started playing cricket. Sponsors of the FCA include Ecolodges Indonesia, the INI RADEF Foundation, Indonesia Air Transport, Bintang Hotel Group, Reef Seekers, Swiss Contact, Hotel Golo, Dive Komodo and the Nature Conservancy. By 2012 however, cricket in Flores was in danger of lapsing due to a lack of local support.

On the large island of Java, the UCC has also played a dynamic and important role in the development of Indonesian cricket by supporting trainers in the regencies of Banten and Bogor.

Response of the Local Community

Although still constrained by funding, equipment and available time, many parents associated with the UCC value the opportunity that cricket is giving their children, not only through outdoor sports activity, but also by including English language training and travel opportunities. One locally based expat who has actively supported the development of cricket for Indonesian people stated: 'Indonesians are natural players of cricket. They come to love the game. Their main strengths are fielding and bowling; their batting is also good but they currently lack patience as a general rule.'

Conclusion

European imperial domination did not leave a legacy of this game of British origins, although references have been claimed of cricket being played in Indonesia as far back as the 1880s. There is evidence that sport has been an integral part of Indonesia's post-colonial transformation even though the Indonesian people's cultural, social and political background has led to different perceptions of sport from generally accepted Western concepts.

In scholarly literature, the term 'cricket' in the Indonesian context will move from the realm of biology to sports and tourism. The game of cricket in Indonesia has grown from being a social activity for expatriates to a recognised sport due to the strong volunteer base of the regional associations, the dedication of CI committee members and corporate sponsors like Rolls Royce, Crown Relocations, Tetra Pak, Ultrajaya, Tunas Group and others. Cricket now has the acknowledgement and support of KONI (National Sports Committee of Indonesia) and the Ministry of Sports and Culture, which included cricket for the first time as a part of the 2010 PON (national games) held in Jakarta.

Cricket Indonesia's regional associations organise leagues in their respective regions for seniors and juniors. Some regional associations also host domestic and international tournaments which attract teams from Australia, Singapore, Malaysia, Thailand, Philippines, China and India. Regional associations have also started introducing women's cricket programmes to schools and some regions hope to soon have enough players to start women's leagues. Jakarta and Bali remain the key centres for the game of cricket within Indonesia, but the game is now also being played in an organised fashion in a number of areas, including Lampung, Kupang, Bogor, Medan, Bandung, Makkasar, Manado, Solo and Balikpapan.

As tourism demand for Indonesia grows over the medium to longer term, cricket will continue to emerge as a new generator of the sports-oriented visitor market segment through spectator and active engagement in the game by visitors to Indonesia. Additionally, and apart from the health benefits, sports such as cricket provide benefits to the complex social fabric of countries such as Indonesia through social and competitive engagement by males and females of all ages, team skills, social skills such as cooperation, communication, learning to deal with winning and losing, social interaction and opportunities for travel and improving language skills.

Acronyms

BICC	Bali International Cricket Club
BIST	Bali International Sixes Tournament
CA	Cricket Australia
CI	Cricket Indonesia
EAP	East Asia Pacific
GANEFO	Games of the New Emerging Forces
GOI	Government of Indonesia
ICC	International Cricket Council
ICF	Indonesian Cricket Foundation
JCA	Jakarta Cricket Association
KONI	National Sports Committee of Indonesia (*Komite Olahraga Nasional Indonesia*)
PCI	Persatuan Cricket Indonesia

POTI   The Indonesian Sports Association (*Persatuan Olahraga Republik Indonesia*)
UCC   Udayana Cricket Club
VOC   De Vereenigde Oost-Indische Compagnie

References

Adams, I. (2002) Pancasila: Sport and the building of Indonesia – Ambitions and obstacles. *The International Journal of the History of Sport* 19 (2–3). See http://dx.doi.org/10.1080/714001759

Airport Technology (2014) http://www.airport-technology.com/projects/ngurah-rai-airport/ (accessed 31 March 2014).

Anon. (2004) Salute King Williams Town! Mighty Champions. In: D.R. Allen and H. Doggart (eds) '*A Breathless Hush.' The MCC Anthology of Cricket Verse* (p. 220). (trans. T. Bafana). Methuen: London

Bali Tourism Board (2012) http://www.balitourismboard.org/ (accessed 14 December 2012).

Bartstra, Gert-Jan (1982) Homo erectus erectus: The search for his artifacts. Current Anthropology 23 (3), 318–320.

Brata, B. and Saepudin, R. (2012) The Effect of Vegetables on Growing Rate in Cricket Gryllusmitratus 10–50 Day Olds. *International Seminar on Animal Industry*.

Bisby, F.A., Roskov, Y.R., Orrell, T.M., Nicolson, D. and Paglinawan, L.E. (2009) *Species 2000 and ITIS Catalogue of Life 2009 Annual Checklist*. CD-ROM; Reading, UK: Species 2000.

BPS Province of Bali (2012) Badan Pusat Statistik, Provinci Bali. See http://bali.bps.go.id/eng/tabel_detail.php?ed=604002&od=4&id=4 (accessed 24 March 2012).

Broadfield, D.C., Holloway R.L, Mowbray, K. Silvers, A., Yuan, M.S. and Ma'Rquez, S. (2001) A new homo erectus from Indonesia. *The Anatomical Record* 262, 369–379.

Cricket Indonesia http://www.cricketindonesia.com/generic/index.php?mid=7 (accessed 31 March 2014).

ILO (2013) *Strategic Plan – Sustainable Tourism and Green Jobs for Indonesia*. Jakarta: International Labour Organisation.

Jakarta Cricket Association (2012) See www.jakartacricket.com/home/index.php (accessed 24 March 2012).

Jakarta Port (2012) http://www.thejakartapost.com/news/2012/12/17/bali-faces-population-boom-now-home-42-million-residents.html (accessed 31 March 2014).

Jones, R. and Shaw, B. (2006) Palimpsests of progress: Erasing the past and rewriting the future in developing societies – Case studies of Singapore and Jakarta. *International Journal of Heritage Studies* 12 (2), 122–138. See http://dx.doi.org/10.1080/13527250500496045

Lutan, R. (2005) Indonesia and the Asian Games: Sport, nationalism and the 'new order'. *Sport in Society* 8 (3), 414–424.

Masaki, S. (1979) Climatic adaptation and species status in the lawn ground cricket. *Oecologia* 43 (2), 207–219.

Otte, D. (1992) Evolution of cricket songs. *Journal of Orthoptera Research*. Philidelphia, USA: Academy of Natural Sciences.

Pauker, E.T. (1964) *Ganefo I: Sports and Politics in Djakarta*. Santa Monica, CA: The Rand Corporation. Also in Asian Survey 5 (4), 171–185. See www.jstor.org/stable/2642364

Picard, M. (1990) "Cultural tourism" in Bali: cultural performances as tourist attraction. *Indonesia* 49 (1), 37.
Ricklefs, M.C. (2001) *A History of Modern Indonesia since c. 1200* (3rd edn). Stanford, CA: Stanford University Press.
Singapore Cricket Club (2011) www.scc.org.sg (accessed 4 June 2011).
UNWTO (2014) http://www2.unwto.org/ (accessed 31 March 2014).
Vickers, A. (2013) *A History of Modern Indonesia*. Cambridge: Cambridge University Press.
Wilson, A. (2012) Personal communication via email, 12 April.
Wintle M. (2000) *An Economic and Social History of the Netherlands 1800–1920*. Cambridge: Cambridge University Press.

Part 3
The True Costs

Travelling to cricket, either as a participant or as a spectator involves considerable cost and this comes in a variety of forms. While one tends to think of sportspeople as enjoying a highly desirable lifestyle with many perks and advantages, it is becoming increasingly apparent that international sports stars are under heavy and growing pressure. The demands for performances at peak level on a continuous basis place great stress on participants, and as noted earlier, international cricket tours are longer and much more intense, involving far more games than in earlier times. The effects of rapid travel to destinations and then a series of matches in different formats mostly at international level and with shorter periods of rest (or practice) between them pose many problems. Cricketers seem to have a disproportionally high suicide rate, and the English team alone has lost three of its best performers in recent years because of stress-related illnesses. Pearce discusses the issues of how difficult and demanding it is to be on an international cricket tour, and the situation he describes is in sharp contrast to the earlier years of cricket touring. Then, travel to the destination was generally by boat, providing a mostly restful and relaxing experience, the number of serious competitive matches was far fewer and a more social atmosphere pervaded the tour. Players were not competing for their jobs and for sponsors and their travel experiences could be seen as much like that of tourists than is the case for today's professionals.

While on-field rivalries are just that, in general off-field settings and activities have traditionally been much more relaxed and friendly, even allowing for present-day issues of sledging and other ungentlemanly behaviour. Most touring teams enjoy interaction with local residents and travel as tourists when the opportunity arises, visiting sites of general attraction and interest. In the case of matches between India and Pakistan, however, relations have often been tempered by political considerations, both official and unofficial. So difficult had relations between the two countries become that cricket matches between them in their home countries ceased and have only recently resumed on neutral grounds. The fact that matches are now taking place, albeit outside India and Pakistan, reflects the potential role of cricket in bringing different entities together. For spectators however, great difficulties arise as irrespective of the team supported, considerable travel would be involved to support their team against a traditional rival. Additional problems exist in the case of Pakistan because of civil unrest and violence related to other cricketing occasions and the fact that other countries are not willing to tour Pakistan because of security issues. Television coverage does allow Pakistani supporters to see their team in action, a benefit available to cricket fans in many countries, even if live test match cricket in the United Kingdom has become available only on a pay-for-view channel.

One of the most spectacular elements of modern cricket has been the rise of organised groups of fans, in particular the 'armies' of England and India. These groups are often long-haul tourists following their teams and bringing a very different flavour to audiences at international matches. No longer do test matches (outside the West Indies) produce only polite applause and the occasional comment of praise from the spectators. In a manner more reminiscent of football supporters, musical accompaniments and verbal exchanges with opposing team supporters and players (generally in a humorous manner), while often dressed in outlandish costumes are common features of the Barmy Army. As Emery *et al.* note, these groups of supporters have become much more organised over time and now play a major role in travel, accommodation and ticketing arrangements for their members, as well as providing sympathetic support to fellow sufferers when their team is doing badly.

Individuals of course make up the majority of spectators at cricket matches and can experience any number of problems, benefits and surprises while following their team, particularly to far flung parts. As Baum notes, the view from the boundary as an individual is somewhat different to that from the perspective of a member of one of the armies. Some of the travails of even getting to the boundary when one has arrived in a foreign country will be familiar to all tourists who venture off the conventional tourist path. Equally arduous are some of the issues faced by amateur or 'coarse' cricketers, added to which are those of securing a pitch, equipment, sufficient team members and, most importantly, opposition of roughly equally poor ability. One of the great problems for those who frequented the square leg or long on and off boundaries during school cricket matches is finding opportunities to remain active rather than passive in cricket after leaving school. Playing cricket on a street where the boundaries are often house walls and windows and the wickets are painted on dustbins or lamp-posts does not satisfy those in their teens and beyond for long. The decreasing number of cricket pitches and teams and costly equipment make it likely that many early active cricketers unavoidably transform into passive cricket spectators as they mature. The 'cycle' referred to by Wheeller and Maitland may well be from street to school (active) to infrequent visits to grounds to watch matches and finally to Sky and other digital television channels (passive) to watch the whole panoply of cricket in its many forms in an increasing variety of locations. In that cycle cricket enthusiasts are joining fans of many other sports whose enjoyment can no longer be gained from participating in the game they love, either because of lack of opportunity or physical limitations. Perhaps all travellers to the boundaries should give thanks to Kerry Packer and his like.

7 Cricketers as Tourists; Analyses of Culture Shock, Travel Motivation and Learning

Philip L. Pearce

> *I must play wherever I like or die*
> *So spare me your news your views, spare me your homily.*
> *I am a professional cricketer.*
> *My only consideration is my family.*
> *Sixty thousand pounds is what they sold me*
> *And I have no brain. I am an anomaly.*
> *I Found South African Breweries Most Hospitable*, Kit Wright

Introduction

It is the working assumption of this chapter that it is possible to view international cricketers as tourists. It can be immediately noted that they are a very special kind of tourist since both their sporting performances and personal lives are of public interest and exposed to much media scrutiny. In the terms of the United Nations World Tourism Organization (UNWTO) formal definition of tourists, professional sportspeople are included in the international arrival statistics but, in common with other travellers who cross boundaries for work-related purposes, they are outliers in the more generic everyday conceptualisation of the term tourist. The perspective that cricketers are outliers or tenuous cases in our understanding of tourists is of particular advantage to this chapter. Eisenhardt (1989), Diamond (2005) and Yin (2009), among others, have argued that in social science research a focus on outlying cases is often an insightful tool for testing the limits of our models and conceptual frameworks. In this chapter two concepts will be tested and potentially enhanced by a consideration of the cricketer as a tourist. First, the concept of *culture shock*, and its updated and allied counterpart *culture confusion*, will be considered. It will be argued that the experience of cricketers, like that of other travelling sports stars, offers some under-researched areas within the culture shock/confusion concepts.

A second application of another conceptual scheme – the travel career pattern approach to tourist motivation – will also be explored. Again the discussion will consider the ways in which viewing the international cricketer as tourist can both help frame the travel behaviours of those who wield the willow and refresh the core ideas of the concept. In these analyses, examples of cricketers' experiences in international travel will be drawn from autobiographies and biographies, mostly but not exclusively from the writings of and about Australian players. The ways in which cricketers deal with culture confusion and the learning they derive from these experiences will be used to form a better understanding of the dynamics of travel motivation.

The basis for assessing the experiences of the cricketer as tourist will be principally through their own autobiographies. The value and veracity of these accounts for research needs a brief commentary. There is a plethora of such books in the global cricketing panorama. Some are simple accounts of the childhood to adulthood journey of a sporting figure. Such books consist of sporting highlights peppered with the inevitable setbacks due to poor form, injury and selection decisions. For the purposes of this account some of these books provide basic insights into the world of travelling associated with sport. The stories of in-group behaviour may be sanitised for the public but the themes of drinking parties, interactions with locals and exuberant off-field behaviour do find a place alongside the wickets taken, catches held and runs scored.

More thorough and searching self-analyses also appear in the cricket literature. On these occasions some individuals are more reflective and open about their emotional journey and the stress of a sporting life (cf. Gilchrist, 2008). These more searching analyses are of special value to this chapter as they offer more than a success story which will sell quickly while the sports star is in the public eye. De Crop (2004), among others, has suggested that tourism researchers, when using non-traditional data sources and accounts from novels and autobiographies, should cross reference and check accounts wherever possible. In some ways this has been possible with the cricketing biographies and autobiographies as the careers of many cricketers tend to co-occur, or at least overlap, so the same social and cultural travel stories are quite often retold by different participants. In this way the selection of the predominantly

Australian cricketers over the last 30 years can be seen as providing a data source where some consensus and understanding of the processes for individuals can be checked and a commonality of experience inferred. While the examples are based on the Australian biographies and autobiographies, it is at least reasonable to suggest that the global interconnectedness of the sport would produce analogous results from others beyond that national boundary.

Culture Shock and Culture Confusion

In the original formulation of the culture shock concept Oberg (1960) noted that there were strong physical components to the problems international sojourners face when in new countries. These physical dimensions include the contrasts in altitude, temperature, humidity, length of daylight and sunlight levels compared to their home locations. Additionally, there is often exposure to new allergens and to troubling diseases. Substantial dietary challenges are a key part of this physical shock and standards of hygiene, particularly related to food, have assailed many tourists, including cricketers, in international travel. It would be a mistake though to view culture shock as only physical. Oberg suggested that occupationally-based travellers (for example, nurses, doctors, aid personnel, diplomats) who seek to fit into new countries also typically experience a range of interpersonal and social difficulties. These psychological components of culture shock include communication difficulties in operating in other cultures. Allied challenges include managing the daily hassles caused by novel routines and practices as well as dealing with people whose values, attitudes and acceptable behaviours are at least surprising and sometimes confronting (Pearce, 2005; Ward et al., 2000).

In a reformulation of the concept of culture shock, Hottola (2004) argued that shock was too strong a term to describe tourists' intercultural experiences. He observed that tourists, unlike expatriates and engaged professionals, seek to enjoy novel locations rather than be assimilated into them. In particular he noted that for tourists some amusement and pleasure can be derived from embracing the differences found in new settings. Nevertheless, some confusion and bewilderment can sometimes prevail. In Hottola's view the term cultural confusion portrays tourists' experiences better than shock. Cricketers would appear to occupy a mid-range in this analysis. They are working and do need to adapt to local conditions, including playing conditions, although their stay in foreign destinations is usually a matter of weeks rather than years. Additionally, as elite sports participants they do have considerable access to locations and chances to meet people and enjoy a range of positive travel experiences which many regular tourists would envy. These special opportunities may alleviate the stress of cultural interaction although the heightened media attention to sports stars may be a counterweight to these positive forces. The ambiguity here calls for data and it is to the autobiographies we can turn to access relevant information.

A consideration of the way in which cricketers as tourists relate to the cultures and places they visit needs to be located within both a time dimension and an account of which countries are being considered. A useful way in which to view the time dimension is to take the period before the introduction of World Series Cricket (1979–1980) and travel after that time as the watershed in the amount of international touring, the professionalism of the sport and the number of countries visited to play the sport.

In the 1950s–1970s, for example, many English and Australian cricketers in their autobiographies commented on the arduous nature of the tours to less developed countries, notably India and Pakistan. In these early years, teams from England and Australia in particular consistently struggled with the food, visible poverty and the sheer tumultuous nature of life on the subcontinent (Harvey, 1963). Often the hotels they stayed in did not cater well for different food preferences and the standards of hygiene were sometimes low. In a series of interviews former Australian cricket captains Benaud, Lawry and I. Chappell reported that for some of their team mates specific tours were endured as much as enjoyed (ABC, 2009; DVD *Cricketers in the 60s, Cricketers in the 70s*). Poor on-field performances were sometimes due to sick players and stressed officials. Greg Chappell provides an illustrative story from a tour to Pakistan:

> The Ripple hotel was more guest house than hotel... we went down and saw the kitchen that serviced the Ripple. Lunch had just finished and it was empty. I'd never seen anything like it. The hotel was six months old but the bench tops were pitted and rusted, and there was an almighty mess of leftover food, unwashed dishes and tins. I nearly threw up. (Chappell, 2011: 261)

If the cricketers were tourists, they were reluctant tourists and, as is typical of culture confusion victims, large periods of time were often spent in the hotels as places of refuge away from the challenging larger world. The persistence of such challenges is captured in the following view:

> Noise in India is a constant. Traffic, music, hustle and bustle, the hum of a thousand conversations. Your hotel room becomes more than just a place to put your head down between games. Usually it is the quietest spot you will find on the entire trip. (Symonds & Gray, 2008: 69)

These reactions are entirely consistent with Hottola's analysis of culture confusion, where he observes that tourists often cope by oscillating between safe havens and the more challenging new horizons.

In contemporary times, which for the purposes of most of this chapter will mean our focus is on the post-World Series Cricket period, the new levels of money in the international game mean that players tend to stay in superior accommodation and the direct exposure to health hazards is reduced. Nevertheless, as Symonds and Gray reported in the preceding quotation, it can be argued that culture confusion persists in many international contexts. The international touring circuit requires cricketers to perform at all times of the year and adjust to different seasons and conditions. Due to the global development of the tours associated with the sport, the cultural contrasts now operate in several directions. It is not simply those cricketers from developed countries visiting less developed nations who have adjustment difficulties. Players with different religions and personal values are now also prominent on the playing fields. Cricketers from Muslim, Buddhist and Sikh communities can find themselves in cultures where the expression of aggression, the consumption of alcohol and more liberal interpersonal relationships are unlike the norms to be found in their own societies.

In numerous cricketers' autobiographies there are repeated references to the topic of homesickness. This expression is arguably more commonly employed than that of culture shock, both within travellers' writings in general and in the cricketers' accounts, but has received little academic attention. For example, in the *Encyclopaedia of Tourism* the concept of homesickness receives only eight lines in a 600-page volume and there are very limited references to the term in the mainstream journals (cf. Jafari, 2000: 283). Given that this is a popular everyday concept it is quite remarkable that academic studies have not honed in on the topic and explored its multiple elements and effects. It is the identification of these kinds of academic gaps which makes the study of special tourist groups like cricketers potentially important for academic tourism research.

The concept of homesickness can usefully be seen as a companion to culture shock/confusion. The term can be defined as an affective reaction involving elements of melancholy and sadness arising from the contemplation of one's distant family, relationships and regular life in the home base. Homesickness, like cultural confusion, can be debilitating for the cricketer/tourist. It can be bred from the travel routines and fractured relationships which the professional sportsperson experiences. Justin Langer observes:

> Touring is one of the privileges of international cricket; new countries, strange cities and exotic cultures. On the surface this all appears exciting but – and this is no complaint – it can also be a grind physically and

> psychologically. Life on the road simply isn't as glamorous as it sounds, with long stints away from your family and most of your time spent in hotel rooms or at cricket grounds. (Langer & Wainwright, 2010: 224)

Homesickness is a potential companion to cultural confusion. It is externally directed as a reaction towards the remembered relationships and familiar places rather than a response to the stresses of the immediate circumstances. The advent of homesickness appears to take place within the genre of cricketers' autobiographies on at least two occasions. First, it can occur when a young cricketer has to adapt to leaving friends and relatives, and sometimes the family home, in pursuit of international cricketing experience and development. Additionally, once cricketers have become well-established performers and are somewhat older with wives and children there are repeated examples that the players involved deeply miss their partners and key moments in their children's lives. Greg Chappell, distressed at missing the birth of his first child, reports that his second tour of England just could not finish fast enough and that his mind was often elsewhere while batting (Chappell, 2011: 173–174). There are reports too that younger cricketers fret about their relationships, including their links to girlfriends as well as to the comforts of familiar food and their social life.

One element generating homesickness is undoubtedly the demands of tour itineraries and scheduling of matches. In some tours the cricketers can criss-cross a country several times and life becomes a routine of packing and unpacking, jumping onto tour buses and flights and regular moving between hotels. This pace of life may be taken in the player's stride if he is constantly performing well, but for those who play less frequently or who score poorly, or who bowl without effect and drop their catches, then missing home and the emotional support of close contacts can be readily understood. The tourist analogy here is a close one. For tourists who venture overseas but whose itineraries are not ideal and who may not be able to participate in desired activities due to weather, timing or extraneous factors and who have few friends to assuage their annoyance and frustration, then they too are likely candidates for homesickness.

An additional and somewhat speculative component can be inferred in the understanding of homesickness. As physically fit and presumably quite sexually active young men, cricketers travelling internationally have to deal with regular interruptions to their sexual behaviour. The study of the way tourists change or modify their sexual behaviour when travelling is a difficult study topic as issues of privacy and ethical researcher conduct as well as the value of the study topic may be questioned (Bauer & McKercher, 2003). There are debates within sporting communities about the desirability of sexual activity boosting or enhancing performance. Administrative permission for WAGS (wives and girlfriends) to join the players on tours has been varied over recent decades (Langer & Wainwright, 2010). Studies of the importance of intimate relationships to traveller well-being are not common in the tourism field but there is some evidence that absence from close partners is a testing and troubling part of independent travel (Pearce & Maoz, 2008; Bowen & Clarke, 2009). Homesickness may in part be generated by sexual frustration.

It is of particular interest to note that several other developments to the culture confusion/shock concept can be offered by considering the tourist/cricketer experience. A second new element is the extent to which others are monitoring one's cultural and personal behaviour. Symonds and Gray (2008: 60–61) observe that the long gaps between games often means that the sports reporters, dubbed the 'trapparazzi', are often on the lookout for anything controversial and may even engineer some unsavoury encounters. The situation has become acute for any player with a reputation for being flamboyant. Symonds and Gray note: 'The players have become a lot more wary when out in public... The potential for abuse has grown enormously over the past few years, and the number of sportsmen and women who have found themselves in a tricky spot is testimony to that' (2008: 61). Similar remarks appear in the autobiographies and accounts of other Australian cricketers, including Justin Langer, Steven Waugh, Adam Gilchrist and Glenn McGrath (Fitzsimmons, 2004; Langer, 2008; McGrath & Lane, 2008; Gilchrist, 2008).

The former Australian captain Ricky Ponting comments: 'We all talk about how hard cricket is when we're away from home and travelling around the world but when you get something else on your plate as well it makes life a hundred times harder' (McGrath & Lane, 2008: 283).

The notion that others are monitoring the tourist's culture confusion and travel behaviours is of broad interest. The ideas from the cricketers' world may be extended to tourists in general through a technology link. While most tourists are not under the watchful gaze of media and public interests, they are increasingly likely to be connected to their friends and associates through the rich raft of new communication technologies. The co-presence of others through technology represents a more immediate feedback and commentary on one's adaptability and reported problems than was previously the case (cf. White & White, 2007). Culture shock and culture confusion may therefore be seen as more influenced in contemporary times by exposure to the criticism and commentary of others. It is no longer so easy to hide one's cultural mistakes and privately manage confusion and culture shock.

A further way in which the tourist/cricketer experience offers an insight into the culture confusion issue lies in attending to the dynamics of the touring group. The cultural confusion literature is oriented towards individual behaviour and coping. Increasingly, there are clear views that social and group reference systems often shape the individual tourist experience. For the cricketers, this reference group can be a complex mixture of fellow players and tour party officials – some are inexperienced while others are touring veterans. Those with considerable knowledge of other cultures may play a formative role in helping the novices adjust to the new setting and assist the newcomers' focus on performing well while still enjoying the visited location. They can also play somewhat cruel jokes on the novices as a part of the sporting culture of young men with a lot of time on their hands. An implication here for culture confusion studies is to explore in more detail the ways in which travel party assistance and cooperation can modify the individual experience.

The concept of loyalty in tourism studies has stimulated much study. Cricketers, or at least those who remain successful, may return to the same locations several times during their playing career. For cricketers the pleasure of the place in tourism terms may be powerfully influenced by their sporting performances at the site. In another context, De Botton comments 'We cannot enjoy palm trees and azure pools when a relationship to which we are committed is suffused with...resentment' (2009: 41). For the cricketer, a low score or a poor bowling performance may act in the same way and curb enthusiasm for a beautiful setting. By way of contrast, a player may come to love a destination because of the satisfying memories associated with individual and superior team performances.

The cricketers' destination choices are limited and effectively selected by others, but over time a familiarity with the visited places can develop. This repeat travel can generate increased confidence in dealing with the local setting, and previously culturally naïve travellers may become more confident and bolder in their exploration of the local setting. Gilchrist reports 'India...while it was frightening there was something about it that I really loved. I found it intriguing almost addictive...I just soak up all the sights and smells and excitement, the pure joy so many people take in our game. There's nowhere like India to show you how much happiness you can give people by playing your sport' (2008: 173).

The broad implications of this growing familiarity are also of generic research interest. The extent to which culture confusion is an episodic versus graded experience has been debated. Hottola thinks that culture confusion can repeatedly and periodically re-occur, whereas the early culture contact models of Gullahorn and Gullahorn (1963) have always argued for curves of adjustment (Bochner et al., 1979; Furnham, 1984). The closer tracking of individuals and their cultural contacts would appear to be a research option which has not yet been undertaken to resolve this debate. For the cricketers the autobiographical evidence is swayed towards supporting the episodic nature of cultural confusion. Anecdotes about a sudden plunge into dangerous encounters and episodes of ambiguity are not uncommon even amongst the diaries and records of those with much previous travel experience. Langer and Wainwright (2010) recount one such incident:

> The venue, Sabina Park...By lunchtime I was peckish and decided to walk to a burger place I had spotted from the team bus. It was only a few hundred metres away and I was not worried for my safety...a big Jamaican man fell into step beside me. When I say big I actually mean huge...covered in tattoos, probably weighed 140 kilograms and had arms the size of my legs...he said nothing as we walked and I kept my head down, hoping he would go away...I ordered and he fell into step with me as I walked back .When we got back to the hotel he said his first words to me 'That'll be ten dollars.' I looked up at this mammoth man with his hand stretched out... 'What for?' He looked at me impassively. 'Security.' I got back to the safety of my hotel room before trying to work out whether he was protecting me from others or himself. (2010: 106–107)

In this trajectory of increasing familiarity, punctuated by occasional incidents of confusion and doubt, travellers' motivations may change, and it is this concept of a motivational career and progression in cultural contact which will now be addressed.

The Travel Career Pattern (TCP) Model

It has been argued for some time in the tourism literature that an understanding of the tourist experience is facilitated by having a rich and multifaceted view of travel motivation. Hsu and Huang (2008) review a number of approaches and suggest that the proposal that there is a pattern of changing motives which can be likened to a travel career is of value. The TCP (Travel Career Pattern) approach on which they are commenting has been developed and commented on in a series of studies (Bowen & Clarke, 2009; Panchal & Pearce, 2011; Pearce & Lee, 2005; Pearce, 2011a). In essence the TCP approach proposes that, like a career at work, individuals change their travel motivational profile with experience and over time. The model is depicted as having three layers of motives; an inner core which is common to all travel – this basic heart of the model represents common needs for relaxation, the building of relationships and novelty. Two other layers consist of more variable motivations. For experienced travellers there is a second inner set of motives which become more prominent in their overall profile as they travel more – these driving forces include a desire to develop closer contact with local people, to obtain new life perspectives and a push to form closer ties with nature. Inexperienced travellers are less selective in stating their motivational needs and do include these motives but additionally also give considerable prominence to forces in a third and outer layer – here the motives include social status, stimulation, romance and autonomy. In recent renditions of these patterns (a key part of the TCP is that no motive or category of motives works in isolation) it has been argued that there is some evidence in affective neuroscience which supports the primacy of the core motives in influencing all behaviour (Pearce, 2011a: 110–114; Panskepp & Biven, 2010).

The relationship between the careers of cricketers, and implicitly their travel behaviour, can be approached by initially reflecting on the rise of the professional cricketer. O'Keefe (2007: 66–67) satirises the process, but it is a dark humour, familiar to many who have trodden this career path or parts of it:

> You start out as gifted naïve teenager graded in your District Fourth XI. Every summer Saturday afternoon you seem to be at some God forsaken outer suburban oval where flies carry you out to bat in forty degree temperatures. While your mates are getting up to all sorts of shenanigans with chicks from the local surf club, you're asking for middle stump from an octogenarian with Coke-bottle glasses and a hearing aid. Your only female company is a 120 kilogram scorer who has already demolished her second pack of chocolate biscuits and is eagerly waiting to record your dismissal because you sledged her the previous Saturday night...In time your performances justify selection in first grade where snarling thirty five year olds give you multiple send offs when they con the nervous wreck of an umpire to win dodgy LBW decisions in their favour...If you're lucky you get to the next level: first class cricket. Suddenly your every failure is recorded in the national newspapers. You're subjected to turning up to start the obligatory warm-up before sun has risen...If you survive all this you're in the Test team. You get to send lewd text messages, binge drink and learn to duck king hits from 150 kilogram bouncers. Eventually the tabloid newspapers call for your dropping...The Chairman of selectors says you are not being dropped, just rotated for at least six years. You retire abruptly, seek a job in the media and eventually

accept the role of computer analyst for the Nepal national team...A tough ladder to climb you'd agree but better than a real job.

Some patterns pertinent to our interest in cricketers' tourist experiences may be deduced from this 'gruelling' path to be a professional cricketer. The concentration and intense focus required to be nearly any kind of top sportsperson is formidable, leaving many of the aspiring athletes naïve to the wider world in which they will have to display their skills (Chappell, 2011). The pattern seems to be repeated in many sports disciplines with footballers and tennis players openly revealing that their formative years were less about classroom success and more about repetitive rounds of practising skills and honing their natural abilities (Agassi, 2009; Beckham & Watts, 2004).

The lack of concentration on academic success and general worldliness may result in younger cricketers being underprepared international tourists. The importance of the issue is reflected in concerted attempts by national cricket bodies to expose their younger talented players to tournaments in other countries. Undoubtedly this is somewhat helpful, although the close chaperoning of the teenage players and the lack of substantial media interest in players' activities on the minor tours still make these rehearsal experiences less testing and demanding than the full glare of competing and coping at the highest levels of international competition.

The treatment of cricketers as tourists is given a particular life by observing that some of the most successful and experienced cricketers become substantial figures promoting cross-cultural causes and goodwill. In particular, several former players, exposed to new worlds and novel situations as cricketer/tourists, use their public prominence to promote charities, support foundations for hospitals and schools and lend support to many organisations which try to reduce poverty and disease. The list of such cricketer/tourist benefactors is a long one and includes Imran Khan, Ian Botham, Garry Sobers, Vivian Richards, Steve Waugh and Glenn McGrath. There are many others. The interesting questions for tourism studies is how does this transition from the inexperienced focused sports star to internationally aware benefactor take place and what might be the implications and connections to tourism study?

The answers to these queries raise the topic of learning and the dynamics of tourist motivation change. They also introduce, perhaps as one of the lesser themes in tourism study, the moral dimensions of the tourist experience. Falk *et al.* (2011) argue that the topic of learning is a neglected tourism research area. They suggest that an appreciation of what can be learned can usefully be approached by distinguishing among three terms: episteme (theoretical knowledge about the world), techne (practical skills linked to action) and phronesis (the application of experiential knowledge to act in a right and often reflexively aware manner). There are some emerging studies revealing that travellers with continued exposure to new settings do learn technical skills (the techne identified by Falk *et al.*, 2011). For example, Pearce and Foster (2007) demonstrated empirically that young international travellers confidently saw themselves as building their generic skills, such as dealing with money, being more effective communicators and handling crises as a result of their travel. In this same tradition, Scarinci and Pearce (2012), working with a young North American sample of student travellers, identified that such skills were developed after four international travel experiences. Tsuar *et al.* (2010) specified three categories of techne or practical skills in their study of Taiwanese travellers; pre-trip preparation, on-site travel capability and emergency response.

All of these studies suggest that cricketer/tourists like other travellers are very likely to be learning several travel-related skills. Nevertheless, it is arguably the knowledge and phronesis dimensions of learning which matter more to the overall travel motivation profile rather than the building of personal capacities and competencies. In this area of study, Falk *et al.* suggest that while many interpretive and public communication efforts directed at tourists do: 'enhance knowledge (episteme) but recent research suggests that this kind of minimal exposure cultivates phronesis only occasionally and only for some visitors' (2011: 12).

These studies on learning partially help describe the path which may lead cricketers to become more socially aware and change their motivational profile. In an analysis of travellers' written descriptions of their exposure to poverty, Pearce (2011b) reported five emotional reactions in the travellers' accounts. Two of these emotional reactions – a desire to change or assist the visited community and an intention to tell others about the situations the tourists had seen were associated with more involved forms of travel. The desire to act in the right way and to effect change (phronesis) was strong in some of these narratives. For example two representative cases from that study provide a clear view of the impact of travel:

> I walked around this 'middle class' (African) home and thought how much excess I have...Is life easier and better with all of our trappings, of course, does this mean I will get rid of all my excess things when I go home of course not. By maybe just maybe when I walk in Target and drop those unnecessary things into the cart, I will think about all of those whose basic needs are not covered maybe I will think harder about buying that extra pair of jeans which I don't really need and think that could provide 4 years worth of schooling for a child...I hope I will anyway.

And separately:

> I do not expect you will automatically understand (the poverty) but I believe my sharing this with you will indeed spark some anger some pity, some feeling that is not positive but it is necessary to create something positive. (Pearce, 2011b: 10–11)

As Falk (2009) suggests, the process of personal change and learning comes from deeper involvement in a setting and from linking one's travel experiences to personal identity. Cricketers as outlying cases of the range of the tourist concept represent individuals whose central livelihood is linked to being in other places, playing against and in front of representatives of other cultures. For the cricketer/tourist they are not merely spectating and gazing at a culture, they are immersed in components of it through their sporting performances and their ancillary responsibilities.

In these intense environments – cricketers can be seen here as special interest tourists with unique on-site access – it can be suggested that phronesis, the third component of learning suggested by Falk et al. (2011), can sometimes occur. In these situations the moral issues and personal life contrasts between the successful sportsperson and the underprivileged communities are not only registered (this was evident in the Pearce (2011b) studies of tourists' reactions to poverty as cited above) – but also the cricketers have the money, political links and capacity to make a difference. Cricket is a sport supported by many rich and powerful individuals and the opportunity to 'do good' is available to those cricketers who can cultivate these links for community well-being. In terms of the travel career pattern model of motivation the shift from the inexperienced traveller with broad and undifferentiated motivational enthusiasms to the experienced traveller with the strong interest in the visited communities and environment is apparent.

Conclusion

Five implications emerge from these analyses for tourism study and, more specifically, for the treatment of culture confusion, learning and travel motivation. It appears from the evidence provided in the cricketers' autobiographies that culture confusion is episodic. Despite considerable travel experience some of the older cricketers report occasions and episodes where the visited customs and traditions provide challenges which they do not expect and which they are confronting. Little academic attention has been given to the course or trajectory of actual culture shock/confusion experiences.

Instead the pattern of a curve was initially postulated in the literature and the gradual adoption of this model penetrated the studies on foreign students and aid workers. When tourism studies treated culture shock it was rapidly pointed out that the there can be a pleasure in experiencing culture differences since permanent adaptability is not required of such visitors. Nevertheless, the idea persisted that with experience, smooth curves of adjustment and readjustment were probable. That view can be challenged and from the outlying case of cricketer/tourists it seems that Hottola's (2004) view of an episodic and intermittent experience of culture confusion is the more compelling model.

In considering culture shock and confusion the role of fellow travellers has been inadequately considered. The dominant trend in the older literature is to treat the tourist as an isolated person who is directly dealing with the local people and their patterns of living rather than considering the social group in which many tourists (including cricketers) are embedded. Studies of tourist guides as culture brokers represent an exception to this trend (cf. Cohen, 1985) but the role played by immediate others has not been carefully considered. The opportunity exists to document more carefully the way in which tourists rely on each other as well as their guidebooks and electronic resources to manage contemporary cultural issues.

The cricketers' autobiographies reviewed in preparing this chapter identified the feeling of being homesick as an important factor shaping the travel experience of this select group of sportsmen. In reviewing the significance of the homesickness concept it can be conceived as a catalyst to the culture shock issue, making the challenges of travelling internationally seem more significant. Alternatively, while cricketer/travellers may embrace the host culture and locations and find relatively few difficulties in their interactions, the personal and intimacy needs which are a part of their at-home lives may generate feelings of loss and despondency. The emotional qualities of homesickness appear to be underrepresented in the documentation of the tourist experience and future research could benefit from the fresh interest in missing one's home setting.

Studies of tourist motivation in the academic literature tend to be static accounts of tourists' pattern of needs at one point in time. Nevertheless there is recognition that motivation is dynamic (Hsu & Huang, 2008). It has though been challenging and remains a complex undertaking to track how motivation changes with experience (cf. Pearce & Lee, 2005). The value of considering how inexperienced young sportsmen can become moral ambassadors for causes and travel with an altogether broader set of motives towards seeing the contemporary world and its issues is arguably underpinned by their access to finance, key people and administrative resources. Clearly having more generous resources can change a lot of features of the travel experience and perhaps better measures of how much travellers are able to afford to spend on their travels might offer further insights as to how and why motivation patterns change. There is a lot of evidence that in earlier times tourists returned to the same holiday location year after year in an annual ritual of replenishing themselves for their working world (Urry, 1990). It may be that this stable motivational pattern and accompanying destination choices were not so much a desired choice as a forced decision due to resource constraints. Such economic determinism thinking may have been underestimated in the psychological studies of tourist motivation and new questions to ascertain the interaction between experiences and having the financial resources to build on the desires created by previous travel could be added to the travel career pattern approach.

The combative nature of cricket at the highest level has generated much on-field banter and less than polite attempts to gain advantage by commenting on the opposition players and their performance. In the English speaking world, or at least those parts of it where cricket is played seriously, the language of cricket has influenced our analogies and is responsible for an inordinately large number of colloquial expressions and sayings (see, for example, Past Times, 2000). For this researcher, a one-time cricketer in Oxford and in South Australia, with at least some contact with select famous players, two broader final cricket related remarks relevant to the life of a tourism researcher can be offered. Greg Chappell provides the following advice to cricketers (and by analogy researchers): 'talent can only get you so far. After that it is just plain hard work' (2011: 363). And finally there is some generic value in attending to the cynical adage about older sports participants: 'The older I get the greater I was.' It is a reminder to those who now profess tourism studies to recall their own early sporting and research careers with modesty and acknowledge their weaknesses in earlier days (see Chapter 11, this volume). Imbued with such modesty, both past and present, it is possible to suggest that this analysis of cricketers as tourists has offered an interesting spin on some well-worn tracks.

References

ABC (2010) *The Australian Cricket Collection*. Sydney: Australian Broadcasting Corporation.
Agassi, A. (2009) *Open: An Autobiography*. London: Harper Collins.
Bauer, T. and McKercher, B. (eds) (2003) Sex and tourism. In *Journeys of Romance Love and Lust*. Binghampton, NY: Haworth.
Beckham, D. with Watt, T. (2004) *David Beckham: My Side*. London: Harper Collins Willow.
Bochner, S., Lin, A. and McLeod, M. (1979) Cross-cultural contact and the development of an international perspective. *Journal of Social Psychology* 107, 29–41.

Bowen, D. and Clarke, J. (2009) *Contemporary Tourist Behaviour: Yourself and Others as Tourists*. Wallingford, Oxon: CABI.
Chappell, G. (2011) *Fierce Focus*. Richmond, Victoria: Hardie Grant.
Cohen, E. (1985) The tourist guide: The origins, structured and dynamics of a role. *Annals of Tourism Research* 10, 5–29.
De Botton, A. (2009) *The Pleasures and Sorrows of Work*. Harmondsworth: Penguin.
De Crop, A. (2004) Trustworthiness in qualitative tourism research. In J. Phillimore and L. Goodson (eds) *Qualitative Research in Tourism* (pp. 156–169). London: Routledge.
Diamond, J. (2005) *Collapse: How Societies Choose to Fail or Succeed*. New York: Penguin Group.
Eisenhardt, K. (1989) Building theories from case study research. *Academy of Management Review* 14, 532–550.
Falk, J. (2009) *Identity and the Museum Visitor Experience*. Walnut Creek, CA: Left Coast Press.
Falk, J.H., Ballantyne, R., Packer, J. and Benckendorff, P. (2011) Travel and learning; A neglected tourism research area. *Annals of Tourism Research*. doi: 10.1016/j.annals.2011.11.016.
Fitzsimmons, P. (2004) *Steve Waugh*. Sydney: Harper Collins.
Furnham, A. (1984) Tourism and culture shock. *Annals of Tourism Research* 11 (1), 41–57.
Gilchrist, A. (2008) *True Colours*. Sydney: Pan MacMillan.
Gullahorn, J.E. and Gullahorn, J.T. (1963) An extension of the u-curve hypothesis. *Journal of Social Issues* 19, 33–47.
Harvey, N. (1963) *My World of Cricket*. London: Hodder & Stoughton.
Hottola, P. (2004) Culture confusions: Intercultural adaptation in tourism. *Annals of Tourism Research* 31 (2), 447–466.
Hsu, C.H. and Huang, S. (2008) Travel motivation: A critical review of the concept's development. In A. Woodside and D. Martin (eds) *Tourism Management Analysis, Behaviour and Strategy* (pp. 14–27). Wallingford, Oxon: CABI.
Jafari, J. (ed.) (2000) *Encyclopedia of Tourism*. London: Routledge.
Langer, J. (2008) *Seeing the Sunrise*. Crows Nest, NSW: Allen & Unwin.
Langer, J. and Wainwright, R. (2010) *Australia You Little *Beauty*. Crows Nest, NSW: Allen & Unwin.
McGrath, G. with Lane, D. (2008) *Line and Strength*. Sydney: William Heinemann.
Oberg, K. (1960) Culture shock: Adjustment to neo-cultural environments. *Practical Anthropology* 17, 177–182.
O'Keefe, K. (2007) *Turn, Turn, Turn…Please*. Sydney: ABC Books.
Panchal, J. and Pearce, P.L. (2011) Health motives and the Travel Career Pattern (TCP) model. *Asian Journal of Tourism and Hospitality Research* 5 (1), 32–44.
Panksepp, J. and Biven, L. (2010) *The Archaeology of the Mind*. New York: W.W Norton.
Past Times (2000) *Stumped on a Sticky Wicket Sporting Sayings and Their Meanings*. Oxford: Past Times.
Pearce, P.L. (2005) *Tourist Behaviour Themes and Conceptual Schemes*. Clevedon: Channel View Publications.
Pearce, P.L. (2011a) *Tourist Behaviour and the Contemporary World*. Bristol: Channel View Publications.
Pearce, P.L. (2011b) Tourists' written reactions to poverty in Southern Africa. *Journal of Travel Research*, 1 February. doi: 10.1177/0047287510396098.

Pearce, P.L. and Foster, F. (2007) A university of travel. Backpacker learning. *Tourism Management* 28 (5), 1285–1298.
Pearce, P.L. and Lee, U. (2005) Developing the travel career approach to tourist motivation. *Journal of Travel Research* 43 (3), 226–237.
Pearce, P.L. and Maoz, D. (2008) Novel insights into the identity changes among backpackers. *Tourism Culture and Communication* 8 (1), 27–43.
Scarinci, J. and Pearce, P.L. (2012) The perceived influence of travel experiences on learning generic skills. *Tourism Management* 33, 380–386.
Symonds, A. and Gray, S. (2008) *Roy on the Rise*. Prahan, Victoria: Hardie Grant Books.
Tsuar, S., Yen, C. and Chen, C. (2010) Independent tourist knowledge and skills. *Annals of Tourism Research* 37 (4), 1035–1054.
Urry, J. (1990) *The Tourist Gaze: Leisure and Travel in Contemporary Societies*. London: Sage.
Ward C., Bochner, S. and Furnham, A. (2001) *The Psychology of Culture Shock* (2nd edn). Oxon: Routledge.
White, N.R. and White, P.B. (2007) Home and away: Tourists in a connected world. *Annals of Tourism Research* 34 (1), 88–104.
Wright, K. (2000) I found South African Breweries Most Hospitable. *Hoping It Might Be So: Poems, 1974–2000*. London: Leviathan.
Yin, R.K. (2009) *Case Study Research Design and Methods*. Thousand Oaks, CA: Sage.

8 Sport Tourism as a Means of Reconciliation? The Case of India–Pakistan Cricket[1]

John Beech, Andrew Rigby, Ian Talbot and Shinder Thandi

> *Some Contests acted out on humble swards*
> *Are no less Epic-filled than those at Lords....*
> *Unrivalled day! Good Win! Immortal Score!*
> *Peace has its Victories more renowned than War.*
> Tales from Far Pavilions, Morgan Dockrell

Introduction

At the core of sporting activity is always a form of competition. Competition may be between individuals or between teams. The highest level of sporting competition is at an international level as sport governance is based, for historic reasons, along national lines, and such competition dates, for most sports, from the late 19th century. In the period since then, the parameters defining such competition – the changing limits of nation-states – have seen, in addition to localised specific changes such as the reunification of Germany, several more general changes: the redefinition of Eastern Europe at the conclusion of the First World War; the partition of states, such as those caused by the granting of independence to Ireland and to India; and the disintegration of the Soviet Union in the 1990s.

Responses to these changes have varied with respect to revised terms of governance. In the case of the Eastern European successor states which followed the disintegration of the Habsburg Empire, the International

Olympic Committee (IOC) welcomed them if they were countries who fought with the Allies, or banned them for one or two Games if they had been members of the Central Axis (Austria, Bulgaria, Germany, Hungary and Turkey). In the case of Soviet Union successor states, the IOC has been welcoming.

It is in the cases of post-partition states that the most complex, and from a reconciliation perspective, the most interesting cases have arisen. This chapter looks in particular at the reconciliation process as a factor in the cross-boundary support at India-Pakistan international cricket matches (known as test matches, and a series of test matches between two nations being known as a test series). Although India-Pakistan cricket has attracted previous attention (see, for example, Marqusee, 1996) this segment of the sport tourism market, representing post-partition national competition, has not been seriously investigated from the peace and reconciliation perspective before.

Before turning to that sector, it is interesting to note the complexity that partition has introduced to sport governance in another location – Ireland, where partition took place in 1922, with six counties choosing to remain part of the United Kingdom (Northern Ireland) and the remaining 26 counties choosing independence as the Republic of Ireland. This complexity is exemplified by a statement issued by the British Olympic Association (BOA) on 27 January 2004:

> The British Olympic Association (BOA) and the Olympic Council for Ireland (OCI) have enjoyed a close and harmonious relationship for many years over a range of issues including the complex issue of Olympic representation by athletes from Northern Ireland.
>
> Irrespective of the difficult political past sport has played an important role in breaking down barriers and breaching political divides.

Sport in Northern Ireland, particularly when it comes to the issue of international representation, is a complex matter. Citizens from Northern Ireland are entitled to hold either or both Irish and British passports. International representation is achieved through the appropriate governing body affiliated to the respective international federation. In some instances this is an all-Ireland governing body, e.g. boxing, rowing, swimming, tennis and triathlon and in some instances it is through a Great Britain and Northern Ireland body, e.g. archery, athletics, gymnastics, judo and sailing. Additionally in some sports, e.g. hockey, athletes can choose which country they represent at Olympic level at the start of their international career.

Less than a month later (20 February 2004) the BOA felt it necessary to issue a further press release, jointly with the Olympic Council of Ireland (OCI):

> The British Olympic Association (BOA) and the Olympic Council for Ireland (OCI) have engaged in full and cordial discussion following recent media speculation concerning athletes from Northern Ireland.
> In the interests of the athletes concerned and of continuing harmonious relations between the two bodies, the two National Olympic Committees have agreed to retain the status quo that the longstanding practice relating to athletes in Northern Ireland who qualify for participation at the Olympic Games will be maintained. That is to say that an athlete born in Northern Ireland who qualifies for participation at the Olympic Games and who holds a UK passport, may opt for selection by either Team GB or Ireland.

Thus, more than 80 years after partition it is still necessary to clarify the official reconciliation process!

The main focus of this chapter is on cross-border spectator sport tourism in India and Pakistan, and in particular the test series of 1955 and 2004. The India-Pakistan scenario is different from the Irish scenario in that it has been shaped by long periods of closed borders, closed that is to the vast majority of spectators, who could not afford to 'cross' the border by transiting a third country. A scenario similar to that of India and Pakistan exists in Cyprus, with a division between Turkish Cyprus and the rump (Greek) Cyprus. Here cross-border sport tourism is just about to be promoted, in this case with football matches (Anon., 2004). Other contentious cricket tours have included the 1968–1969 England tour of South Africa and the current England tour of Zimbabwe, but, although having strong political dimensions, their contexts do not derive from partition.

The 1955 series was the last for 17 years and has been largely neglected other than by cricket statisticians. The 2004 series has been selected not only because of its currency but because there seem to be the first signs that the occasion of sporting contact will be used as a catalyst of a more reconciliatory relationship between the two nations, a feature distinctly lacking in the intervening cricket confrontations.

The post-part test series of cricket matches, which took place intermittently depending on the state of relations between India and Pakistan, are next reviewed, with particular emphasis on the 1955 series and the 2004 series. A chronology of meetings between India and Pakistan including those which took place in other countries is given in Figure 8.1.

October 16, 1952 – Five years after the separation of the two countries, they were involved in the first test series, which was played in Delhi, India.
March 1, 1955 – The five match test series finishes after five drawn (no-result) games.
February 13, 1961 – After 12 successive draws in their last 15 test appearances, this was the last test match, also played in Delhi, between the two nations before the 1971 war broke out.
October 16, 1978 – Faisalabad saw the resumption of the India–Pakistan Series exactly 26 years after its inauguration and more than 17 years after the last encounter.
November 3, 1978 – Indian captain Bishan Singh Bedi called his batsmen from the field (when 23 runs were required from 14 balls with eight wickets in hand) in protest against the persistent short-pitched bowling of Sarfraz Nawaz in the one-day game at Sahiwal, Pakistan. The latter's last four deliveries were all bouncers, which were not called wides (i.e. illegal) by Pakistani umpires.
October 31, 1984 – The Sialkot, Pakistan, one-day match and the remainder of the series were cancelled immediately after the assassination of Indian Prime Minister Indira Gandhi.
February 22, 1987 – Pakistan's President General Zia-ul-Haq watched part of the second day of the Jaipur test as part of his 'Cricket for Peace' mission.
October 23, 1989 – Pakistan's only appearance in the one-day international match in the city of Mumbai, India, the headquarters of Shiv Sena, a Hindu nationalist movement, not against India but versus Australia during the MRF Nehru Cup.
December 14, 1989 – The Jinnah Stadium in Sialkot witnessed the last test match day to be staged between the two countries in Pakistan for 14 years. It produced a record 33rd drawn game which yielded a record of 75% of matches in a no-result state.
December 20, 1989 – By resorting to tear gas and baton charges, Karachi's police converted crowd disturbances into a full-scale riot after Pakistan was precariously placed at 28 for three off 14.3 overs. Indian captain K. Srikkanth was manhandled during the fiasco.
October 22, 1991 – The Shiv Sainiks dug up the Wankhede stadium strip in Mumbai in order to prevent Pakistan from playing in the city.
March 4, 1992 – Due to the format of the championships, India and Pakistan met each other for the first time in the World Cup after a long gap of 17 years since its inception. Batsman Javed Miandad mockingly mimicked wicket keeper Kiran More's frivolous appealing by leaping up and down.
September 14, 1997 – In the second match in Toronto the heavily built Inzamam ul Haq was reportedly taunted about his size by a spectator Shiva Kumar Thind using a megaphone. 'Aloo', the Hindi word for potato, was reportedly used as an offensive word. Inzamam charged into the stands wielding a bat, handed to him on the boundary by the 12th man, to accost his tormentor.
February 20, 1999 – The last test match for five years between the two nations was played in Kolkata, during the Asian Test Championships.
April 4, 1999 – The last one-day international to be played between the two nations in India, at Bangalore. Like the last test in India (won by Pakistan by 46 runs), this match resulted in a 123-run victory for Pakistan.
March 1, 2003 – The last match between the two nations for two years – either in tests or one-day internationals – was held during the World Cup and was termed 'the mother of all battles' and 'the match of the championships'. India registered a win by six wickets.
March 29, 2003 – India cancelled the International Cricket Council (ICC) scheduled tour of Pakistan, which was to start from the second week of April. In retaliation, Pakistan also called off their tour to India in 2004.
October 22, 2003 – The Vajpayee government gave a green signal for the resumption of India–Pakistan cricket ties, giving permission to the Indian team to visit Pakistan in March, 2004. The proposed tour, comprising three tests and five one-day matches, would largely boost the Pakistan Cricket Board's financial situation.
March–April 2004 – India's tour to Pakistan. India won the test series 2-1, their first ever series win in Pakistan, and won the one-day matches 3-2.

Figure 8.1 Chronology of India v. Pakistan cricket matches

Historical Background from 1947 to the 1965 War

The new international border between India and Pakistan, drawn up in 1947 following independence, drew a line between the neighbouring cities of Lahore, in Pakistan, and Amritsar, in India. Before the transfer of population in August 1947 amidst scenes of unspeakable murder and mayhem, both cities had possessed large minority populations. Lahore, which became the capital of the Pakistan Punjab, was denuded of its large Hindu and Sikh population. Amritsar similarly lost its large Muslim population. The policing of the Wagah-Attari border on the road from Lahore to Amritsar became a symbol of the newly independent states' national sovereignty (Purewal, 2003). Whereas once day trippers, students and businessmen regularly moved between the cities, first permits and later passports and visas were required for travel. The border was closed at a time of international tension between the 'distant neighbours'. The vexed Kashmir dispute brought both countries to the brink of war in July 1951. Air-raid precautions were introduced in both cities and there was a flight of population from Amritsar. The border was not reopened until February 1953. A further 20 months passed before the Lahore–Amritsar railway link was restored.

In a foretaste of the use of cricket in 2004 to normalise relations, the India–Pakistan test series of January–February 1955 provided an occasion for opening the border. Around 5000 Indians attended the drawn third test that commenced in Lahore on 29 January at the Bagh-i-Jinnah ground. On the opening two days, the ground was packed with 40,000 spectators an hour before the first ball was bowled. Many of them had to be accommodated in temporary seating. Offices closed as people crowded around radios to listen to the commentary. According to the figures cited in *Dawn*, the leading English language newspaper, 22,000 Indians visited Lahore in a five-day period. Nearly half of these were Sikhs (Anon., 1955b). A hundred buses had been laid on to carry visitors from Wagah to the Lahore Railway Station. *Dawn* gave prominence to the fact that 200 high school and college girls entered through the Wagah border on the morning of 2 February and 'roamed around the city unescorted in small batches' (Anon., 1955b). While the motives for the reporting of such comments are obvious, such sentiments appear genuine as:

> It is such a great pleasure to be back in Lahore. It has the same old look and has been an immense joy to meet many of my classmates. They have been so nice to me. I wish the old days were back. (A Hindu lady who had studied in the city before Partition, Anon., 1955a)

Lahore has not changed much. It is so different from what fanatics in East Punjab want us to believe. I could probably live here ages and not feel a stranger – so good my Muslim friends are to me. They have welcomed me back home with open arms. (A former Hindu resident, Anon., 1955a)

Similar scenes occurred when the border was opened from 20–26 January 1956 to allow some 6000 Indian visitors to see Pakistan play a Marylebone Cricket Club (MCC) 'A' team in an unofficial test match, again at Lahore's Bagh-i-Jinnah ground. The customs post at Wagah was kept open from 6 am to 9 pm daily and the staff increased threefold so that no visitor was detained more than 'five minutes for the necessary formalities' (Anon., 1956b). The 21 January was declared a public holiday in Lahore. The next day, Indian dignitaries were publicly honoured in a meeting and a *mushaira* (poetry recitation) at the Lahore Town Hall (Anon., 1956a).

The previous April, it had been the turn of hockey to provide an opportunity for goodwill visits. The East Punjab Police Hockey Team played a series of exhibition matches in Montgomery and Lahore. Special five-day permits were issued to Indian visitors, 7000 of whom crossed the border at Wagah on 20 April in fleets of buses and on bicycles and in cars. 'The old walled city of Lahore bears a festive look', *Dawn* reported, with buntings and welcome slogans hanging in various localities, especially Gowalmandi and Anarkali (Anon., 1955c). These localities had been major centres of Hindu residences and businesses in the pre-partition period. Free food and accommodation were provided and 'even the tongawallas [drivers of horse-drawn carts] refused to charge a fare for their Hindu and Sikh passengers' (Anon., 1955d). Many of the visitors were curious students from Amritsar, but there were numbers of pre-partition residents, including Sikhs who were seen walking the Mall with their old Muslim friends and busily shopping in the famous Anarkali market. At an official reception hosted by the Pakistan branch of the Indo-Pakistan Joint Trade Board, its convenor M.K. Mir declared that if India and Pakistan created 'unbreakable ties of friendship, they could march on the road of progress' (Anon., 1955e).

The temporary opening of the border to mass tourists in 1955–1956 has now been largely historically forgotten, perhaps because it does not fit in with official accounts that stress the animosities between the two countries. Individuals interviewed in Amritsar in 2000 as part of a study on partition (Talbot, forthcoming) did however personally remember the remarkable scenes of the time. While the upper classes can overcome the hurdles of obtaining a visa for travel across the border, at all but the most tense times, these are usually insurmountable for ordinary people. Greater 'people-to-people contact' (sometimes referred to as 'Track II diplomacy') is vital if true harmony is to be established. It remains hostage, however, to political developments. Rather than ushering in a new era, the opening of the border in 1955–1956 was followed by a period of estrangement arising from the Kashmir issue and the 1958 military coup in Pakistan. The downward spiral culminated in the 1965 War when tanks rumbled across the international border in the Punjab.

Change in Political Climate

If there is one sport on the sub-continent that has enduring powers to create bonds between people by transcending caste, class, religion and gender, it is cricket. The gentleman's game remains a secular religion in the Indian sub-continent. Cricket could also arguably be considered the greatest enduring legacy of the British Empire. It took just five years after partition, in 1952, for the first test to be played between the newly independent states of India and Pakistan. Over time, however, growing hostilities between the two countries, especially over the disputed territory of Kashmir, politicised the game and India–Pakistan cricket matches were left to the vagaries of foreign relations between the two countries and to the whims of politicians and political parties.

The 2004 India–Pakistan test series would not have taken place had there not been a series of confidence-building measures initiated by both Prime Minister Vajpayee of India and President Musharraf of Pakistan. The current phase of India–Pakistan peace talks, which climaxed in the cricket tour, have their roots back in May 2003. It was then that the two countries decided to send back High Commissions and restore normal civil aviation and diplomatic links, which had been severely soured by the terrorist attack on the Indian Parliament on 13 December 2001. By the end of 2003 a further series of confidence-building measures had been agreed – these included restoring air and rail links, bus services and ferry links. The crucial turning point was the South Asian Association for Regional Cooperation (SAARC) summit on 6 January 2004 in Islamabad, Pakistan. Here both Vajpayee and Musharraf agreed to begin a composite dialogue in February to resolve all issues, including the disputed territories of Jammu and Kashmir, and President Musharraf assured Prime Minister Vajpayee that territory under Pakistan's control would not be permitted to support cross-border terrorism. In the forthcoming months, there were several ministerial-level meetings and in keeping with the earlier tradition of 'cricket diplomacy' the Samsung Cup cricket series was finally endorsed. Although the Board of Control for Cricket in

India (BCCI) and some players expressed concern about security issues and the cricket itinerary, they were eventually assured that there would be full protection. The cricket tour finally began on 10 March. Before leaving for Lahore the Indian cricket team paid a courtesy visit to the Indian Prime Minister Vajpayee, who urged them not only to win matches but also hearts.

The 2004 *Dil Jeet Lo* (Win Hearts) Tour

An India–Pakistan cricket match conjures up images of thrills and primal outpouring of emotions, enthusiasm and energy, pageantry and patriotism and the sheer, undiluted spirit of sport. In those moments we may think everything else has been forgotten – the 1947 Partition, the Hindu–Muslim riots, three India–Pakistan wars and Kashmir. At that juncture all that matters is that two cricketing giants are matching their skills in the sporting arena and a sub-continent of crazed enthusiasts is watching every moment with bated breath. The duel represents a clash of egos, the clash of ideals and the clash of history. We are in fact witnessing a proxy war, or to use Orwell's (1945) term 'mimic warfare', fought with much national pride and passion, where the losing team is dishonoured both in the eyes of the nation and its neighbour.

In cricketing terms the 2004 tour thoroughly lived up to this expectation – tickets for all the matches had been well over-subscribed and hotels, theatres and eating places were bursting to the seams during match days. The matches were telecast live to Indian and Pakistani audiences and were enthusiastically watched by diaspora communities of South Asia as well. India won the one-day series 3-2 and the test series 2-1 to win the Samsung Cup. This was India's first ever series victory over Pakistan on opposition soil.

Since 1947, and until this series, there had been 47 test matches and 86 one-day internationals between the two teams. The results of these encounters make interesting reading. Pakistan had won 52 of the one-day internationals (most of them played outside the sub-continent, many in the Gulf state of Sharjah) whilst India won only 30 and four ended with no result. In the test matches, however, the picture is quite different. Whilst Pakistan had won nine and India only five, 33 ended in draws, strongly indicating the caution exercised in developing a strategy of avoiding defeat rather than of winning. There could be no other sure way of bringing shame on one's nation than a defeat in a test series!

This was India's first cricket tour of Pakistan for 14 years. It involved playing five one-day internationals and test matches. The two most violence-prone Pakistani cities – Karachi and Peshawar – were denied a test match and had to be satisfied with one-day matches. The tour, lasting from 10 March to

17 April, largely shut down the two countries with an estimated match-day TV audience of 600 million – four times the audience for the American Super Bowl. The Pakistan embassy only issued 10,000 visas for visiting Indian fans but the numbers wanting visas were ten times more than that. Many tried and succeeded in using different excuses to gain entry, such as business and religion (as pilgrims to Sikh holy shrines) as a way of getting a visa.

Played under the shadow of the gun, especially amidst tight security in Karachi and Peshawar, the tour concluded without any major law-and-order incident. Numerous news reports and personal accounts recall the jovial atmosphere at grounds, the sportsmanship shown to both teams and the tremendous warmth and hospitality extended to Indian visitors. The powerful images on television and in the print media conveyed how the fans of two teams could enjoy the sport with a brotherly mindset, dispel myths of the 'Other' and identify with and emphasise commonalities rather than differences. The fact that the tour did not generate any security issues is itself a remarkable aspect. This showed the tremendous cooperation and goodwill generated by all sides for the tour to succeed. The Pakistani security establishment, with cooperation from their Indian counterparts, successfully coordinated an unprecedented security operation. According to Basu, 'Safe houses were identified to shelter the cricketers in the event of danger to their lives, helicopters were on standby for evacuation, flights were delayed on purpose, dummy convoys moved on the roads and elite commandos stood guard around the clock' (Basu, 2004). (If only such cooperation and meticulously detailed planning could be extended to building the peace process!)

It was not only the cricket fans who triumphed in this series, the tour acted as a major boost to the region. The Pakistan Cricket Board had signed sponsorship deals worth US$21 million – another $1.5 million was expected from the sale of tickets, hospitality boxes and vending rights. TV advertising revenues shot up. Gambling syndicates in Mumbai, Karachi and Dubai made a killing and re-distributed incomes between thousands in South Asia. Hotel occupancy rates and revenues in cities that were hosting the matches were at an all-time high – a great relief to the tourist sector after the collapse of tourism post 9/11 and due to the general rise in terrorist attacks in Pakistan. According to a Pakistan International Airline (PIA) official, airlines would generate US$500,000 in revenue during the Indian tour. Cinema theatres were showing matches for those unable to get the limited tickets. Their capacity was much higher than usual for film viewing. Thus not only was the tour a success in terms of Track II diplomacy, it was also extremely beneficial for reviving the sluggish tourist industry.

The question of whether this success can lead to a longer-term reconciliation is less clear however.

Can Cricket Have the Potential to Build Lasting Peace?

Historically sport has always been described in terms of war. Games are often described as 'battles', and teams are often said to have been 'routed', 'slaughtered' and 'demolished', and often using terminology associated with macho-male aggression. 'Sport is an unfailing cause of ill-will', George Orwell argued. In an essay written towards the end of the Second World War in 1945, he elaborated:

> I am always amazed when I hear people saying that sport creates goodwill between the nations, and that if only the common peoples of the world could meet one another at football or cricket, they would have no inclination to meet on the battlefield. Even if one didn't know from concrete examples (the 1936 Olympic Games, for instance) that international sporting contests lead to orgies of hatred, one could deduce it from general principles. (Orwell, 1945)

The real point Orwell was making was that all sport was competitive, and involved winning or losing, and thus involved impact on pride. A sporting encounter between nations, by implication, took on bigger proportions, as it involved national pride – much as war would. He referred to this as 'mimic warfare'. There are many historical rivalries which exist in sport between countries – the Ashes (test series between England and Australia), also in cricket, England–Scotland or Brazil–Argentina in football – but none are quite so fierce and filled with 'ill-will' as any sporting tie between India and Pakistan.

Despite the political rhetoric, posturing and clash of nationalisms and strong emotions, the 2004 tour has demonstrated amply that there are strong reasons for encouraging further sporting and other cultural links between India and Pakistan. The Orwellian argument that sport between nations is like war has some backing in terms of both evolutionary psychology and game theory. Sport and war are both good examples of zero-sum games. Since only two parties are involved, for one to gain something, the other must lose. Both cannot gain from the encounter, just as both India and Pakistan cannot win the same match. To gain something, one must defeat – and thus, humiliate, as national pride is involved – the other.

But can we use such sporting paradigms to reflect on how civilisation and societies evolve over time? By way of contrast one could strongly argue that economic and social progress is a non-zero-sum game. If two countries cooperate with each other they both stand to benefit, and in fact as Adam Smith so poignantly put it 'it is not from the benevolence of the butcher, the brewer or the baker that we expect our dinner, but from their regard to their self-interest' (Smith, 1776). Thus economic and social progress result from the fruits of mutual exchanges – if the increased people-to-people contact (albeit initially through cricket) generates trust and greater intensity in exchange, it can only lead to non-zero-sum benefits. Economic analysts and some political leaders see the potential of development of the north-west region only through increase in intra-regional trade and they seriously question the economic viability of maintaining the Wagah border.

It is to the credit of Musharraf and Vajpayee that they were beginning to recognise that war (and sport until recently) functions on a different paradigm from society. War and war-mongering lead to the creation of a specific mindset in which, as Glover has argued, individuals are degraded and dehumanised and persons are stripped of their personhood (Glover, 2000). Sport, especially cricket, can act as a catalyst in creating more interaction and cooperation. By increasing people-to-people contact (and thus depoliticising cricket and halting the dehumanising elements of sport as war) people of India and Pakistan can see and feel themselves as humans again and feel empathy towards each other. Over time, if this leads India and Pakistan to cooperate more in every sphere – economic, social, cultural, political – both stand to make major gains. The proposal for a SAARC's South Asian Free Trade Area by 2006 will be an important marker. It may be an important route for them to take if they are to leave behind their Third World status (Aftab, 2004).

The Reconciliation Perspective

Reconciliation work refers to those activities, initiatives and processes that are primarily concerned with bringing peace. Gandhi shared this view, asking for cricket in Bombay during the 1930s to be banned as he saw it as enhancing communal tensions about a restoration of relationships between those divided by conflict and enmity. As such, reconciliation work can embrace initiatives aimed at changing people's perceptions of themselves and former enemies such that new constructive relationships might be created. Reconciliation work can also focus on bringing about those socio-economic and political institutional changes deemed necessary for the creation of a new culture of reconciliation between those that were once divided.

Considered in this manner, reconciliation refers primarily to a process. The attempt to restore relationships can take place at any point during a destructive conflict, as people seek to establish bridges across the conflict lines, but it is an activity more commonly encountered during the post-settlement phase of a conflict when the space available for such activities is expanded.

Insofar as reconciliation involves the restoration of fractured relationships, a common element in many reconciliation initiatives throughout the world is the attempt to create 'safe spaces' within different institutional spheres in order that encounters might take place between those that have been divided. Underpinning such efforts is the assumption that through dialogue enemies might begin to see each other in a new light. The demonisation of 'the other' that is part and parcel of most cycles of division and conflict can be undermined as people begin to relate to each other as fellow human beings and thereby develop a degree of mutual understanding. Sporting occasions can fulfil such a role, acting as safe spaces for such encounters.

John Paul Lederach has attempted to identify three key sectors that can be significant in the kind of *horizontal* interactions across lines of division that are at the heart of any reconciliation project (Lederach, 1999). Using a pyramid as a diagram he identifies the top leadership engaged in formal negotiations at the pinnacle, with grass-roots community-based leaders at the base. He attributes particular significance, however, to the encounters between what he terms 'middle-range leaders' – those whose structural location within their respective societies allows them access not only to the grass-roots but also to the top leadership. Lederach emphasises the importance of coordination between the different levels in reconciliation processes:

> The challenge of horizontal capacity is how to foster constructive understanding and dialogue across the lines of division ... The challenge of the vertical capacity is how to develop genuine recognition that peace-building involves multiple activities at different levels of leadership, taking place simultaneously, each level distinct in its needs and interdependent in effects. (Lederach, 1999: 33)

If we were to adopt Lederach's three-fold distinction between key sectors in reconciliation processes, with particular reference to the role of sport in healing the wounds of conflict, especially at the international level, we might identify the top leadership within the respective countries who have adopted a peace agenda and are genuinely seeking a rapprochement, we could identify the actual sportsmen and women as middle-range actors – people with the capacity to influence their supporters at the grass-roots and who also have access to the top leadership. We might categorise the sports tourists as people coming from the grass-roots sector.

So, the question is: how significant is sports tourism in promoting reconciliation? Although previous cricket encounters between India and Pakistan might suggest that sport has served to divide the communities further by tending to reinforce dichotomous social imagery, based on the reasoning above it is suggested that sports tourism can make a contribution to reconciliation between divided nations and communities to the extent that it is an integral part of a broader process of reconciliation being pursued between the different sectors of the respective societies. Indeed, this has been recognised by those with a particular interest in the 2004 cricket test series between India and Pakistan. Former Pakistani captain Imran Khan commented: 'When the two countries are trying to become friendly, trying to ease tensions, then cricket plays a healing role, cricket becomes a cement in bonding the two countries together' (Jawad, 2004).

If sports tourism takes place as part of a more-or-less-orchestrated series of confidence-building measures (CBMs) in the context of a sustained commitment to ease tensions by the political elites of the parties to the conflict, then such encounters can serve to undermine stereotypes and are more likely to result in the humanisation of 'the other' and the promotion of cross-border links and relationships that can feed into the process of détente and wider peace-building. A significant factor in this overall process is that if top-level leadership and middle-level opinion-leaders are stressing the importance of friendly relations with an erstwhile enemy, then this can create the space for encounters across the lines of division, making it safe for those at the grass roots to echo such sentiments and act upon them in terms of holding out the hand of friendship to the other.

The March/April 2004 test series between India and Pakistan was part of a series of measures aimed at promoting contact between people; others included the restoration of transport links and the upgrading of diplomatic missions. These occurred in the context of a ceasefire in Kashmir in November 2003, at a time when both countries were under pressure from the US and each had its own reasons for pursuing détente. As this was a tour designed not just as a sporting contest but as one to 'win hearts' (Basu, 2004), the test matches themselves became a powerful symbol and representation of the ongoing reconciliation process, and the sports tourists became participants in this.

However, it is completely unrealistic to think that sporting contacts between players and respective sets of supporters can heal the wounds of division if the political leadership of the respective communities are concerned to keep such wounds raw. Hence, if sports tourism takes place in a context of worsening relations between parties to the conflict, then there is the possibility of such encounters leading to a worsening of relations and confirmation of the demon-like status of 'the other'. Expressions of distrust and enmity made by significant leaders and opinion-makers can legitimise and create the space for expression of similar attitudes at the grass-roots level. In such circumstances, encounters can merely serve to confirm the stereotypes. In such cases there is a strong likelihood that such encounters, far from being occasions for dialogue, might become opportunities to display one's colours and reaffirm one's hatred and animosity towards the historic enemy, and to reproduce the old memories of division and contempt that continue to divide the communities. In such circumstances the victory of one's own side becomes a confirmation of national superiority – the team one is supporting becomes the embodiment, the carrier of a nation's stature and prowess. Defeat of course has the opposite effect – an extreme example of this from the world of sport is the so-called Football War fought between El Salvador and Honduras (14 July–18 July 1969). Although there were other more significant factors which caused the war, the invasion of Honduras by El Salvador was triggered by a contentious outcome in an early round of the World Cup.

Of course, there are different types of sports tourism. In the particular example of the Indo-Pakistan cricket series we are looking at a situation where citizens of one country visited the territory of a former enemy. But the history of Indo-Pakistan cricket should alert us to the fact that, although tests between the two countries in the normal sense came to a halt in 1961, and for 17 years they did not visit each other's countries, they did continue to play each other at the Olympics, the Asian Games and other international tournaments. So, there is the sports tourism which involves the travel of supporters from either side of a conflict line to a 'neutral' venue. Sporting encounters in such contexts can take on a powerful symbolism, such as when the representatives of North and South Korea marched alongside each other in the opening parade of the Sydney Olympics in 2000 or when the US football (soccer) team played Iran in the 1998 World Cup in France. Maybe on such occasions personal friendships are established across the boundaries, as people become aware that beyond their identity as citizens of states in conflict they also share commonalities such as a love of sport. But without the sustained commitment of relevant political elites, then such acts of bridge-building are likely to remain relatively insignificant in terms of their impact on the broader process of reconciliation.

At the same time, such occasions for encountering the enemy can have a longer-term significance as examples of 'prophetic dialogue' that can lead eventually to changes in public opinion and political agendas. Thus, sports tourists encountering the enemy in the safe spaces of an international cricket competition, the Football World Cup, or the Olympics can have experiences that undermine old demonic stereotypes. The parties to such encounters are themselves links in chains of influence within their own societies. They can tell their stories on their return, influence those with whom they interact at home, and thereby contribute to what might be an imperceptible change in public opinion which might find expression at some stage in pressure on political leaderships to commit to a peace process from the top to complement the peace-making from below embodied in the sports tourism.

Conclusion

The cross-border contact occasioned by the large-scale sport tourism associated with cricket test series, notably those of 1955 and 2004, suggests that such contact may be a significant contributory factor in the reconciliation process. The 1955 series failed to achieve this potential because of the broader political context, but the 2004 series may have been more effective, if the broader political rapprochement is sustained. That rapprochement is currently driven by an increasing level of cultural links on a semi-formal basis in spite of reservations by governments at a more overtly political level. The desire of peoples, and thus of sports tourists, for reconciliation is evidenced iconically by the formalised visitation arrangements at the Wagah border (Nayar, 2004) necessitated by the scale of visitation.

Contacts such as those described prompt a call for a research agenda which extends to other places where partition or other redrawing of a border has taken place. Cyprus, with its current return of football contact, the successor states to the former Federal Republic of Yugoslavia, and, perhaps in the not-too-distant future, even North and South Korea are worthy possibilities for further study.

Note

(1) This chapter is included with kind permission of the editor and publisher of *Tourism Recreation Research*. It was originally published in that journal in 2004, Vol. 30 (1), 83–91.

References

Aftab, M. (2004) Can Safta lead to a South Asian economic union? *Dawn* (Karachi). See www.dawn.com/2004/01/19/ebr8.htm (accessed 22 November 2004).
Anon. (1955a) *Dawn* (Karachi), 2 February, p. 8.
Anon. (1955b) *Dawn* (Karachi), 4 February, p. 6.
Anon. (1955c) *Dawn* (Karachi), 20 April, p. 8.
Anon. (1955d) *Dawn* (Karachi), 21 April, p. 1.

Anon. (1955e) *Dawn* (Karachi), 24 April, p. 5.
Anon. (1956a) *Dawn* (Karachi), 21 January, p. 7.
Anon. (1956b) *Dawn* (Karachi), 26 January, p. 8.
Anon. (2004) Greeks and Turks to meet again after 40 years. *Daily Times* (Pakistan). See www.dailytimes.com.pk/default.asp?page=story_10-1-2004_pg2_23 (accessed 20 November 2004).
Basu, I. (2004) *The Indo-Pak Series 2004: Winning Games and Hearts*. Delhi: Rupa and Co.
Dockrell, M. (1984) A famous victory. *Tales from Far Pavilions*. London: Pavilion Press.
Glover, J. (2000) *Humanity: A Moral History of the 20th Century*. New Haven, CT: Yale University Press.
Jawad, R. (2004) Former skipper says cricket can heal wounds of India-Pakistan rift. *Daily Times* (Pakistan). See www.dailytimes.com.pk/print.asp?page=story_11-3-2004_pg2_1 (accessed 22 November 2004).
Lederach, J.P. (1999) Justpeace. In *People Building Peace* (pp. 27–36). Utrecht: European Centre for Conflict Prevention.
Marqusee, M. (1996) *A War Minus the Shooting: A Journey Through South Asia During Cricket's World Cup*. London: Heinemann.
Nayar, K. (2004) The melting of wax: A candle-lit vigil at Wagah is now a people's movement. *Outlook India*, 13 September.
Orwell, G. (1945) The sporting spirit. *Tribune*, December.
Purewal, N. (2003) The Indo-Pak border: Displacements, aggressions and transgressions. *Contemporary South Asia* 12 (4), 539–556.
Smith, A. (1776) *An Enquiry into the Nature and Causes of the Wealth of Nations*. London: Methuen.
Talbot, I. (forthcoming) *A Tale of Two Cities: Lahore, Amritsar and the Partition of India*. Oxford: Oxford University Press.

9 On the March with the Barmy Army

Paul Emery, Warwick Frost and Anthony Kerr

> *Whan that Aprille with his sonne bright*
> *The chille of March hath halfway put to flighte,...*
> *Thanne longen folke to and watch crickette*
> *And see the batter cope with greene wickette...*
> *And thus we gan to riden on our weye*
> *To see the cricket for the next five day*
> Prologue to the Teste Matche Tales, Simon Barnes

Context

- *Event* – Boxing Day test match (fourth test of five); Australia v. England, day one of five.
- *Aim* – To win the Ashes (again). Held every four years, this fiercely fought contest is the pinnacle of any English cricket season. At this stage, the series is tied one all. England need one win in the last two matches to retain the Ashes.
- *Location* – Melbourne Cricket Ground, the historic coliseum of Australian Cricket, venue for the first ever test match and ultimate battleground.
- *Perspective* – Match-day experience of a Barmy Army member.

The Army in Action

Our English cultural heritage dictates that we, a 10,000-strong army of English cricket followers, must politely start the day by introducing ourselves to the 85,000 crowd present. 'With his back to the play and his

Figure 9.1 Two members of the Barmy Army

oversized red-and-white top hat crowning his all-England outfit' (Hedge, 2010), our 'general' and match-day leader (aka Vic Flowers, Figure 9.1), leads us in singing the Barmy Army anthem:

> Everywhere we go, people want to know,
> who we are, where we come from,
> so we tell them,
> we are the England, the mighty mighty England.
> We are the army,
> the barmy barmy army.
> Barmy Army, Barmy Army.

Having continued this for a full five minutes, and as if others in the stadium would like to know more or simply wish to join us, our flag-waving leader continues

> We are the army,
> the Barmy Army,
> and we are mental and we are mad,
> we are the loyalest Cricket supporters
> that the World has ever had!

Our loud vocal and colourful demonstration of the 'new laddism' culture (Parry & Malcolm, 2004) is a sharp contrast 'to the conservatism and restrained manners of the cricket establishment' (Morgan, 2007: 365). Fuelled by alcohol, we will continue such chants throughout the day and night. Every Australian cricket fan now knows us, I can imagine our reputation of gallows humour, patriotism and fervour, has reached these shores well before our physical arrival (see Baum, Chapter 10, this volume for a comparison with other English supporters in India).

But oh dear, the day starts badly on the hallowed turf against the old enemy. England have already dropped two catches in the first three overs. We are not perturbed in the slightest. As experienced cricketing foot soldiers, we have seen it all before. Last time we were here, we were thrashed 5-0 and the Boxing Day test was over in three days! On that final day three years ago we were still singing 'We get three dollars to the pound' followed up by 'we're going shopping in the morning'. Indeed, self- as well as opposition-ridicule are a natural part of the Barmy Army existence.

As Parry and Malcolm (2004) explain, regardless of sporting outcome, the Barmy Army is motivated by three aspects; fun, influence, and a strong sense of nationalism. Fun is clearly evident by our colourful match-day appearance and long-established rituals. This includes what we wear, dressing up in fancy dress costumes or wearing something that just relates to the home country, painting body parts, creating humorous placards, waving large flags and exuding passion through songs, reposts and individual banter with anyone who is prepared to listen (see Figure 9.2).

On-field influence on the other hand, is achieved through 'slogans and choruses directed at individual players of the England team and collectively, and in even greater contrast to the traditions and norms of cricket spectatorship, irreverent, insulting and even crudely abusive chants and songs directed at opposition fans and players' (Parry & Malcolm, 2004: 80).

Representing a new variant of English national identity (Parry & Malcolm, 2004), we have other 'lieutenants' who take responsibility for bonding the troops and igniting nationalistic behaviours. First there is 'Billy the Trumpet' (aka Bill Cooper), our travelling trumpet player who, for example, leads renditions of the English national anthem. The vuvuzela, the notorious South African trumpet which dominated the 2010 Football World Cup, is banned.

As we sing 'God Save our Gracious Queen', we collectively point to the Australian fans emphasising the final lines 'Long to reign OVER YOU, God Save YOUR queen'. Indeed the strong sense of nationalism shines through in everything we do. Engaging with the uniqueness of the destination, in this case Australia, we specifically focus on our Commonwealth history. Fans

Figure 9.2 Barmy Army members in 'uniform'

comically dress as members of the royal family, or even as convicts as we sing 'You all live in a convict colony', to signify Australia's penal history.

There's also 'Union Dave', he's the Army's fund-raising 'lieutenant'. His role is to engage in charity work and mix with the locals. For example, he played in the recent 'bashes', a cricket series between the fans of England and Australia, which raised £37,500 for the charitable McGrath Foundation.

It is lunchtime now, and another beer beckons. While in the queue, I smile as I read one Barmy Army placard that reads 'The Hurley bird catches the Warne', referring to the recently publicised relationship between English actress Elizabeth Hurley and the Australian spin guru, Shane Warne.

Thoughts draw to home and gloatingly I text my brother in England, informing him that Australia have had a shocker and are 58-4. Oh and by the way, I also attached the video of us singing 'Jerusalem', another famous song of English significance, while performing Swanny's (English bowler Graeme Swann) latest dance craze, 'the sprinkler', against a backdrop of blue skies. Surely he gets the message... I'm in heaven!

Play resumes and our giant gladiator Chris Tremlett comes in to bowl. Swanny in the slip cauldron takes the catch, and there is the back of the under siege but highly respected opposing captain Ricky Ponting. As he slowly trudges back to the pavilion, we unleash the lyrics to the old Beatles hit of the same name:

> Yesterday, Ponting's troubles seemed so far away, Now Doherty is here to stay, McGrath and Warne were Yesterday, Suddenly, They're not half the team they used to be, Will he lose Ashes number three, Yesterday came suddenly.

As highly committed cricket fans (Weed, 2006) our barbs directed towards the opposition are both insightful and contemporary. Once again Tremers bowls and Matt Prior gets his sixth catch of the day. It is 3.14 pm and the old enemy all out for a low 98! Holding a replica Ashes urn skyward a Marylebone Cricket Club (MCC) attired Barmy Army man shouts 'Ricky – you're getting sacked in the morning!!'

As Australia take to the field, the barracking intensifies, as last night's carefully rehearsed songs await every Australian player. Mercilessly barracking the out-of-form Mitchell Johnson, we pump out another song. 'He bowls to the left, he bowls to the right, that Mitchell Johnson, his bowling is shite.' And to cue he bowls yet another wide!! Who says we cannot influence the game?

After an exhausting and memorable day, Australia are all out for 98. England are 157 for no wicket! I cannot wait to read tomorrow's Australian headlines. When can I buy the commemorative clothing just to reminisce and prove that I was there? Can life really get any better than this?

That is the experience of one of the authors of this chapter. Across in the Members' Pavilion sits another author, conforming to its dress regulations. There is no singing, nor merriment. It is the worst day of test cricket he has ever seen. Our third author misses all, instead, scuba diving off Easter Island.

Origins and Scope

What was the origin of the Barmy Army and how has this new type of sports fan changed the landscape of planning tourist activities? Ironically, it was *The Sydney Morning Herald*, an Australian newspaper, that bestowed the name 'Barmy Army' on the mass travelling English spectators of the 1994–1995 Ashes tour. On this tour, the England team were beaten by just about everyone – Australia A, Australia B, and even the Under 19s. Yet despite these losses, the touring English fans continued to support their team, demonstrating a jovial and happy experience. The media labelled this group of excessive fans the 'Barmy Army'; 'Barmy' because they could not understand why any fan would follow a losing cricket team half-way around the world, and 'Army', because of the large numbers that clearly did. Initially bonded by a common nationality, camaraderie, hedonistic lifestyle and a passion for the game of cricket, an organised but cohesive and clearly identifiable group of fans emerged (Parry & Malcolm, 2004).

The Barmy Army constitute a very different target audience in comparison to both the less emotional and more conservative older traditionalists of English cricket and the historical working-class fans of English professional football. As Bates (2012) explains: 'The Barmies, many approaching middle age and of uncertain sleekness and sobriety... [possess] the wherewithal to be able to afford several weeks in Australia.' This is similarly reflected in the leadership of the group that was cofounded by three socially privileged and ex-public schoolboys – Dave Peacock (National Power manager), Paul Burnham (British Airways executive) and Gareth Evans (chartered surveyor). Registering the trademark name of 'Barmy Army' in 1995, its primary aim remains today to help cricket fans watch and support the England Cricket team play all over the world (Barmy Army: Our History, 2012).

Despite the military connotations of the Barmy Army name, Sengupta (2011) argues:

> there's nothing war-like about the fans themselves – they are gentle and friendly, and their cricket-watching ethos is based firmly on humour and encouragement. They take great pains to distinguish themselves from the English football fans, who have a long history of hooliganism.

As one of the founders suggests, The Army at any one game or for that matter at any place and time, evolves spontaneously, being made up of whoever wants to join in (Peacock, 2001). While it possesses a current membership base of 5000 (Barmy Army: Our History, 2012), it is not unusual for between 40,000 and 75,000 fans to make the trip to Australia (Sengupta, 2011). With members specifically benefitting from block seating, priority tickets, discounted tour prices, branded merchandise, participation in Barmy Army events and access to general cricket networking opportunities, pre-, match and post-match Barmy Army activities are inclusive and open to all.

From its origins of being principally a small and potentially deviant English cricket team supporters' club, relative to the traditionalists, the Barmy Army has quickly evolved into a powerful organisation that is now 'welcomed at grounds all over the world' (Barmy Army: Our History, 2012). Actively discouraging unsavoury behaviour, the Barmy Army possesses an excellent reputation among players, cricket administrators and stadium managers alike. Endorsed by the former Australian cricket captain Ricky Ponting, 'the Barmy Army is the best sporting crowd in the World. I don't care what sport you are talking about, or what country – they are unbelievably good supporters' (quoted in Barmy Army membership email, 2011).

Opportunities to leverage the strength of the brand are numerous. As a prime atmosphere-generator of the new world of commercialised international cricket, the Barmy Army have quickly developed their resource base and their power to influence has extended the cricket arena. Their contribution to the match-day experience is grass-roots, spontaneous and authentic, in sharp contrast to the increasingly contrived razzamatazz provided by cricket boards, venues, broadcasters and sponsors. Individual businesses have for more than a decade paid the Army to stand close to their advertising hoarding boards on match-day, and agreements are typically made with public houses to freely host the Army's significant social drinking habits. England players similarly acknowledge and welcome the Barmy Army support, both on and off the field (Hedge, 2010). For example, after the 2010–2011 Melbourne Ashes victory, the players joined the fans in the designated Barmy Army bar of the night, and as one fan memorably recalled his story: 'My finest night on tour. They downed beers and Jaegerbombs with us and sang the songs we had written about them!' (Sengupta, 2011). Cricket administrators, such as the England Cricket Board, have additionally formulated strategies of co-option and commercial incorporation, as have television companies who now work cooperatively with the Barmy Army as they attempt to capture and transpose the stadium atmosphere to their television viewers (Parry & Malcolm, 2004).

The Barmy Army has become more than a national fan club, rather it is an international cricket forum that has been instrumental in raising cricket's profile, particularly to a younger mass audience. With authentic, spontaneous and co-created match-day experiences, the sport tourism field has entered a new era of experience management, where a unique interaction of activity, people and place (Weed, 2006) must be appropriately managed to feed the experience-hungry sports fan.

The Opposition – The Swami Army

In contrast to the Barmy Army, which has been entertaining British cricket fans in Australia since the mid-1990s, the Swami Army was only formed during India's 2003–2004 tour of Australia (Swami Army: About Us, 2012), but made a major contribution to crowd atmosphere in the 2011–2012 season. Swami is a Sanskrit word that means teacher or guru and the Swami Army is intent on supporting their cricketing heroes and bringing a little piece of Bollywood to Australian venues (Mercer, 2012). Founded by ten Australian-born Indian supporters, and touted as India's equivalent of 'The Fanatics' (an Australian multi-sport supporters group), the Swami Army now boasts 3500 members and has an official website, a social media presence, uniform and merchandise line. According to the fan group, whose members support Australia in all other sports except cricket, its aim is to support the Indian team but also to enhance the viewing experience for all cricket supporters 'in an enjoyable, family-friendly environment, dhol player and all!' (Swami Army: About Us, 2012).

While the Swami Army concept began as a play on the name of their British counterparts, it is set to be a worldwide movement as 'regiments' have been established in the United Kingdom, US, Singapore, United Arab Emirates (UAE) and South Africa. As one of the group's founders, Sumit Grover, explained, 'The Barmy Army is the benchmark of any sporting group in the world. But there are 1.2 billion of us, so we should have no trouble getting the numbers and making a bit of noise' (Lynch, 2011).

Corporatising Cricket Tourism

A different approach to cricket tourism is provided by a company set up by Cricket Australia – the controlling body for cricket. This is the Cricket Australia Travel Office (www.crickettraveloffice.com.au). For matches played in Australia, it offers tickets and packages (and most other major sporting codes have a similar arrangement). When Australia plays overseas, it runs tours. These are much more staid than those of the Barmy Army or Fanatics. However, by being a business division of Cricket Australia it has certain advantages over its competitors. For example, on a tour to New Zealand in 2010, it included:

- VIP attendance at team training
- A golf day with current players
- A question and answer session with team management and selectors

These tour companies provide security for the traveller. There have been a number of well-publicised scams involving mega sporting events. For both the 2008 Beijing Olympics and the 2010 Football World Cup, bogus websites tricked fans into paying for tickets online which were then never supplied. For Australians, security is provided by the Australian Cricket Travel Office having to be licensed by government under the uniform scheme of Travel Agents Acts in all states and territories. In addition to strict standards and regulation, this ensures that all tourists are covered by the Travel Compensation Fund if the operator fails to provide services (Frost, 2004).

Next to the tickets, there is also appeal in the range of exclusive functions and experiences provided as part of the tour. In the examples noted above, participants on the Fanatics tour to the Football World Cup travelled with a well-known former player and the Cricket Australia group to New Zealand were invited to watch practice sessions and play golf with the players. These opportunities for the fans to socialise with their sporting heroes are an example of MacCannell's Backstage Experiences. Tourists, MacCannell (1976) argued, are increasingly seeking special experiences where they are allowed to venture backstage or behind the scenes. This provides them with a more satisfying experience, as they have gained insights which the average person fails to gain. Going backstage, mingling with present and former players, provides satisfaction and status.

Brand, Community and Fellowship

According to FutureBrand, any organisation that 'seeks a relationship with its audience can be considered a brand' (Kleinman, 2001: 5) and as such can differentiate its product from those of key competitors. Furthermore, as sport has become more commercialised, professional clubs, and their respective leagues, have adopted branding principles (see Bauer *et al.*, 2005; Bihl, 2002; Burton & Howard, 1999; Chadwick & Holt, 2007; Couvelaere & Richelieu, 2005; Gladden *et al.*, 2001; Kerr & Gladden, 2008; Richelieu & Pons, 2006). As Pons (2008: 1) explained, strong brands have 'the potential of transcending the sports arena (event) by building a "brand community" and a reputation for the sports product'. Therefore, we have seen sport organisations increasingly develop their own brands in the battle for the hearts and wallets of consumers.

Muniz and O'Guinn (2001: 412) explain that brands now transcend geographic boundaries and so we have seen the rise of the brand community, or 'specialized, non-geographically bound community, based on a structured set of social relationships among admirers of a brand'. These communities have been documented for many popular brands such as Apple, Volkswagen, Swatch and Nutella (see Brown *et al.*, 2003; Cova & Pace, 2006; Muniz & Schau, 2005; Ouwersloot & Odekerken-Schroder, 2008) and can be found in cyberspace as 'virtual' communities. Given the emotional attachment that supporters have with a favourite team brand (see Kerr & Emery, 2011), one wonders whether the likes of the Barmy Army constitute a bona fide brand, and hence brand community.

There is some evidence to suggest that the likes of the Barmy Army, Swami Army and the Fanatics are a form of brand community, although their dedication is arguably centred on a national sporting team rather than the Swami Army brand as such. That said, the England and Wales Cricket Board consistently leverage the national team's 'brand' in order to secure revenue from television rights and sponsorship (Fernandez, 2010; Wilson, 2011). Furthermore, those who consider themselves members of these communities appear to exhibit the three traditional markers of community: a shared consciousness; rituals and traditions; and moral responsibility (Muniz & O'Guinn, 2001).

A shared consciousness exists as individuals often make a critical distinction between fellow brand users and those of other brands (Muniz & O'Guinn, 2001). Respective army members congregate together, such as when the Swami Army had a 1400-seat section at the Melbourne Cricket Ground or in customised blue jerseys 'commandeered a section of the Sydney Cricket Ground, festooning it with banners and with saffron, white and green colours of the Indian flag' (Mercer, 2012). A brand community also exhibits evidence of rituals and traditions. These usually revolve around shared consumption experiences with the brand, and through constant interaction with fellow brand users, community and brand meaning are reproduced (Muniz & O'Guinn, 2001). These can be seen with the worldwide supporters of the English Premier League's Liverpool FC who, regardless of their nationality or geographic location, know the significance of, and words to, 'You'll Never Walk Alone' as 'true' devotees to the brand (Kerr & Emery, 2011). In a similar vein, the Swami Army is famous for its Bollywood-inspired cricket chants while the Barmy Army party has not started until Vic Flowers leads his troops with another raucous rendition of 'Everywhere We Go'. Finally, brand communities have a sense of shared moral responsibility whereby the community seeks to integrate and retain members and share information about the product (Muniz & O'Guinn, 2001). The Swami Army encourages supporters of the Indian team (through its Facebook page or website) to become official members so as to participate in official overseas tours and join them in reserved areas of Australia's cricket venues.

Although the Swami Army, as opposed to their European equivalent who registered the Barmy Army name and formed a company, Barmy Army Limited (Ronay, 2006), is a brand in its infancy, there are plans to extend the brand to foreign markets. Tourism authorities in host nations should welcome these supporter groups and seek to capitalise on the rise in cricket tourism. While the Barmy Army helped to inject $317 million into the

Australian economy during the 2006–2007 Ashes series (Salvado, 2007) and 'invaded' the UAE (playing Pakistan) and Sri Lanka in 2012 (Barmy Army: Overseas Tours, 2012), the Swami Army hopes to organise official tour groups to 'all corners of the globe... to follow their passion with like-minded people' (Swami Army: About Us, 2012). Both the Barmy and Swami Armies are working hard to develop a brand that is recognised beyond its own shores and a social network that strengthens and provides an outlet for a member's passion for their team; an identity that is clearly important to its members. For many individuals, sports serve as 'anchors of meaning' (Jarvie & Maguire, 1994: 152) and so support for an organisation, as in the case of the Barmy Army, Swami Army and the Australian Fanatics, is often consistent with an important identity.

Towards Some Sociological Understandings

Social identity theory was developed in the 1970s to understand human behaviour in group situations and explains why individuals identify with groups to which they feel they belong (Tajfel, 1978; Tajfel & Turner, 1986). According to Tajfel (1981: 255), one's social identity is 'that part of an individual's self-concept which derives from his knowledge of his membership of a social group (or groups) together with the value and emotional significance attached to that membership'. The theory has proven to be a useful lens by which to examine sport fandom and identification with a favourite sport team (for example, Branscombe & Wann, 1991; Donavan *et al.*, 2005; End, 2001; Fink *et al.*, 2002; Gwinner & Swanson, 2003; Jacobson, 2003; Kerr, 2009; Wann & Grieve, 2005).

Sport can often act as a vehicle of identity and allows supporters to classify themselves accordingly (MacClancy, 1996). The role of sport spectator for some supporters, in particular those involved with the Barmy Army, is a defining part of one's self-identity and for these individuals participation as a sport tourist is important (Weed, 2002, 2006). As Derbaix *et al.* (2002: 513) explain, 'since he is to cheer, to shout and to sing, the good fan is not only a spectator but also an actor of the game'. As a result, those that identify strongly with a team (for example, the English national cricket team) tend to invest more time and money in support of that team. This can be reflected in their membership of an organisation such as the Barmy Army or by wearing clothing that signifies their inclusion in a particular group (for example, a Swami Army replica cap or customised Indian jersey). The latter, wearing clothing that identifies one as a faithful supporter of the team or a subgroup of it (that is, a fan club), is a form of symbolic consumption. These material possessions are ultimately used to show their support for the team as supporters raise scarves, wave flags and display banners (Derbaix et al., 2002). Such behaviour reinforces a supporter's identification with a favourite team and can lead to a more salient identity as a team fan (Arnett & Laverie, 2000; Wilde, 2004). Indeed, supporters can often be seen wearing team merchandise in the wake of a memorable victory in order to 'bask in the reflected glory' of their triumph (Cialdini et al., 1976).

Spectator sports are often used to construct identities and affirm a sense of community (Donnelly & Young, 1998; Klein, 1984; Melnick, 1993; Stewart & Smith, 1996). Indeed, Eastman and Land (1997) suggested that participation in these communities, and the resultant opportunities for social interaction they provide, is a primary motive for the sports fan. Although traditional notions of community have been limited to a team's geographic location, group members often share common features such as ethnic or national characteristics that significantly distinguish them from members of other groups (Burdsey & Chappell, 2003; Cohen, 1985). In this particular context, Swami Army organiser, Amit Grover, was born in Australia to Indian parents and so feels a strong connection to the sub-continent but says in every other sport 'his allegiance is to those wearing the green and gold' (Swami Army adds spice to India's campaign Down Under, 2012). Indeed, even their tribute to Tendulkar has an Australian flavour, sung to the tune of the iconic 'Waltzing Matilda'. Likewise, English migrants and expats, who for most of the time may be thoroughly Australian in many ways, choose to spend Boxing Day surrounded by members of the Barmy Army. Such dilemmas of who to barrack for in a settler society versus the motherland sporting contest date back as far as the first English cricket tour of Australia in 1861–1862 (Frost, 2002).

Social identification is important in the creation of brand equity, especially for service brands, and sport teams, as service brands, generate high levels of consumer identification (Underwood et al., 2001). While the Barmy Army, Swami Army and Fanatics are at different stages in their brand development, social identity provides a mechanism to tap the 'emotional connection between the consumer [for example, cricket supporter] and the service brand [for example, Barmy Army]' (Underwood et al., 2001: 2). For brand managers, such as Sumit Grover, the opportunity exists to grow membership, enhance the game-day experience for fellow fans and develop a multinational brand, while making a valuable contribution as sport tourists supporting the Indian cricket team wherever they may 'take guard'.

Those on these cricket tours are more than spectators. They are sports fans who follow and support a particular team or sport. Such fans have a strong, lifelong attachment to their team (Wann et al., 2001). They may be viewed as a subset of the increasing devotion to serious leisure (Stebbins, 1992) and as similar to other fans linked to events, such as the Trekkies who attend Star Trek Conventions (Kozinets, 2001). They are not casually attracted to the tour as a leisure option, nor are they interested in other general tourism substitutes. Their sport, team and the event is the 'main game', which consumes them (Jones, 2000; Parry & Malcolm, 2004). Company names like the Fanatics and Barmy Army highlight the obsessive (possibly irrational) nature of these fans.

These fans travel and spectate as a group. A key part of the appeal of the Barmy Army is that members have organised large block bookings of seats for their groups. For the duration of the tours there is a strong group bond, reinforced and defined by customs, behaviours and self-identifying signs. These include singing, chanting and the wearing of clearly marked and colour-coded clothing. This group identity has been identified in other studies of leisure groups, such as the 'Short-Lived Society' of passengers on a cruise ship (Foster, 1986) and the 'Sudden Community' of attendees at an alternative festival (Kozinets, 2002). There is a strong attraction in regressive or childlike behaviours, with group regimentation reminiscent of school, uniform clothing, singing and games. It is an area which needs further research, but it may be that these groups offer a comforting return to childhood for their adult market. (One might compare such behaviour with that of rugby players on tour, particularly the English team at the 2012 World Cup in New Zealand, which elicited severely negative coverage in the media.) There is also a strong suggestion that participation in these groups at sporting events allows an outlet for subversive and disrespectful behaviour, the rites of reversal which Falassi (1987) noted as one of the key ritual structures of events. Such a reversal of entrenched rites and ceremonies opens up the potential for conflict with others (including conservative fans, security and venue administrators).

Conclusion

The rhetoric of tourism privileges certain experiences as profound, high status, even life-changing (Frost, 2010). Ecotourism, wildlife watching, adventure travel and gourmet tours are positioned as exclusive, worthy and highly desirable. The rapidly growing phenomenon of fan-led supporter tour groups such as the Barmy Army introduces a new style of emotionally charged tourism. As a tourism experience, it is certainly profound, providing a strong sense of positive communitas. Developed by fans rather than the increasingly corporatised and formulaic cricket boards, these groups provide a sense of authenticity and grass-roots engagement for fans. They suggest changing directions in how spectators might behave and consume the cricket experience. Cheap airfares and transnationalism are fuelling a Brave New World of cricket, where home ground advantage is no longer supported by the crowds. As seen in Australia in the summers of 2010–2011 and 2011–2012, full houses may be dominated by large sections of carnivalesque tourists barracking for the touring team and against the home team.

References

Arnett, D.B. and Laverie, D.A. (2000) Fan characteristics and sporting event attendance: Examining variance in attendance. *International Journal of Sports Marketing & Sponsorship* 2 (3), 219–238.

Barmy Army (2012) Overseas tours. See http://barmyarmy.com/tours/ (accessed 28 March 2012).

Barmy Army (2012) Our history. See http://barmyarmy.com/about/index.php?m=history (retrieved 28 March 2012).

Barnes, S. (1989) *Prologue to the Teste Matche Tales in A Ls Recherche du Cricket Perdu*. London: Macmillan.

Bates, S. (2012) England's Barmy army revel in new-found respectability in Melbourne. See http://www.guardian.co.uk/sport/2010/dec/28/england-australia-ashes-barmy-army (retrieved 28 March 2012).

Bauer, H.H., Sauer, N.E. and Schmitt, P. (2005) Customer-based brand equity in the team sport industry. Operationalization and impact on the economic success of sport teams. *European Journal of Marketing* 39 (5–6), 496–513.

Bihl, M. (2002) Are teams brands? 3 June. See www.brandchannel.com/brand_speak.asp?bs_id=36 (accessed 31 July 2006).

Branscombe, N.R. and Wann, D.L. (1991) The positive social and self concept consequences of sports team identification. *Journal of Sport and Social Issues* 15 (2), 115–127.

Brown, S., Kozinets, R.V. and Sherry, J.F. (2003) Teaching old brands new tricks: Retro branding and the revival of brand meaning. *Journal of Marketing* 67 (July), 19–33.

Burdsey, D. and Chappell, R. (2003) Soldiers, sashes and shamrocks: Football and social identity in Scotland and Northern Ireland. *Sociology of Sport* (online). See http://physed.otago.ac.nz/sosol/v6i1/v6i1_1.html (accessed 28 December 2005).

Burton, R. and Howard, D. (1999) Professional sports leagues: Marketing mix mayhem. *Marketing Management* Spring, 37–46.

Chadwick, S. and Holt, M. (2007) Utilising latent brand equity as a foundation for building global sports brands. *Developments in Marketing Science* 30, 90–98.

Cialdini, R.B., Borden, R.J., Thorne, A., Walker, M.R., Freeman, S. and Sloan, L.R. (1976) Basking in reflected glory: Three (football) field studies. *Journal of Personality and Social Psychology* 34 (3), 366–375.

Cohen, A.P. (1985) *The Symbolic Construction of Community*. Chichester, UK: Ellis Horwood Limited.

Couvelaere, V. and Richelieu, A. (2005) Brand strategy in professional sports: The case of French soccer teams. *European Sport Management Quarterly* 5 (1), 23–46.

Cova, B. and Pace, S. (2006) Brand community of convenience products: New forms of customer empowerment – The case of 'my Nutella The Community'. *European Journal of Marketing* 40 (9–10), 1087–1105.

Derbaix, C., Decrop, A. and Cabossart, O. (2002) Colors and scarves: The symbolic consumption of material possessions by soccer fans. *Advances in Consumer Research* 29, 511–518.

Donavan, D.T., Carlson, B.D. and Zimmerman, M. (2005) The influence of personality traits on sports fan identification. *Sport Marketing Quarterly* 14, 31–42.

Donnelly, P. and Young, K. (1988) The construction and confirmation of identity in sport subcultures. *Sociology of Sport Journal* 5, 223–240.

Eastman, S.T. and Land, A.M. (1997) The best of both worlds: Sports fans find good seats at the bar. *Journal of Sport & Social Issues* 21 (2), 156–178.

End, C.M. (2001) An examination of NFL fans' computer mediated BIRGing. *Journal of Sport Behavior* 24 (2), 162–181.

Falassi, A. (1987) Festival: Definition and morphology. In A. Falassi (ed.) *Time Out of Time: Essays on the Festival* (pp. 1–10). Albuquerque: University of New Mexico Press.

Fernandez, J. (2010) Jaguar seals sponsorship deal with England and Wales Cricket Board, 9 June. See www.marketingweek.co.uk/news/jaguar-seals-sponsorship-deal-with-england-and-wales-cricket-board/3014424.article (accessed 28 March 2012).

Fink, J.S., Trail, G.T. and Anderson, D.F. (2002) An examination of team identification: Which motives are most salient to its existence? *International Sports Journal* Summer, 195–207.

Foster, G. (1986) South Seas cruise: A case study of a short-lived society. *Annals of Tourism Research* 13 (2), 215–238.

Frost, W. (2002) Heritage, nationalism, identity: The 1861–62 England cricket tour of Australia. *The International Journal of the History of Sport* 19 (4), 55–69.

Frost, W. (2004) *Travel and Tour Management*. Sydney: Pearson.

Frost, W. (2010) Life-changing experiences: Film and tourists in the Australian outback. *Annals of Tourism Research* 37 (3), 707–726.

Gladden, J.M., Irwin, R.L. and Sutton, W.A. (2001) Managing North American major professional sport teams in the new millennium: A focus on building brand equity. *Journal of Sport Management* 15, 297–317.

Gwinner, K. and Swanson, S.R. (2003) A model of fan identification: Antecedents and sponsorship outcomes. *Journal of Services Marketing* 17 (3), 275–294.

Hedge, M. (2010) Barmy Army general leads his troops. See http://www.couriermail.com.au/news/barmy-army-general-leads-his-troops-story-e6freomx-1225976861892 (retrieved 28 March 2012).

Jacobson, B.P. (2003) Rooting for laundry: An examination of the creation and maintenance of a sport fan identity. Doctoral dissertation, University of Connecticut.

Jarvie, G. and Maguire, J. (1994) *Sport and Leisure in Social Thought*. London: Routledge.

Jones, I. (2000) A model of serious leisure identification: The case of football fandom. *Leisure Studies* 19 (4), 283–298.

Kerr, A.K. (2009) 'You'll Never Walk Alone'. The use of brand equity frameworks to explore the team identification of the 'satellite supporter'. PhD dissertation, University of Technology, Sydney.

Kerr, A.K. and Emery, P.R. (2011) The allure of an 'overseas sweetheart': A Liverpool FC brand community. *International Journal of Sport Management and Marketing* 9 (3–4), 201–219.

Kerr, A.K. and Gladden, J.M. (2008) Extending the understanding of professional team brand equity to the global marketplace. *International Journal of Sport Management and Marketing* 3 (1–2), 58–77.

Klein, A.M. (1984) A review of soccer madness. *Sociology of Sport Journal* 1 (2), 195–197.
Kleinman, M. (2001) Man Utd tops Euro brand value table. *Marketing*, 5.
Kozinets, R.V. (2001) Utopian enterprise: Articulating the meanings of Star Trek's culture of consumption. *Journal of Consumer Research* 28 (1), 67–88.
Lynch, J. (2011) The Swami Army ready to fire in enemy territory, 22 December. www.theage.com.au/sport/cricket/the-swami-army-ready-to-fire-in-enemy-territory-20111 221-1p5ot.html (accessed 28 March 2012).
MacCannell, D. (1976) *The Tourist: A New Theory of the Leisure Class*. New York: Schocken.
MacClancy, J. (1996) Sport, identity and ethnicity. In J. MacClancy (ed.) *Sport, Identity and Ethnicity* (pp. 1–20). Oxford: Berg.
Melnick, M.J. (1993) Searching for sociability in the stands: A theory of sports spectating. *Journal of Sport Management* 7, 44–60.
Mercer, P. (2012) India's 'Swami Army' brings Bollywood colour to cricket, 4 January. See www.bbc.co.uk/news/world-asia-india-16406146 (accessed 28 March 2012).
Morgan, M. (2007) 'We're not the Barmy army!': Reflections on the sports tourist experience. *International Journal of Tourism Research* 9, 361–372.
Muniz, A.M. and O'Guinn, T.C. (2001) Brand community. *Journal of Consumer Research* 27 (March), 412–432.
Muniz, A.M. and Schau, H.J. (2005) Religiosity in the abandoned Apple Newton brand community. *Journal of Consumer Research* 31 (4), 737–747.
Ouwersloot, H. and Odekerken-Schroder, G. (2008) Who's who in brand communities – And why? *European Journal of Marketing* 42 (5–6), 571–585.
Parry, M. and Malcolm, D. (2004) England's Barmy Army: Commercialisation, masculinity and nationalism. *International Review for the Sociology of Sport* 39 (1), 75–94.
Peacock, D. (2001) *The Ashes 2010/11 – The Inside Story*. Lace DVD.
Pons, F. (2008) Editorial. *International Journal of Sport Management and Marketing* 3 (1–2), 1–2.
Richelieu, A. and Pons, F. (2006) Toronto Maple Leafs vs Football Club Barcelona: How two legendary sports teams built their brand equity. *International Journal of Sports Marketing & Sponsorship* May, 231–250.
Ronay, B. (2006) Crass and corporate – Why the Barmy Army are no laughing matter, 1 December. See www.guardian.co.uk/sport/2006/dec/01/ashes2006.cricket7?-INTCMP=ILCNETTXT3487 (accessed 28 March 2012).
Salvado, J. (2007) Ashes series a big hit for economy, 5 June. See www.theage.com.au/news/cricket/ashes-series-a-big-hit-for-economy/2007/06/05/1180809490461.html (accessed 28 March 2012).
Sengupta, R. (2011) Got to be Barmy to be in this army. See http://www.livemint.com/2011/03/04191621/Got-to-be-Barmy-to-be-in-this.html (retrieved 28 March 2012).
Stebbins, R. (1992) *Amateurs, Professionals and Serious Leisure*. London: McGill.
Stewart, R.K. and Smith, A.C.T. (1996) Sports watching in Australia: A conceptual framework. Paper presented at Advancing Management of Australian and New Zealand Sport, 22–23 November, Lismore.
Swami Army: About Us (2012) See www.swamiarmy.com/history/ (accessed 28 March 2012).
Swami Army adds spice to India's campaign Down Under (2012, January 8) See http://sports.ndtv.com/cricket/features/specials/item/183633-india-vs-australia-swami-army-adds-spice-to-indias-campaign-down-under (accessed 28 March 2012).
Tajfel, H. (1978) Social categorization, social identity and social comparison. In H. Tajfel (ed.) *Differentiation between Social Groups* (pp. 61–76). London: Academic Press Inc.

Tajfel, H. (1981) *Human Groups and Social Categories*. Cambridge: Cambridge University Press.

Tajfel, H. and Turner, J.C. (1986) The social identity theory of intergroup behaviour. In S. Worchel and W.G. Austin (eds) *Psychology of Intergroup Relations* (Vol. 2, pp. 7–24). Chicago, IL: Nelson-Hall Publishers.

Underwood, R., Bond, E. and Baer, R. (2001) Building service brands via social identity: Lessons from the sports marketplace. *Journal of Marketing Theory and Practice* 9 (Winter), 1–13.

Wann, D.L. and Grieve, F.G. (2005) Biased evaluations of in-group and out-group spectator behavior at sporting events: The importance of team identification and threats to social identity. *The Journal of Social Psychology* 145 (5), 531–545.

Wann, D., Melnick, M., Russell, G. and Pease, D. (2001) *Sports Fans: The Psychology and Social Impact of Spectators*. London and New York: Routledge.

Weed, M.E. (2002) Understanding cricket crowd behaviour. Paper presented at the 12th Commonwealth International Sport Conference, Manchester, UK.

Weed, M. (2006) Sports tourism and the development of sports events, 13 December. See www.idrottsforum.org/articles/weed/weed061213.pdf (accessed 28 March 2012).

Wilde, N. (2004) Fashion accessory, social identity or tribal uniform? In S. Butenko, J. Gil-Lafuente and P.M. Pardalos (eds) *Economics, Management and Optimization in Sports* (pp. 121–130). Berlin: Springer-Verlag.

Wilson, A. (2011) England and Australia risk Ashes overkill with 11 tests in seven months, 28 June. See www.guardian.co.uk/sport/2011/jan/28/england-australia-ashes-2013-cricket (accessed 28 March 2012).

10 An Ethnographic View from the Boundary: India vs England, The Fourth Test, Nagpur, December 2012

Tom Baum

> *The die is cast- my fate is sealed-*
> *To India I'm away:*
> *I'm scoring in a wider field_*
> *I'm going to Bombay.*
> *Adieu, dear Kent and M.C.C.!*
> *Bat, ball and stumps., Adieu!*
> *I go whence comes the proud Parsee_*
> *Last bright recruit for you!*
> *I Am Going to Bombay*, Anon.

Introduction

As the extensive bibliographies associated with contributions elsewhere in this book highlight, cricket is a sport which has stimulated countless journalistic (for example, Cardus, 1937; Agnew, 2011), autobiographical (Flintoff, 2009), diarised (Lillywhite, 1860; Ranjitsinhji, 1898/1985; Tufnell & Hayter, 1998; Waugh, 2001), anecdotal (Edmunds, 1987), poetical (Lowe, 1927), fictional (Bright-Holmes, 1988; Aspinall, 2012; Karunatilaka, 2012) and frequently eccentric (Bell, 2008; Curr, 2012) depictions of cricket-as(or in)-travel. These accounts date back to the very early days of international cricket and address major tours and events as well as the exploits of club and leisure cricketers on their travels (for example, Headlam, 1903; Coleman, 1990). The playing of cricket, by the very nature of its colonial origins, represents a map of major playing countries that substantially mirrors the red of the former British Empire. Indeed, the only substantial cartographical gap here is North America, in particular Canada, where sports participation has been influenced far more by proximity to the United States than by colonial sentiment. Thus, the playing of international cricket invariably involved, and still involves, long-distance travel, extended periods away from home and, in its early days, travel fraught with considerable risk and adventure. Contemporary efforts, not least by the International Cricket Council (ICC), seek to expand participation in the game to countries with no traditional affiliations to the sport, often through engagement of the diaspora from traditional cricketing countries (see Noakes & Wilson, Chapter 6, this volume). The travels and travails of cricket, therefore have provided a rich source of writing, some focusing primarily on sporting endeavours while other sources stray over far wider territory and represent an experience of the country, not just of sport (see for example, Margusee, 1997; Simkins, 2011).

The language of cricket is interesting in the context of this book and this chapter. Any team travelling away from home in order to play one or, generally, more matches and including an overnight stay are deemed to be on tour and its participants, tourists. At international level, use of the word 'tourists' as an alternative to Australians, Indians or English, etc has been common practice in the media since the early days of such tours, certainly much before the United Nations World Tourism Organization (UNWTO) attempted to define 'a tourist' along (sort of) similar lines. By contrast, the home team have always been known as the hosts, conjuring up some notion of civilised hospitality rather than competitive international sport. One of the first uses of the terms 'tour' and 'tourists' in the context of cricket relates to the 1868 visit by a team of Australian Aboriginal cricketers to England, some 10 years before their first white counterparts, and the sporting and social issues raised by touring and hosting such a team are both fascinating and challenging (Mulvaney & Harcourt, 1988).

This chapter was neither intended or planned and, therefore hopefully has endearing features which outweigh evident limitations. I make no claim that this piece stands comparison with some of the great cricket travelogues. It is a snapshot experience based on two days' play, very much a Twenty20 of cricket writing alongside the studiousness, depth and timelessness of a full test match series, represented in much of the best cricket writing (this analogy, of course, is challenged by the irony that the match I attended produced some of the slowest play in recent test cricket history). The chapter aims to express my personal experiences as a short-term cricket tourist and to relate these to tourism, its organisation and management. Theoretically, therefore, what is considered here has a genus in the academic consideration of travelogues and wider writing about tourism in fact and fiction (Krist, 1993; Holland & Huggan, 1998; Dann, 1999). It also has links to the emerging field of sports tourism and the contribution which writers such as Gammon and Robinson (2003), Deery *et al.* (2004) and Smith and Stewart (2007) have made to our understanding of those who travel to watch rather than to play.

Methodology

Ethnography is a research method which is primarily applied within social anthropological research. One of the key methods of enquiry in ethnographic research is participant observation (Brewer, 2000). The ethnographic approach to social research is no longer purely that of the cultural anthropologist and it is suggested that, in definitional terms, ethnography is a particular kind of knowledge inquiry based on rigorous observation, requiring an incremental process of continuous engagement by the observer with a group of people or social context with whom the researcher has the ability to engage at a personal level (Olson, 1991). Ethnography is an approach that provides access to data often inaccessible through traditional methods, while fostering the emergence of details which, despite their sometimes seemingly mundane status, can provide powerful insights into the subject of interpretation of the researcher and its audience (Holt, 2003). Autoethnography is an extension of ethnography in that it assumes personal engagement and familiarity with the field of study from the researcher (Ellis *et al.*, 2011). It is an approach to research and writing that seeks to describe and systematically analyse personal experience in order to understand cultural experience (Ellis, 2004; Holman Jones, 2005).

This chapter reports what might be called serendipitous autoethnography. It represents serendipity in the sense that planning for this piece of research took place just a few days prior to its execution and was inspired by an unexpected opportunity for the researcher to be in the proximity of the event in Nagpur, India. It is autoethnographical in the sense that the researcher has had a passion for cricket, as a (mediocre) player, a relatively passive supporter and spectator and as a father-of-player, for over 50 years. This latter role, watching the exploits of a far better player than I ever was, represents a journey which started in our back garden in Scotland when our son was three, traversed junior club cricket (with coaches from three continents) across the West of Scotland and on to the national stage from Under 12 through to Under 19 levels. As tourists and virtual tourists we followed his exploits at home, in England and Ireland, elsewhere in Europe, South Africa and Sri Lanka, and this junior cricketing odyssey culminated in the 2014 Under 19 World Cup in the United Arab Emirates. I have also attended test and one-day internationals in Australia, England and Scotland but this was a first-time experience of cricket in India and, therefore, cultural unfamiliarity with the context of the test match, beyond media representation, is an important starting point for this account.

The opportunity allowed me to attend days two and three of the test match. For the uninitiated, a test match in cricket is scheduled to run over a period of up to five (usually) consecutive days and, therefore, the planning of most cricket tours around tests for spectators travelling overseas allocates this as a minimum period within the host destination. In my case, on day one, while participating in a workshop in New Delhi, I monitored the progress of the match via the internet. On the fourth day, I was en route back to Europe, and day five saw me following things from home and my office.

This study depended on talking to and observing the behaviour of people, both local and visitors, at the match, on the way to the match and in my hotel. I talked to fans from both sides at the match: where language permitted (my Hindi is non-existent), I talked to those working at the game in security and catering and to tuk-tuk drivers. I communicated with some of the many motorcyclists weaving their way in and out of the traffic after a day's play, using sign language. I did have the opportunity to talk to some of the players in the hotel after a day's play, the English side as tourists in the original cricketing sense and the Indians as their hosts. I chose not to do so as this would have been unacceptably intrusive and, in any case, my bottom-line priority was always going to be the success of the tourists on the field and anything that distracted them from this would have been unforgivable. I did, by chance, get the opportunity to speak with one of the English back-room support staff or tourists over coffee and this gave me a sense of the experience of all-inclusive, tightly managed tourism which the players experience during the tour. Finally, I also talked with a tour group leader from England, playing a dual role as part-organiser of the travel and also a committed, 'hardcore' follower of England's cricket fortunes.

Before the Event

The research context was woefully ill-researched, a factor of time but also the absence of readily accessible information. The challenge faced can be classified as

- a tourist-in-Nagpur challenge, highlighting matters such as access transport, accommodation and local facilities; and
- a cricket tourist-in-Nagpur challenge, how to obtain tickets, which tickets to choose, locating the ground and getting there.

Nagpur is not a major tourism destination for international visitors, despite its vaunted location in the centre of the country. Given my tight window of opportunity and limited options for direct flights between New Delhi and Nagpur (most options route via Mumbai), one realistic option in each direction, with different airlines, were identified. In the not-too-distant past, this would have been problematic and expensive but the age of single fare pricing has arrived in India, as elsewhere, and booking was relatively easy, even if in the end I retreated to the kind ministrations of a travel agent after trying to book with a non-Indian address. My flights, 5.45 am on the outbound and 10.30 pm on the return, gave me a maximum window in Nagpur for just one night in a hotel. These flights gave me a taste of, on the one hand, the country's ailing, state-owned legacy carrier and, on the return, one of the range of new, start-up low cost airlines. Travelling in economy class and with the exception of a rather mediocre snack on the first flight, there was little discernible difference between the two, both offering free checked bags and allocated seating. I did look at train options as an alternative to flights but the actual length of the journey, unfortunately, put paid to that notion.

To book accommodation, I resorted to two or three of the online consolidators and soon found that options were limited, maybe the result of the cricket circus in town. Low-cost options were available in the range of 1,000–2,000 rupees (£12–£25) as well as one internationally branded property, located close to the airport and on the right side of town for the cricket stadium. This, however, was on offer for 8000 rupees (c. £100) but included breakfast and free wifi. Given the time constraints for my visit and seeing that it was for just the one night, I opted for four-star luxury!! This profligacy proved a worthwhile investment, although my initial attempts to contact the hotel did not bode well – emails requesting advice on transfers from the airport and to the cricket stadium going unanswered. Arriving at the hotel from the airport – in a local taxi when, in fact, the hotel offers complementary transfers which I did not know about – I find that I am sharing the accommodation with the two teams, so elaborate security is in place and the enthusiasm of staff and local well-wishers outside the property, particularly for the Indian team, is palpable and rises to a loud crescendo as they leave for the stadium.

I arrive at my hotel early – about 7.30 am – and am delighted to be able to check in and access my room immediately. I am clearly getting maximum value for my one night's stay. I ask the same questions as I posed in my email: transport to the ground and, more importantly, match tickets. I am assured that they are bound to be available at the ground. Suitably persuaded, a quick shower and I am ready to roll.

I was not going to have time to enjoy the non-cricket attractions of Nagpur but, in any case, did find out that they do not appear to be a local priority. The city's tourism website (http://nmcnagpur.gov.in/en/city-information.html) lists the highlights of Nagpur as

- Nagpur city's foundation was laid by The Gond King of Deogad, 'Bakht Buland Shah', in the year 1703.
- Nagpur is well-known for its oranges. It is also called the 'Orange City'
- The Nagpur District's area is 9,890 sq. km.
- According to the 2001 census, the population of this region is 34,36,765.
- Nagpur District consists of 13 Districts or Tehsils and 1969 small villages.
- Nagpur was the capital of Central Provinces and Berar State till 1960.
- On 1 May 1960, it became the Second Capital of Maharashtra State.
- Nagpur has completed 300 years of establishment in the year 2002. A big celebration is planned to mark this event.

Despite the laudable highlights of the history and role of any city, there is little here to entice the uncommitted visitor. Just before the game, Paul Collingwood (https://twitter.com/Colly622, 12.12.12), a former England player now working as a media commentator, predicted a match played to the finish inside three days. What, I asked myself, would travelling cricket tourists do with their free time if his predictions came true, a concern echoed by a number of those attending on day two (at a time when the game appeared to be swinging strongly in England's direction) – 'what can we do in this place on Sunday and Monday if the game is over?' I wonder whether the Indian tourism authorities talk to their cricket counterparts at BCCI about the tourism potential of international cricket? I talked with those England fans who had remained in Nagpur and it is clear that, of the four test match venues for the 2012 tour, Mumbai and Kolkata are where most visitors want to be and that many fewer attended the first test in Ahmedabad (a 'dry' or alcohol-free city) or the fourth in Nagpur. As with all tourism-related decisions, it comes down to a matter of priorities – is the choice in favour of maximising the tourist dollar (which would certainly have flowed into venues such as Delhi and Chennai) or does it give priority to the equitable distribution of games across the country, always taking likely weather conditions into consideration?

At the Event

For me, no game of cricket in India could be complete without a tuk-tuk ride and this was on my mind in considering transfer options to the Vidarbha Cricket Association (VCA) Stadium, in this case, a journey of about 12 km. A hotel car would have made life easy but did not feel authentic – as well as being considerably more expensive!! So, on both days, I headed out from the hotel and to the main road in anticipation of hailing a tuk-tuk. However, the kindly hotel security guards would have none of that and insisted on calling a contact of their own 'Just 10 minutes sir', 'Just 10 minutes, sir' before it eventually arrived and I agreed to pay what they considered to be an outrageous amount for the fare.

Driving out of Nagpur to the stadium on the highway to Hyderabad, you soon leave the city and head through scrubland, broken by small roadside communities. Leaving the city, the sign says 'Happy Travels' where in the UK we might have expected 'Travel Safely'. Maybe this reflects the differing philosophical outlook of people in India compared to those in the West. In India, safety would be an unrealistic aspiration so they just accept the inherent dangers of a helmetless family of three on a motorcycle; cars, tuk-tuks and trucks avoiding the drain on their batteries which using headlights entails at night; and traffic lights playing a cautionary rather than mandatory role. If you can do all this and remain happy, what more could you want?

The Vidarbha Cricket Association Stadium, with its towering light pylons, stands tall in the shimmering dust and haze of a flat landscape. The access road from the highway is hugely rutted and demands high levels of skill from my tuk-tuk drivers to negotiate potholes, motorcyclists and pedestrians, all in large numbers. On my first day, my driver displays a special pass which permits access though two layers of the security cordon. I am about to pay him but first ask where I can obtain a ticket. A look of horror appears – 'Tickets in the city – you want me to take you?' (well, horror disappears at the prospect of a triple run!!) – so much for the advice received in my hotel! Then he says – 'I will ask' and off he goes, to return with the good news that a five-day pass in one of the shaded stands is available for Rs 750 – now that is pricing from which Lord's and The Oval could learn!! Unlike some international cricket venues (reputedly in the Caribbean), to its credit the Vidarbha Cricket Association does not operate differential pricing for locals and international visitors. My book of tickets entitles me to five days' access – I have already missed day one, so the stubs for days one and two are carefully removed and I pocket the rest for my visit the next day...or so I think!

When I do return on day three, the stubs for days four and five (which I will not use) are intact but where is the necessary stub for day three? Nowhere to be found. I turn my pockets out under the supervision of a smiling security guard who just shakes his head. 'No third day', he repeats. 'I know, what shall I do?' Another smile. I plead/smile and this seems to work because eventually, with a shrug, he waves me in. Again, I am sure this could not happen elsewhere but I am so relieved.

So back to my first visit to the ground, and I head in to find my seat, with the time fast approaching the start at 9.30 am. Test cricket, traditionally, is bound by rigid laws on the timing of the start, the lunch break, the tea break and the close of play (widely casualised to 'Stumps'). As a child, the start of play was always 11.30 am (perhaps to allow gentlemen sufficient recovery time from the night before) and stumps was at 6.30 pm before the invention of the 24-hour clock. This has now changed to an 11.00 am start in England but, nonetheless, 9.30 am did seem very early.

The Vidarbha Cricket Association Stadium was opened in 1988 and has a capacity of 45,000. At no point was it anywhere near as full as that – reports put attendance at 20,000 on my second day, a Saturday. The stadium is concrete and functional and does not have the picture-book charm of some, admittedly much smaller, grounds around the world. The noise generated by a non-capacity crowd was awesome so a full house would be worth hearing. India does not get such crowds for test cricket any more but shorter forms of the game can certainly fill a stadium such as this. Equally impressive as the noise was the total silence when national superhero Sachin Tendulkar was bowled very cheaply on my first afternoon. As an England supporter, there was never any sense of a threat from Indian fans, who engaged in light-hearted banter throughout the play.

Seating is totally mixed and in my area are families, groups of students, armed soldiers with their full hardware kit (it is disconcerting sitting a couple of seats along from three upright rifles) and members of the Barmy Army (see Emery *et al.*, Chapter 9, this volume). This is the name given to England's cricket following on overseas tours and it is a group that can swell to several thousand for matches in desirable locations. In Nagpur, it is best described as a hardcore Barmy Platoon, just a fraction, I am told, of the numbers at the two previous games. My own seat is located high in the gods, out of the sunshine and directly behind the bowler's arm. I am satisfied. When I arrive, few of the seats are taken and I soon learn, from Baz and Alf, two engineers who have taken a few days out from a project in Hyderabad, that there are no checks for actual seating, provided that you are, broadly, in the correct area. The seat I select is upholstered and comfortable if a little worn and I make this my home for the next two days.

Catering at the ground showed no compromises to the possible expectations of visitors – a staple of samosas, ice cream and gooey cake, all brought to your seat at regular intervals!! The highly spiced samosas and ice cream make a fabulous and filling combination which sees me through playing hours. Water in sealed bags is complementary but you cannot bring your own in through the multi-layered security.

The cricketing public in Nagpur stay the course and few seem to leave early. On the first day there I wondered what this would mean for me and my hopes of catching a tuk-tuk back to the hotel. I need not have worried. Those vehicles permitted access close to the stadium were waiting close by and their enthusiastic drivers vying for custom from us tourists, no doubt able to agree fares much higher than local hosts would have negotiated. So local travel was painless and, even at such inflated prices – Rs 300 (£4) for 12 km – worthwhile, both as a transaction and an experience. The real travelers among my new friends in the stands walked out to the main road where tuk-tuks could be hired for 'far less', or even buses could be caught!

Talking to My Fellow Spectators

Domestic tourists?

All the Indian spectators I talk to are from Nagpur and the surrounding district or are working in the city. This suggests that test cricket in India does not contribute to domestic tourism in any tangible way. This may reflect the distances involved in travel in India as it certainly is in Australia where state 'ownership' of each match is reflected in the visitor profile. By contrast, in England, ticket purchases, while regionally skewed, are much more national in complexion.

In Nagpur there are exceptions of those attending from out of town but these are foreigners, mainly English, but at least two Australians as well – I talk to a number working in Hyderabad, Lucknow, New Delhi, Pune and similar locations. While their loyalties may be clear, they are domestic travellers in the strict sense and so occupy a contrary position in any attempt to classify spectators at the game. Their position, perhaps, can be likened to that of 'local poms', the English who have settled in Australia but have not switched their sporting loyalties and attend matches making their affinities clear.

International tourists?

As I have already noted, the travelling support for England had greatly thinned by the time the circus came to Nagpur so it is difficult to gauge much about the majority of the Barmy Army. Those that remain have been to all four tests and have created time in their lives to do so on the back of self-employment and the ability to pack work commitments into other times of the year. Those in Nagpur have distinguished service records in the Barmy Army, in some cases having not missed a test match, home or on tour, for a number of years. They are seasoned travellers to and in India, plan the best options for flights, trains and hotels well in advance and tend to be in control of their own itineraries, even though they may go through one of the specialist sports events travel agencies that offer packages to wherever England play. Less experienced campaigners tend to buy into pre-constructed itineraries from these companies and probably did not make it as far as Nagpur.

The Barmy Army, as Emery *et al.* note (Chapter 9), has a very clear code of conduct for its members and has adopted a wide range of identifiers and 'badges', such as a fanzine (a copy of which, *The Corridor of Uncertainty*, I purchased from Jeff at the game for Rs 150), t-shirts and other identity paraphernalia. Prior to Nagpur, I had seen the Barmy Army in action in grounds in Australia and England and had noticed how commentators, on radio and TV, tended to include all travelling supporters to away series under that banner. 'The Barmy Army expresses its approval' or 'That shot has silenced the Barmy Army'. Does that now vest membership of the Barmy Army on me? Am I like some latter-day Napoleonic War conscript who wakes up after a heavy night out to find himself in the army or navy at Her Majesty's pleasure? I wonder idly whether my excited response to key events in the match could lead Jonathan Agnew of the BBC to exclaim 'That wicket/stroke/diving save has certainly won the approval of members of the Barmy Army'. This would mean that I am in, I am part of the Barmy Army. When I raise this conundrum with fellow spectators (genuine members of the Barmy Army), they are not very sympathetic...

I encourage my fellow foot soldiers to talk about their travel experiences. The older hands enjoy India and the sub-continent generally because it is 'more authentic'. They lament the tendency for games in the Caribbean to increasingly be played in tourist hot spots (Antigua, St Lucia) instead of more traditional venues because there is less contact with 'genuine' local cricket followers and, indeed, at some locations, tourists outnumber hosts in the crowd by some considerable number. This is not the case in India where, despite declining interest in test match cricket, locals are always in the majority. The tourists also enjoy the challenges of travelling in India and want to be 'close to reality'. So they tend to stay in lower-cost accommodation, close to the heart of the venue city, travel as a group, using trains where this is practical and enjoying local food and, undoubtedly, Indian beers beyond the Kingfisher and Cobra found in their local Indian restaurants back home. There my 'admission' to having checked into the teams' four-star hotel was met with knowing smiles – clearly, I was (rightly) being categorised as a mere cricket tourist alongside their battle-hardened cricket traveller status, thus placing me at the heart of both a sociological (Cohen, 1974) and status-identity (Peregrine, 2012) debate, but in the specific context of cricket.

One of their group leaders, Mick, is a seasoned veteran of many similar tours to wherever England play. His role is that of both spectator and local organiser on behalf of the company he runs, organising trips 'mainly in sports I enjoy like cricket, but we'll try our hands at anything, really'. My own limited experience is confirmed – organising things in India from a distance is a real challenge. Scheduling, ticketing and practical, on-the-ground arrangements (accommodation, local transfers) are all subject to multiple uncertainties and change, 'But we always get there'. All the coordination and management of tours is driven from the UK end with little direct interest or engagement from potential Indian counterparts or competitors. The experience is very different to that in Australia or South Africa where all arrangements can easily be sub-contracted locally. I cannot help wondering whether Indian tourism is missing the opportunity to add value to cricket tours by its passivity here. Mick sees this as reflecting the way many travel businesses in India view the UK travel market to much of India (other than Goa) as polarised into either backpackers or those aspiring to five star luxury. Cricket tourists do not fit into either category so they are not able to handle their needs.

The original tourists, the players, do not see themselves as tourists at all. They are working so, by technical definition, are business tourists. By public pronouncement, they value the support which the Barmy Army and others (me?) give – the 12th man – but in reality want to stay within their team cocoon and avoid direct engagement with their fan base. Honestly, I don't blame them!!

Conclusions

What, then, does this account of a two-day trip to Nagpur add to the wider discussion of cricket and tourism in this book? The autoethnographical experience of cricket tourism at the fourth test in Nagpur says some things about the characteristics of modern tourism – serendipity in choice of destination (I had never considered a visit to Nagpur prior to this trip); the influence of major events on destination choice, taking us to places that, as in my case, would have been unlikely location choices were it not for the event; short lead time for planning (just a few days); combination with other tourism motivations (business tourism); and the linking of high-end (four-star hotel) consumption with budget travel (low-cost airline, tuk-tuks for local transport). At the same time, this account is also contrary to the experience of many cricket tourists whom, as Emery *et al.* (Chapter 9, this volume) note, generally travel within organised groups to international venues – I relied on my own dynamic packaging and a fair bit of chance to end up in the team hotel, locationally convenient to both airport and cricket stadium.

This book addresses a range of themes, linking travel, tourism and cricket from diverse perspectives. There is an emphasis on place. Butler talks about the historically constrained geography of cricket and speculates on if and how the traditional boundaries of the international game can be pushed out, both informally (as Noakes & Wilson encapsulate, Chapter 6) and under the aegis of the ICC through their tournaments and wider proselytisation (Chapter 1). White focuses on place in the sense of a location where the memory is revered (the birthplace of the Ashes) but which is very much a footnote location in current cricketing terms (Chapter 3). Both Caldwell and Ali (Chapter 4) and Parrett (Chapter 5) focus on the role which stadiums play in giving identity to cricket as a sport – something by no means unique to the game as the role of Old Trafford (Manchester), Villa Park (Birmingham) and the Santiago Bernabéu Stadium (Madrid) testify in footballing terms. Caldwell and Ali focus on the most iconic of places in cricketing terms, Lord's in London (itself a third location for the ground in its long history) while Parrett's interest is in the newly built Rose Bowl in Southampton, replacing the County Ground which had served as the home of cricket in Hampshire for 115 years prior to its closure in 2000 and where, incidentally, I gained my first experiences as an enthusiastic follower of the professional game in the 1960s. The Vidarbha Cricket Association Stadium in Nagpur is very much in the mould of the Rose Bowl, replacing the older Vidarbha Cricket Association Ground in the downtown area as an international venue but retaining its cricketing purpose as a location for state and other representative cricket. Maybe time will overrule contemporary sentiment but it is challenging to see how the new generation of cricket stadiums (Nagpur, the Rose Bowl), impressive though they may be in scale and design, can ever achieve the revered status of some of cricket's truly iconic and quirky locations – Lord's, certainly; Sabina Park; the Sydney Cricket Ground; the St Lawrence Ground in Canterbury with its famous tree within the boundary ropes, an oddity that it shares with the City Oval in Pietermaritzburg in South Africa. This is me waxing nostalgic, something which Wheeller and Maitland have already done to far better effect earlier in this volume (Chapter 2).

Place in cricket, however, is far more about people and culture than it is about concrete. Emery *et al.* talk about the cultural context of the cricket tourist, both in a locational sense and in terms of the created culture of the commodified cricket follower as part of the Barmy Army (Chapter 9). Pearce talks about international cricketers as tourists which, indeed they are (Chapter 7). Thus, my observation in the restaurant of 'our' hotel (the teams and myself) in Nagpur is that the downtime behaviour of international cricketing celebrities (those that deigned to join us rather than avail themselves of room service) is not that much different from those who pay to follow their every movement on the cricket field. Culturally, cricket is not, generally, a confrontational sport from a spectator perspective – unlike football, for example, where fan rivalries in the more concentrated environment of a 90-minute game do not really allow for exchange and personal engagement. Thus, my experience of Nagpur was one of spending leisurely time, during the many more soporific moments of the match, talking about cricket and travel to fellow visitors from abroad but also to welcoming local supporters.

I return to one of my starting points to conclude this discussion – the language used in cricket which describes international players as tourists and their local opponents as hosts. These descriptors, when cricketing tours were elongated experiences over months in England, India or Australia, were apt because the teams would generally spend much time together, travelling by train or ship in consort between matches, maybe whiling away the extended down-time between matches over cards, golf, dinners or within the homes of their hosts or, in the case of professionals, rather more 'earthy' interaction in the bars and other night venues of their host cities. Today, the complexity of the contemporary game of Twenty20, one-day and test matches, means that specialists in one form of cricket or the other are constantly on the move, availing of modern travel arrangements to fly in and fly out of tours on a just-in-time basis. Thus, internal tour cohesion is lost as few players are there for the full duration while their opponents likewise chop and change on demand. Tours are also much shorter. The England tour of India in 2012–2013, indeed, was, in fact, two tours during which test matches and Twenty20 internationals were played in November and December (requiring, in fact, two virtually different squads for these games); players returned home or headed elsewhere in search of alternative remunerative opportunities or for family and health reasons; and then the one-day squad (with perhaps a 60% overlap of players from that touring earlier) travelled back to India for a further series in January. The challenges for logistics and tour management in the face of such fragmented arrangements are daunting and of a totally different order to the requirements of a four to five-month tour in the 1930s, based on much more stable player participation. The roles of both tourists and hosts are clearly substantially different from the times when the words were first applied in a cricketing context. Indeed, it may be time to park such language and accept that modern cricketers are business travellers in every sense, their local opponents likewise transitory in their movements. The real tourists in the hedonistic sense of the term, therefore, are their mobile followers, the Barmy Army and their counterparts from other countries.

Postscript – The Result (If It Matters)

The fourth test between India and England in Nagpur ended in a tame draw and I watched the final rites of the game from the comfort of my home. The outcome sparked mass celebrations from those remaining of the Barmy Army – and why not? The draw gives England their first series win in India for 28 years... From afar, I am delighted and feel that I have played my small part as the England captain lavishes praise on the travelling supporters... or tourists!

References

Anon. (1986) *India's Hambledon Men*. Bombay: Tyeby Press.
Agnew, J. (2011) *Aggers' Ashes*. London: Blue Door.
Aspinall, P. (2012) *The Tour*. Leicester: Matador.
Bell, A. (2008) *Batting on the Bosphorus: A Skoda-powered Cricket Tour through Eastern Europe*. London: Canongate Books.
Brewer, J.D. (2000) *Ethnography; Understanding Social Research*. Buckingham: Open University Press.
Bright-Holmes, J. (ed.) (1988) *Lord's and Commons: Cricket in Novels and Stories*. London: Andre Deutsch.
Cardus, N. (1937) *Australian Summer*. London: Jonathan Cape.
Cohen, E. (1974) Who is a tourist? A conceptual clarification. *The Sociological Review* 22 (4), 527–555.
Coleman, V. (1990) *The Village Cricket Tour*. Barnstable: Chilton Design Publishers.
Curr, A. (2012) *Cricket on Everest: The Inspirational Story of the World's Highest Cricket Match*. Leicester: Matador.
Dann, G. (1999) Writing out the tourist in space and time. *Annals of Tourism Research* 26 (1), 159–187.
Deery, M., Jago, L. and Fredline, L. (2004) Sport tourism or event tourism: Are they one and the same? *Journal of Sport and Tourism* 9 (3), 235–245.
Edmunds, F. (1987) *Another Bloody Tour: England in the West Indies, 1986* (new edn). London: Fontana.
Ellis, C. (2004) *The Ethnographic I: A Methodological Novel about Autoethnography*. Walnut Creek, CA: AltaMira Press.
Ellis, C., Adams, T. and Bochner, A. (2011) Autoethnography: An overview. *FQS. Forum Qualitative Social Research* 12 (1). See www.qualitative-research.net/index.php/fqs/article/view/1589/3095 (accessed 13 December 2012).
Flintoff, A. (2009) *Ashes to Ashes*. London: Hodder and Stoughton.

Gammon, S. and Robinson, T. (2003) Sport and tourism: A conceptual framework. *Journal of Sport and Tourism* 8 (1), 21–26.

Headlam, C. (1903) *Ten Thousand Miles through India & Burma: An Account of the Oxford University Authentics Cricket Tour with Mr. K.J. Key on the Year of the Coronation Durbar.* London: Dent.

Holland, P. and Huggan, G. (1998) *Tourists with Typewriters. Critical Reflections on Contemporary Travel Writing.* Ann Arbor: University of Michigan Press.

Holman Jones, S. (2005) Autoethnography: Making the personal political. In N.K. Denzin and Y.S. Lincoln (eds) *Handbook of Qualitative Research* (pp. 763–791). Thousand Oaks, CA: Sage.

Holt, N.L. (2003) Representation, legitimation and autoethnography: An autoethnographic writing story. *International Journal of Qualitative Methods* 2 (1), Article 2. See www.ualberta.ca/~iiqm/backissues/2_1/html/holt.html (accessed 13 December 2012).

Karunatilaka, S. (2012) *Chinaman*. Delhi: Vintage Books.

Krist, G. (1993) Ironic journeys: Travel writing in the age of tourism. *The Hudson Review* 45 (4), 593–601.

Lillywhite, F. (1860) *The English Cricketers' Trip to Canada and the United States.* London: F. Lillywhite.

Lowe, R.H. (1927) *A Cricket Eleven: An Anthology of Cricket Short Stories with Verses.* London: Gerald Howe Ltd.

Margusee, M. (1997) *War Minus the Shooting: Journey through South Asia During Cricket's World Cup.* London: Mandarin.

Mulvaney, J. and Harcourt, R. (1988) *Cricket Walkabout. The Australian Aboriginal Cricketers on Tour, 1867–68* (2nd edn). London: Macmillan.

Olson, G.A. (1991) Clifford Geertz on ethnography and social construction. *Journal of Advance Composition* 11, 245–268.

Peregrine, A. (2012) Are you a tourist or a traveller? *The Daily Telegraph* (Travel), 3 August. See www.telegraph.co.uk/travel/familyholidays/9448828/Are-you-a-tourist-or-a-traveller.html (accessed 18 December 2012).

Ranjitsinhji, K.S. (1898/1985) *With Stoddart's Team in Australia.* London: Constable.

Simkins, M. (2011) *The Last Flannelled Fool: My Small Part in English Cricket's Demise and its Large Part in Mine.* London: Ebury.

Smith, A. and Stewart, B. (2007) The travelling fan: Understanding the mechanisms of sport fan consumption in a sport tourism setting. *Journal of Sport and Tourism* 12 (3–4), 155–181.

Tufnell, P. and Hayter, P. (1998) *Postcards from the Beach: Phil Tufnell's Alternative 1998 West Indies Tour Diary.* Manchester: Willow.

Waugh, S. (2001) *Ashes Diary 2001 With Highlights from Australia's Remarkable Tour of India.* Sydney: Harper Sports.

11 Recollections of a Coarse Cricketer: Ninety Nine Percent Boredom, One Percent Terror

Richard Butler

> *As a fielder batsmen love me...*
> *I'm each bowler's favourite batsman,*
> *And each batsman's favourite bowler...*
> *Popularity*, Morgan Dockrell

In his brilliantly perceptive and hilarious book *The Art of Coarse Golf*, Michael Green (1967) notes that golf is the only sport which refuses to recognise the vast majority of its players because most do not belong to a club and thus do not have a handicap. While there are many similarities between cricket and golf, that is not one of them, as anyone can call themselves a cricketer even if their only experience is keeping score at school, and thus can feel a member of the fraternity and share a love of willow and leather. However, there are vast differences between those fortunate enough to be able to honestly wear a red and yellow striped tie and the rest of us, and to most followers, the members' room at Lord's is as out of bounds as the Royal and Ancient clubhouse at St Andrews is to non-members of that body. I do recall being a guest of the now defunct Canadian Airlines (formerly Canadian Pacific) which invited me to a game at The Oval (perhaps the second most iconic cricket ground in England after Lord's) one afternoon in the late 1990s. The invitation included a buffet in one of the rooms overlooking the ground from where we were able to watch Alec Stewart and the rest of the Surrey team have a successful innings. Interestingly, and perhaps shamefully, few of those attending were interested in cricket, all having been invited because of their status in Canadian Airlines' frequent flyer programme and many spent most of their time at the buffet or the bar rather than on the balcony. A sunny afternoon, access to many parts of the pavilion and the chance to watch a county game at The Oval with splendid hospitality was something to remember with an affection for Canadian Airlines that lasted long after their demise.

Other similarities between cricket and golf include the attitudes of their elites towards women, which remain generally anachronistic and chauvinistic, and various elements of snobbery and gamesmanship (see Potter, 1964). In some ways cricket is also similar to Marmite (or Vegemite to Antipodean cricketers), in that one either likes the thing intensely (even if not being an active participant) or one cannot understand why anyone would bother watching, or playing (or eating) it. In my own case, I have played some pretty low standard cricket, and prefer Bovril to Marmite or Vegemite as both a drink and on toast. My cricket experience began formally in high school, which, by British standards at the time (late 1950s–early 1960s) was large (700+ pupils) and of the direct grant variety (a sort of minor public (and therefore private) school). En route to school on my bike I daily passed Edgbaston Cricket Ground, a test ground and the home of Warwickshire County Cricket. Sports, as befits the heritage of such schools (mine was founded in the 16th century by Edward VI) were important; Tuesday and Thursday afternoons were reserved for generally compulsory inter-house team sports (primarily cricket in the summer and rugby in the winter) and Saturday afternoons (classes were held on Saturday mornings of course, to make up for the sports afternoons) for matches by the elite school teams against other schools. During school house league competitions members of the school first teams were not allowed to participate, and were only active in the knock-out competitions towards the end of each season. During the period that A.C. Smith (of Warwickshire and England) was captain of the school XI, this limitation on his play was much appreciated by the other houses. It was a tradition of the school to award a cricket bat to anyone in the school XI scoring a century in an inter-school match. These were awarded at the Monday morning school assembly following the match, and my recollection is of Smith regularly collecting his bat throughout his last term at school. Obviously other schools found him as difficult to remove from the wicket as his schoolmates in the inter-house matches.

My standard of cricket was such that Saturday afternoons were always free. I did get house and school 'colours' but in shooting, which was done on the school range at lunch times, evenings and Friday afternoons during cadet periods. Thus my cricketing experience, while frequent and considerable, was at a low standard. I regularly made the house 4th XI (there being four teams per house), but in my penultimate season I graduated through the thirds to a couple of matches for the 2nd XI. I am reminded of another similarity with golf (or at least *coarse golf*) in that players at such a standard always remember clearly when they do something at a high (for them) standard, such is the infrequency of these occurrences. A great drive from the tee, or actually getting out of a bunker towards the green in golf, or in my case of cricket, taking two hard and high catches at cover in the first of my 2nd XI matches, earning a compliment from the house master the following day. That particular day, however, was rather marred by the fact that after those catches I had returned an errant ball from a match taking place on a neighbouring pitch and in the process hit a player on the fielding side on the head with my throw. Luckily he did not lose consciousness but it did become the cause of both barracking and a 'talking to' from the umpires of both matches. My second appearance for the 2nd XI was far less successful: no catches and out first ball to one I attempted to glance off my legs down the leg side only to see middle and leg stumps cartwheel out of the ground. My only justification was that the bowler was a former fast bowler from the school XI who was recovering from injury. My only other school cricketing highlight was being a member of the house 4th team which ran up 207 runs for four wickets one afternoon and then dismissed the other team for 10. While we were as suitably satisfied as gloating 13-year-olds could be, generally we agreed it would have been better to have batted second and saved ourselves two or three hours in the afternoon.

Cricket disappeared for several years after school as I was certainly not good enough to make a university team, so I chose football instead, the experience continuing when I joined the University of Western Ontario as a staff member, playing both outdoor and indoor five-a-side varieties of the game. Indeed, the geography department mixed five-a-side team won the intramural competition, playing as 'The Moving Boundary' (allusions to both geography and cricket). Cricket in Canada was rather rare. Perhaps partly because of the climate, cricket did not develop in Canada as it did in Australia, South Africa or the Indian sub-continent, and thus there are few organised teams and competitions. The climate did not easily allow for high-quality pitch production in most parts of the country, the playing season would generally be short, and so at Western, as in many other places, no formal cricket pitches existed. The lack of pitches meant that the few games that took place were usually played on coconut matting laid over grass, which substituted for a normal bowling wicket. What it lost in appearance and reality it made up for somewhat in

Figure 11.1 Coarse cricket Canadian style

relatively unchanging inconsistency of bounce, giving neither team an advantage in winning the toss (see Figure 11.1).

I did have one memorable cricket experience at Western, despite the lack of teams, equipment and pitches, purely because one of the geography doctoral students played for the university cricket team (which was made up almost entirely of West and East Indian players). Winston, our Bajan colleague, was able to arrange not only the loan of equipment and the coconut matting, which he assured us played true (he lied convincingly) but also provided an opposing team which included many of his colleagues from the university team. We chose to play on Queen Victoria's Birthday (21 May 1972), a national holiday in Canada, and duly pitched tents, brought food and drink and families and managed to field 11 players of considerable variety and experience as far as cricket was concerned. Several Brits, including an elderly Cambridge don well-versed in the principles if not the execution of cricket, two Americans with baseball experience, an Indian with considerable cricketing experience and talent, a South African, a German, and one true Canadian. To even things up, given that we were playing a team which included several of the official university team, members of our team were allowed two innings each, played consecutively, so when one of our team was out for the first time, they simply carried on until they were out a second time (usually fairly soon after the first occasion). In many ways it was a stereotypical performance by our team, the Brits managed to survive for some time and actually scored some runs, our two Americans were both dismissed by being caught all four times at bat, near what would have been third base in a baseball game or midwicket in this case, and as the Canadian played the ball rather like a hockey puck with expected results, our subcontinental player ran out of partners. Our bowling performance was surprisingly effective however, limiting our opposition to 115 runs, mainly due to the inconsistencies of the surface of the pitch and the inability of the experienced opposition to play in a manner appropriate to a by-then rather alcoholic and laid-back celebration of the birth of the former Queen, Empress and overall Head of the Empire. My two wickets were typical, the first batsman being puzzled by the second bounce of the ball which crept under his bat and resulted in him being stumped, the other victim, who, on receiving one of the few balls I have ever managed to properly spin, walloped it straight back over my head but luckily directly at a cunningly placed long-on at the boundary, generally hidden by myself when bowling. In the end the opposition hung on to win by seven runs in a gentlemanly fashion, which was decent of them as they had had to provide all the equipment, including the pitch. Talk of making it an annual event does not seem to have materialised as the second match has not yet taken place despite 40 years having passed.

At this point I felt my cricket experience was over, but when returning to Britain on a sabbatical I discovered that my old ski club had spawned a cricket team (sort of). Various members had assorted friends scattered across Scotland who were in cricket teams who wanted casual opponents and so another rag-tag and very casual team was concocted. One problem, which is common to all amateur 'casual' teams is organisation, particularly actually getting seven people together at the right place and on time with a wicket and equipment. We were playing a precursor of Twenty20 cricket with a Duckworth-Lewis twist, with teams consisting of seven players, and the winning team being the one which had the best score when the total of runs scored was divided by wickets fallen. In theory this required considerable strategic skills by the two captains, whether to go for runs or to safeguard wickets, but as the overall standard of most teams was certainly at coarse cricket level, most players proved unable to implement any particular strategy. Being on sabbatical and therefore having nothing better to do in my friends' opinion, I was not only welcomed to the team but appointed captain, which meant arranging the team and travel details. Most of our games were in and around Glasgow on city parks, played on weekday evenings with a minimum of kit and rarely any umpires. Members of the batting teams took on that responsibility in turn and as one would expect from 'gentlemen', there were rarely disputes, perhaps partly because there was ample opportunity for revenge and partly because there was rarely anyone keeping score.

The highlight of that season was an away game at Aberfeldy, a Perthshire village at the edge of the Scottish Highlands. This was the highlight for several reasons; it meant a car journey of some distance, thus making the game a day-long event at a weekend, the pitch was in a beautiful park setting in a natural bowl in the centre of the small town, which meant there was an audience (a new and terrifying experience for most of us) of several score people for a while (until they saw the actual standard of play perhaps), and best of all, the host team was a pub team. This meant that they were true hosts, their splendid attitude being that as the other team had taken the trouble to travel to their ground, it was their responsibility to provide refreshments. Given we had a number of designated drivers (had we realised what good hosts they were we would undoubtedly have contracted the bus company used by the ski club) we were moderate in our overall consumption, but the post-match discussions were lively and did bring forth one rather lengthy statement (much abbreviated here) by one of our team members, a former semi-professional cricketer, about the behaviour of youth in general. The problem he declared, was that modern day youngsters were often ill-mannered and anti-social in behaviour and the main reason for this was that they had not played cricket. He explained that behind the anti-social behaviour was boredom. Going on to expand this insight, he argued that for most amateur cricketers an average game involved several hours of standing around while in the field, watching mainly only one or two others actually being actively involved with the ball, and then probably an equal amount of time would be spent sitting in a pavilion while the other members of his team were batting. Activity in the field would come suddenly and often unexpectedly, most terrifyingly in the form of a skied ball coming towards you that had to be caught while everyone else watched your performance (most low-level coarse cricketers are rarely trusted in the slips or to bowl) and then, whether successfully executed or not, another long period of inactivity would ensue. (The all too often brief period of batting could be equally fearsome when facing fast, and often inaccurate bowlers.) My team-mate's argument was that if all young people had to play cricket for a period of years at school or elsewhere, and thus became used to spending long hours of inactivity while holding a watching brief on reality (the game), they would never be bored again, with a consequent reduction in vandalism and anti-social behaviour. The combination of the hospitality and the late hours prevented further discussion of the role of cricket in juvenile behaviour modification, but the logic of his thesis is appealing, if only in part because if the idea was adopted it could result in an increase in participation in cricket.

 My penultimate personal involvement with cricket beyond watching games or highlights on television was attending a match between a visiting

England test team and the Governor-General's XI in Canberra in the company of that noted tourism academic, Michael Hall. Of particular interest was the participation in the host team of Shane Warne but the anticipation of seeing him in action was tempered by the news that no alcohol was allowed to be brought into the ground. This was rather frustrating news to the two new temporary members (one a new Canadian and one an Aussie resident) of the English Barmy Army (see Emery *et al.*, Chapter 9, this volume) and necessitated bringing a large brown bag along with sandwiches and the other elements of a sunny weekend's picnic. The fizzy contents of the brown bag, along with two plastic glasses, were concealed behind the basket placed amid the above-ground roots of some large unknown Australian tree that stood beyond the midwicket boundary and sampled during an increasingly warm and blurry afternoon, and used to celebrate an English victory if memory recalls correctly (although it may not). It did also result in a yet-to-be-published children's story about Dickie and Mikie, a bottle of fizzy pop, some mild misbehaviour and a famous cricketer called Shady Wall.

Given other commitments, and living in semi-rural Scotland, I had anticipated my first-hand experience of cricket was probably over and television would provide my only contact with the game. However, while at a conference in Christchurch, New Zealand, I was very kindly given a ticket to a one-day international between England and New Zealand by Sarah Williams, the Channel View publisher representative and this book's commissioning editor. The match was at Eden Park in Auckland, and as I was staying with my daughter and her family in north shore Auckland the opportunity was too good to miss. Thus on match day I set off along with my son-in-law's father, with his son agreeing to join us later and drive us home. On a beautiful sunny day we caught the Devonport Ferry to central Auckland, a delightful 10-minute experience and a great way to go to work. We then walked a few minutes to the railway station, which, like those in many ex-colonial towns, was an impressive 19th-century building (a former post office), to get our tickets to the ground. To my surprise we got tickets to Kingsland, not to Mount Eden, which I naturally thought would be the station for Eden Park, but turned out to be the station for the prison. One wonders if some members of the Barmy Army are still in Auckland if they got off at that earlier stop. At the station there was a member of the railway company selling wristbands as return tickets for $5.00, and had we not had the offer of a lift home, we would have purchased these. However, on buying our single tickets we found the price was only $1.80, so a sharp bit of sales by the railway company there, making $1.40 off each gullible tourist.

The narrow gauge journey was more reminiscent of the above-ground sections of the London Tube than a rail journey, and we soon arrived at

Kingsland, and decided to have lunch before the match. The local bars and restaurants were busy with Barmy Army and other fans and a very hospitable atmosphere pervaded the local main street. After a very enjoyable lunch a five-minute walk got us to Eden Park, a large stadium which had been extended for the Rugby World Cup the previous year. We had seats in the North Stand, which fortunately for us, remained in the shade for the duration of the match, while those in the other stands who were without hats or sunscreen gradually turned a light shade of beetroot. The playing area itself was small, essentially an oval rugby pitch in size, and unlike many cricket grounds, had no signs of previous wickets but a beautiful expanse of uniform green apart from the 'drop-in' wicket. Having only been to live matches where the traditional red ball was used, it was novel to see sightscreens being black instead of white. One other intriguing aspect of the ground was the visibility of several British organisations advertising around the ground. Their rationale for advertising in New Zealand, even given the presence of England supporters, seemed a little unclear, in particular the advertisements for Grand National tickets and Dementia UK.

We arrived with New Zealand having scored two runs for no loss of wickets, but things soon changed. A devastating spell of bowling by Finn, who at one stage had the remarkable figures of seven overs for seven runs and two wickets, saw New Zealand slump to 11 for three wickets and thus to some extent the result was determined early in the match. This was the third and final match in the one-day series, and the score was one game all, and like the other two games, it seemed clear that the team batting second was likely to be the winner. New Zealand's batting began to improve, although the run rate remained below five an over, until Taylor and first Elliott and then McCullum came together. Taylor had scored a century in the previous match and was a crowd favourite, while his skipper had scored over 70 in each of the other matches at a very fast rate. For a few overs the Kiwis in the crowd were clearly in the ascendancy until Elliott was run out and then Taylor was given out caught behind. That decision was sent to the fourth official and a very long delay ensued. The crowd grew increasingly restive until the decision was announced as 'Out', and then broke into a chorus of boos and jeers, as Taylor's departure seemed likely to see an early end to the innings. However, Brendon McCullum decided attack was the best form of defence and as in previous games rapidly took the English bowlers on, ruining Finn's figures with 16 off one over. The warning flashed repeatedly on the big scoreboards during his innings to the effect that spectators should 'Keep an eye on the ball!', as the short boundaries began to be breached repeatedly. The New Zealand skipper again reached the seventies before being caught just short of the boundary and the New Zealand innings ended with the score of 185.

Figure 11.2 Kwik cricket at Eden Park

The break between innings was quite fascinating as no sooner had the players disappeared than out ran about 200 children, both boys and girls, to play 12 games of Kwik Cricket, a child's version of the game, involving plastic wickets, balls and bats (Figure 11.2). The crowd cheered heartily at each boundary in their part of the field, a fairly frequent occurrence as they were playing in the outfield, and were much more receptive of the juniors than of a local DJ and two go-go dancers performing for a video on another part of the pitch. The various comments on both his appearance and performance were somewhat derogative to say the least. Like most of the audience we decided to partake of some refreshment, and visited the offerings available within the stadium, deciding to pass on the 'donuts' being sold at the seats. The choice was fairly similar to the offerings at most stadiums these days, hamburgers (and, inevitably in New Zealand, lamb burgers), hot dogs, sandwiches and a variety of quite decent pies, with a limited choice of desserts. Beer seemed expensive, $8 for a very small bottle, most commonly sold in fours, held together at the necks by a paper surround which nevertheless generally survived the journey back to the seats as far as we could see.

Perhaps not surprisingly the noise level began to increase as the interval drew to a close, the warnings about the danger of balls began to reappear on the screen, along with images from the Tui 'box'. Tui is a New Zealand beer (and pie) producer with the slogan 'Distracting the boys from the task at hand since 1889' and their television advertisements in conjunction with the cricket showed various players getting hit in the groin by balls. Its website (www.tui.co.nz) requires users to confirm they are over 18, and has various sections including one labelled 'Cool Shit', offering screensavers, wallpaper and other images. At the ground the Tui 'box' is a small golf-cart like structure seating about eight people, shaped like a groin protection 'box', from which various pieces of advice are forthcoming at irregular intervals. During the interval, several inflatable plastic balls began to float around the stands to great cheers from the crowd, and the locals began to cheer even more loudly as occasional members of the English supporters were escorted from the west and south stands by the stewards. (I am assuming they were English supporters from the fact that they were seated in areas behind flags of St George and from the comments of the Kiwi supporters.)

Interest in the balls and the refreshments was such that people were still standing, eating and stretching without apparently noticing that the match had restarted for several minutes. As England began their innings the pace of the game became faster, Cook and Bell scoring at better than six an over until Bell's dismissal just short of the 50 partnership. After that things began to slow down, or perhaps it was my appreciation beginning to wane, but the run rate dropped (albeit remaining faster than New Zealand's had been) and the crowd seemed at times to be more excited about the progress of the inflatable balls and the musical accompaniment at the end of each over, the Monkees' 'Daydream Believer' gaining a massive cheer and sing-along. The greatest cheer, however, was for a young lady in very short shorts who caused the English batsmen to stand away from the wicket when she walked up the aisle beside the sightscreen in the South Stand. Each time an inflatable blew onto the outfield and was returned by the New Zealand fielders there were also great cheers, but when one of them, Rutherford, refused to be distracted when one fell near him, a chorus of boos went up. Eventually at the end of the over he picked it up and threw it back to great cheers and some comments from the Barmy Army to the fact that at least he could hold a ball that size (as he had dropped a catch previously). As the match progressed the New Zealand bowlers took wickets, making the end result a little more respectable from their point of view. Root was cheered in with some apprehension by the locals as he had been in devastating form in the previous one-day match but here was much more restrained, and it was Morgan who hit out more strongly and effectively. In the end the inevitable result was a five wicket win for England and the crowd began to disperse.

We had received a text indicating our lift had not materialised and thus we resolved to return by train and ferry. Joining the rapidly dispersing very good-natured crowd we made our way to the station, avoiding the one drunk we saw, a middle aged Englishman (whose boater was being held by his embarrassed partner) emptying his stomach against a lamppost. The station was jammed solid, so busy that we could not reach the ticket machine, and we began regretting we had not bought the overpriced wristbands. We decided to board the train and get tickets at the other end, New Zealand train staff being much more understanding according to my companion, than those in the UK. To our amazement the first train managed to take all those waiting at the station, and to cap our good fortune, two young New Zealanders offered us their seats on the train. Obviously we looked our age, and we gratefully accepted their offer. On arrival at Auckland not only were there no staff present, there were no visible ticket machines and the counters were closed, so we left the station rationalising that we had intended to pay, and our free trip served New Zealand Rail right for ripping off visitors with their overpriced wrist bands. An ice cream on the ferry home on a still warm evening brought the outing to a close. Overall a very civilised, pleasant and friendly experience, marked by easy, efficient and cheap travel and a congenial atmosphere in a very attractive setting on a beautiful summer afternoon and evening. Undoubtedly the absence of any language or logistical problems helped in this, as did travelling with a local and thus avoiding a visit to the jail, as would have been likely given the names of the railway stations!

So much for my personal experiences of cricket. Unlike my co-editor and some of the other contributors to this volume, my personal exposure and travel to cricket of a high standard has thus been very limited, although certainly not unmemorable, but my participation in the game at lower, perhaps the lowest, levels has equally certainly been enough to confirm my status as a coarse cricketer.

References

Dockrell, M. (1984) Popularity. *Tales from Far Pavilions*. London: Pavilion Books.
Green, M. (1967) *The Art of Coarse Golf*. London: Hutchinson.
Potter, S. (1964) *The Theory and Practice of Gamesmanship*. Harmondsworth: Penguin.

Stumps

Richard Butler

> *The act of 'drawing stumps' marks the end of play in a cricket match. In its abbreviated form this is often referred to simply as 'stumps'. Both expressions are used metaphorically and often in a light-hearted sense to mean reaching the end of something.*
> Stumped on a Sticky Wicket (2000: 53)

In light of the quotation above, it seems appropriate to title the last entry in this volume 'Stumps' to signify the conclusion of the volume. Cricket has contributed many terms and phrases to the English language, the volume cited above includes 20 such terms and even then is not totally comprehensive. It is reflective of the underlying significance of the game to many English speakers that such terminology is in common usage. As several of the contributors to this volume have noted, to its supporters and devotees cricket is more than a game, which explains in part the increasing numbers of supporters who are travelling to cricket matches, particularly international ones, and the appearance of the 'Armies' of supporters in many parts of the world.

In this volume we have focused on illustrating and commenting upon the spectator side of cricket, particularly in the context of travelling to watch the game in its variety of forms, as well as noting issues related to the pressures upon participants exerted by such travel and the problems of providing and maintaining the grounds at which the sport is practised and watched. Cricket in the 21st century is probably stronger in terms of sizes of audiences than at any time in its history, reflecting the variety of forms of the game now being played, the media interest and coverage of the game, and the frequency of matches, particularly at the international level. Despite this, there is no doubt that elements of the game are under great pressure and suffering accordingly. The rapid rise in popularity of Twenty20, particularly in the Indian sub-continent, now mirrored by the 'Big Bash' in Australia, is often blamed for a decline in interest in both the one-day limited over version of the game in particular and also for a decline in the quality of batting, especially in test matches. The pressure to accumulate runs at a high rate per over (upwards of ten runs or more an over in some matches) compared to three or four runs per over in test matches is held to mitigate against players being able to build a lengthy innings such as the double and triple hundreds witnessed in test matches in the early and mid-20th century (although the outstanding Twenty20 New Zealander Brendon McCullum recently scored a triple century in a test match against India).

Whether such thoughts are accurate or not, there is no doubt that the ways in which the game has developed, while welcomed by many, are seen as simply 'not cricket' by some. Much as one may sympathise with proponents of what might have been a gentler and quieter more traditional form of the game (the antics of W.G. Grace, the 'Bodyline' series, and the emergence of 'sledging' aside), it is clear that the dynamic nature of the game in the last few decades has revolutionised both the playing and spectating aspects of the game, increasing the numbers of participants and spectators and the media appeal of cricket throughout the world. Travelling to the boundary has widened from being an essentially domestic and even local event, supporting one's county, state or other local team, to become an international global element of tourism. The numbers of cricket supporters travelling internationally to matches are greater than those for any other sport, with the exception of events such as the Olympics or the World Cup of football. Cricket is somewhat unique in that supporters travel to a series of matches which have little real significance compared, for example, to a World Cup of football. While there are now world championships in the varied forms of cricket, test match series are still the major draws for international travelling supporters, with the Ashes series representing the pinnacle of such events.

The nature of such support has changed radically over time as the chapters in this volume dealing with the 'Armies' of supporters clearly demonstrates. While the authorities at Lord's, the 'home of cricket', ban both musical instruments and fancy dress, at least on their website (www.Lords.org), the reality is a little different, depending on one's definition of fancy dress at least. The Barmy Army may be a little more subdued on its home grounds than at the Gabba or in Melbourne or Sydney, but the Australian contingent are clearly recognisable abroad in what is scarcely their everyday wear. Thus we can expect travelling to the boundary to continue and most likely to continue to grow as long as international matches deliver excitement and a high standard of cricket between well-matched sides. Too many 'whitewashes' may reduce the drama but probably not the need for stronger support. One can remain hopeful that grounds remain full even as 'stumps' draws near, although the situation may not be as exciting as Sir Henry Newbolt (1892) described:

There's a breathless hush in the Close to-night-
Ten to make and the match to win-
A bumping pitch and a blinding light,
An hour to play and the last man in (Newbolt, 2007).

References

Anonymous (2000) *Stumped on a Sticky Wicket: Sporting Sayings and Their Meanings.* Oxford: Past Times. www.Lords.org (accessed 12 November 2012).

Newbolt, H. (2007) Vitai Lampada. In D.R. Allen and H. Doggart (eds) *'A Breathless Hush...' The MCC Anthology of Cricket Verse* (p. 40). Methuen: London.

Subject Index

Amateur 1, 2, 15, 23, 27, 32, 100, 172, 173
Army 8, 10, 13, 15, 30, 100, 136–139, 140–148, 160, 162, 163, 165, 166, 174, 175, 177, 180
Ashes 9, 11, 12, 18, 30, 35–38, 40–49, 50, 52, 53, 56, 58, 59, 61–69, 80, 129, 136, 139, 140, 142, 146, 164, 180
Australia xvii, xviii, 1, 4, 5, 7–11, 13, 18, 23, 27, 29, 30, 35–42, 45, 46, 49, 50, 52–56, 58–62, 64–70, 88–93, 95, 104–106, 109, 117, 123, 129, 136, 138–149, 154, 156, 161–163, 165, 170, 174, 179, 180

Bodyline 13, 29, 58, 180
Brand/branding 40, 43, 48, 49, 81, 92, 141, 142, 144, 145, 147

Caribbean xviii, 159, 162
Colonial/colony 4, 5, 6, 7, 27, 35, 41, 42, 50, 52, 54, 55, 56, 58, 59, 66, 68, 69, 85, 86, 94, 139, 154, 174
County xi, 2, 10, 12–14, 21, 23, 30, 36, 73, 75, 76, 78, 79, 81, 164, 169, 180

England xviii, xv, 1–11, 13–16, 18–22, 24, 25, 26, 28–31, 35, 37, 41, 42, 43, 47, 49, 50, 52, 56–59, 61, 62, 65, 66, 68, 69, 76, 77, 79, 100, 106, 108, 122, 129, 136–139, 140–142, 145, 153, 154, 156, 158, 160–163, 165, 166, 168, 169, 174, 175, 177, 178
Experience xviii, 7, 10, 12, 13, 14, 19, 22–25, 30, 31, 38, 40, 42, 46, 49, 53, 54, 60, 61, 63, 64, 66, 68, 88, 91, 92, 99, 100, 104–117, 133, 136, 138, 140, 142, 144, 145, 147, 148, 149, 154, 155, 156, 161–165, 168–173, 178

Fan 1, 4, 8, 23, 30, 31, 40, 42, 49, 52, 54, 58, 59, 61, 64, 65, 67, 68, 69, 70, 78, 81, 100, 101, 128, 138–148, 156, 158, 160, 162, 163, 165, 175

Gentleman/men 11, 14, 57, 160, 172

Heritage 11, 12, 19, 21, 25, 38, 40, 42, 49, 50, 55, 64, 136, 169
History xvii, 6, 12, 18, 19, 21, 29, 36, 38, 41, 44, 45, 49, 52, 53, 57, 62–66, 68, 76, 82, 85, 86, 127, 133, 138, 139, 141, 155, 158, 164, 179
Home (Home of) 4, 8, 9, 11–15, 22, 24, 26, 29, 30, 32, 35, 39, 45, 52, 53, 54, 56, 57, 58, 62, 65–69, 73, 75, 81, 86, 100, 105, 107, 108, 109, 114, 116, 125, 134, 138, 139, 149, 154, 156, 160, 163–166, 169, 174, 178

Image 1, 2, 5, 6, 7, 27, 35, 41, 42, 50, 52, 54, 55, 56, 58, 59, 66, 68, 69, 85, 86, 94, 139, 154, 174
India/Indians xviii, 1, 5, 6, 7, 8, 10, 11, 13, 14, 15, 23, 30, 56, 60, 69, 88, 89, 91, 92, 95, 100, 106, 110, 120–132, 138, 142–147, 153–163, 165, 166, 170, 171, 179
Indigenous 1, 9, 12, 43
Innings 19, 169, 171, 175, 176, 177, 180

Legacy 11, 27, 50, 52, 58, 59, 94, 126, 157
Local 1, 4, 9, 13, 15, 23, 36, 39, 74, 75, 78, 80, 81, 82, 88–93, 99, 104, 105, 110, 112, 116, 139, 156–159, 161, 163–166, 175–178, 180
Lord's 2, 9, 11, 12, 14, 15, 21, 22, 26, 35, 36, 52–69, 75, 159, 164, 168, 180

Media 2, 9, 11, 27, 30, 36, 41, 50, 53, 54, 63, 74, 88, 89, 103, 106, 109, 112, 113, 122, 128, 140, 143, 148, 154, 156, 158, 179, 180
Melbourne xvii, 10, 15, 43–46, 48, 64–66, 68, 70, 89, 91, 93, 136, 142, 145
Mumbai 123, 128

Nationalism 38, 39, 40, 55, 65, 120, 138, 149
New Delhi 123, 156, 158, 161
New Zealand xviii, 5, 7, 45, 60, 88, 89, 93, 143, 144, 148, 174–178
Nostalgia 11, 14, 18, 19, 21, 26, 28, 52–56, 59, 60, 62–69

Oval(s) 12, 14, 35, 36, 88, 92, 93, 112, 164, 175

Pakistan 7, 8, 11, 69, 100, 106, 120–130, 132, 133, 146
Players 2, 4, 6, 8, 9, 10, 11, 13, 14, 15, 18, 23, 24, 28, 29, 30, 35, 36, 53, 73, 79, 80, 89, 90, 91, 93, 94, 95, 99, 100, 104, 106–110, 113, 117, 127, 132, 138, 142, 143, 144, 148, 156, 163, 165, 168, 170, 171, 172, 176, 177, 180
Professional 2, 4, 10, 13, 14, 15, 23, 30, 32, 35, 74, 79, 82, 90, 103, 105, 106, 107, 112, 113, 141, 144, 164, 165, 173

Religion 107, 126, 128
Revenue 23, 48, 69, 75, 128, 145

Security 11, 100, 111, 127, 128, 143, 148, 156, 157, 159, 160, 161
Scotland 8, 9, 28, 129, 155, 156, 172, 174
South Africa 5, 7, 8, 10, 60, 69, 79, 88, 103, 122, 138, 143, 156, 163, 164, 170, 171

Spirit/Spiritual 12, 21, 23, 24, 35, 54, 56, 127
Sponsor/Sponsorship 6, 36, 74, 81, 82, 85, 89, 94, 95, 99, 128, 142, 145
Sport/Sporting xvii, xviii, 2–6, 12, 14, 18–22, 24, 26–28, 30, 35–42, 46, 50, 52–57, 59, 63–67, 73–79, 81, 82, 85–87, 92–96, 100, 101, 103–107, 109, 110, 113, 115–117, 120–122, 127–134, 138, 140, 142–144, 146–148, 153, 154, 155, 161–165, 168, 169, 179, 180
Sri Lanka 7, 60, 77, 93, 146, 156
Stadium 8, 55, 67, 74–77, 80, 81, 82, 87, 123, 137, 142, 157, 159, 160, 161, 164, 175, 176
Supporters 3, 4, 10, 13, 14, 15, 23, 24, 30, 35, 37, 64, 68, 100, 131, 132, 133, 137, 138, 141–147, 162, 165, 166, 175, 177, 179, 180
Sydney xviii, 29, 42, 65, 67, 68, 117, 133, 140, 145, 164, 180

Television 3, 6, 9, 10, 15, 26, 28, 39, 41, 82, 100, 101, 128, 142, 145, 173, 174, 177
Test 2, 4, 7, 8, 9, 10, 11, 13, 14, 15, 18, 19, 21, 26, 30, 35, 36, 38, 41, 42, 45, 52, 53, 56, 58, 59, 61–67, 69, 74, 77, 79, 80, 100, 104, 106, 109, 112, 113, 121–127, 129, 132, 134, 136, 138, 139, 140, 147, 153, 154, 156, 158, 160–166, 169, 174, 180
The Oval 12, 14, 35, 36, 37, 45, 62, 159, 164, 168
Tours 1, 2, 4, 10, 13, 18, 24, 35, 37, 63, 65, 81, 89, 90, 99, 100, 106–110, 113, 122, 123, 126–129, 132, 140–144, 146, 147, 148, 154, 156, 160, 162, 163, 165
Tournament 22, 80, 89, 90, 91, 93, 95, 113, 133, 164
Tradition/Traditional 2, 3, 4, 6, 9, 10, 14, 18, 21–24, 27, 36, 38, 42, 49, 52, 53, 55, 56, 58, 62–65, 68, 69, 79, 99, 100, 104, 114, 115, 126, 139, 141, 145, 147, 154, 155, 160, 162, 164, 175, 180

Travel xii, 1–6, 13, 15, 18, 19, 20, 27–31, 35, 36, 37, 40, 47, 64, 87, 94, 95, 99, 100, 103–117, 124, 125, 133, 138, 140, 143, 144, 148, 154–159, 161–166, 172, 173, 178, 179, 180

Twenty20 xii, 2, 4, 6, 9, 10, 12, 14, 15, 21, 22, 23, 30, 36, 69, 78, 80, 91, 93, 154, 165, 172, 179

War 13, 21, 24–27, 42, 84, 86, 89, 120, 123, 124, 126, 127, 129, 130, 133, 141, 162

West Indies 5, 6, 7, 19, 79, 100

Wicket 10, 14, 15, 21, 23, 73, 101, 104, 123, 136, 140, 162, 169, 170, 172, 174–179

World Cup 1, 8, 9, 10, 41, 123, 133, 138, 143, 144, 148, 156, 175, 180

For Product Safety Concerns and Information please contact our EU Authorised Representative:

Easy Access System Europe

Mustamäe tee 50

10621 Tallinn

Estonia

gpsr.requests@easproject.com